I0812760

IMAGES
*of America*

# CASS COUNTY

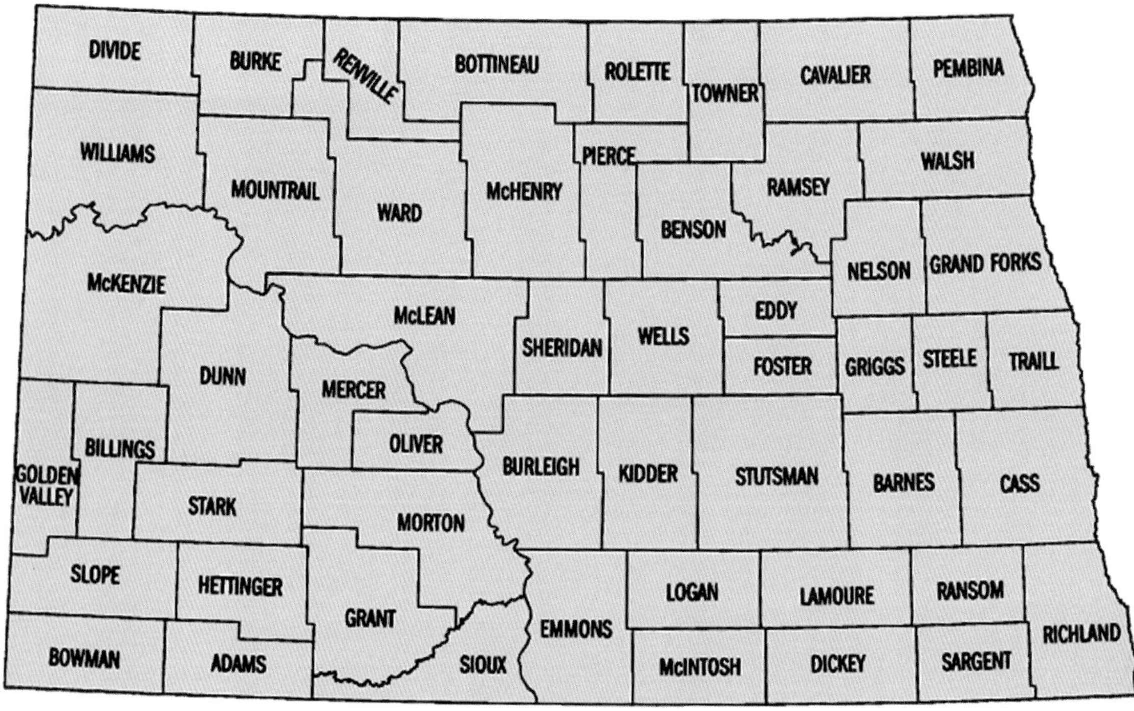


The land that is North Dakota was part of the Louisiana Purchase except for the Red River Valley, which was acquired by the United States in 1818. Some of the land that is North Dakota was part of Missouri Territory in 1818, Michigan Territory in 1834, Wisconsin Territory in 1836, Iowa Territory in 1838, Minnesota Territory in 1849, Nebraska Territory in 1854, and finally Dakota Territory in 1861. North Dakota officially became a state on November 2, 1889. There are 53 counties in the state.

*On the cover*: The Red River Valley is known for agricultural abundance and extraordinary flatness; this photograph gives an indication of both of those characteristics. The name of the man in the cover photograph and the location of his farm are unknown, except that they are somewhere in Cass County. Farming was not about machinery and technology, which were used on bonanza farms in large numbers and are still used today. It was about people and their connection to the land. With less than two percent of the American population currently involved in agriculture, the anonymous person standing alone in his wheat field represents the everyman farmer, when people were still tied to the land and proud of their work. This man could be virtually any farmer in Cass County at virtually any time in the late 19th or early 20th century—the golden age of agriculture. (North Dakota Institute for Regional Studies.)

IMAGES
*of America*

# CASS COUNTY

Tim Hoheisel and Andrew R. Nielsen

ARCADIA
PUBLISHING

ISBN 978-0-7385-4145-7

Published by Arcadia Publishing
Charleston, South Carolina

Printed in the United States of America

Library of Congress Catalog Card Number: 2006933898

For all general information contact Arcadia Publishing at:
Telephone 843-853-2070
Fax 843-853-0044
E-mail sales@arcadiapublishing.com
For customer service and orders:
Toll-Free 1-888-313-2665

Visit us on the Internet at www.arcadiapublishing.com

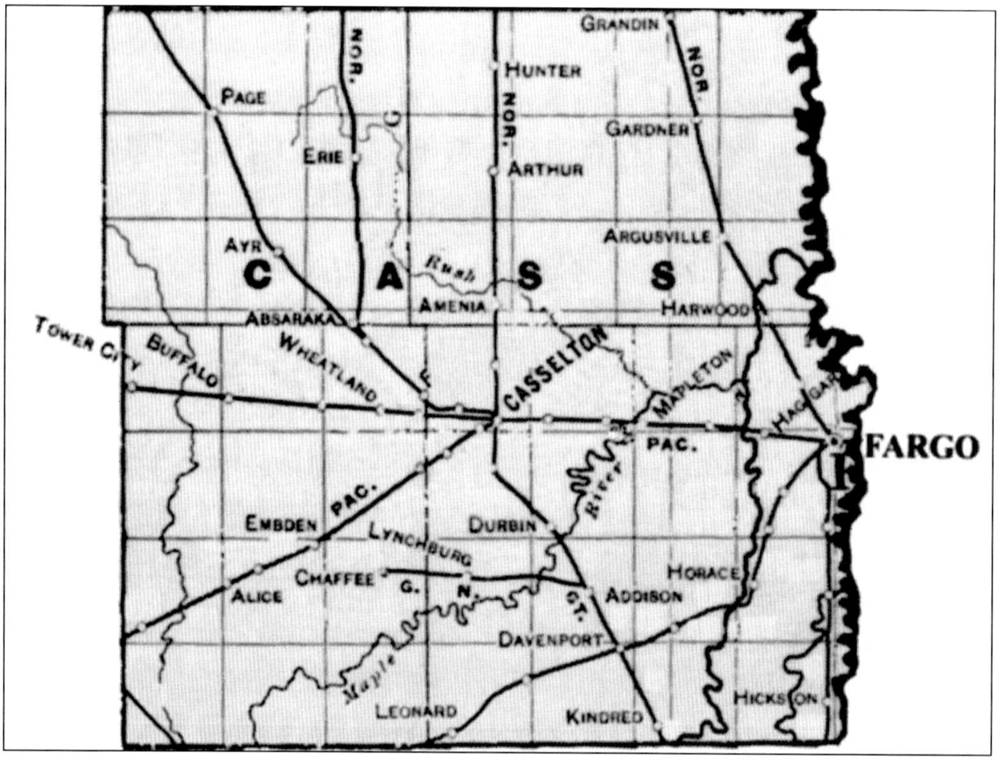


Cass County was organized in 1873. Fargo was selected as the county seat but was not officially organized until 1875. There are 50 townships in Cass County and currently 26 towns. Townships include Amenia, Arthur, Ayr, Barnes, Bell, Berlin, Buffalo, Casselton, Clifton, Cornell, Davenport, Dows, Durbin, Eldred, Empire, Erie, Everest, Fargo, Gardner, Gill, Gunkel, Harmony, Harwood, Highland, Hill, Howes, Hunter, Kinyon, Lake, Leonard, Maple River, Mapleton, Noble, Normanna, Page, Pleasant, Pontiac, Prosper, Raymond, Reed, Rich, Rochester, Rush River, Stanley, Tower, Walburg, Warren, Watson, Wheatland, and Wiser.

# CONTENTS

# ACKNOWLEDGMENTS

This book would not have been completed without the hard work of Andrew Nielsen. When I was the executive director of the Cass County Historical Society, I hired Andrew to be the assistant curator. Together we selected the photographs that appear in this book. We even agreed on the photograph that should grace the cover. Thanks to Andrew for his hours of hard work on this project while simultaneously finishing his bachelor's degree in history at Minnesota State University Moorhead.

Most of the photographs in this book are from the Cass County Historical Society collection at the Institute for Regional Studies at North Dakota State University in Fargo. We also used photographs from several other collections as well. Thanks to archivist John Bye and his staff at the institute for their friendly assistance.

Much thanks goes to you, the reader, for buying and reading our humble pictorial history. The mission of the Cass County Historical Society is to collect, display, and interpret artifacts relevant to the history and cultural heritage of Cass County and the Red River Valley. This book fulfills all three underlying aspects of the mission—collecting, displaying, and interpreting.

Part of the proceeds from the sale of this book, including all author royalties, go to support the operation of Bonanzaville and the Cass County Historical Society. The success of the organization depends on your support, and it is important that you know how greatly that support is appreciated. We hope you appreciate this latest installment of historic photographs of Cass County, North Dakota.

Thank you to anyone and everyone else who assisted us on this project but are not mentioned by name here—your help was also valued.

For more information on the Cass County Historical Society, call (701) 282-2822 or visit the Web site at www.bonanzaville.org. For more information on the Institute for Regional Studies at North Dakota State University, call (701) 231-8914 or visit the Web site at www.lib.ndsu.nodak.edu/ndirs/.

Tim Hoheisel
Fargo, North Dakota
November 2006

# INTRODUCTION

In 1976, the Cass County Historical Society published a 944-page book entitled *Rural Cass County: The Land and the People*. The book was a detailed history of the county, its towns, townships, and its people, featuring extensive family histories. It is now out of print, and the only way to get a copy of it is to stumble across one at an auction or garage sale. Much of the information for the text of this book was taken from *Rural Cass County*. Other books about agriculture and bonanza farming, the Northern Plains, and some pictorial histories about the city of Fargo are available and still in print. There is not, however, a book that is available and in print on the history of Cass County. This slim volume, the first book on Cass County history since 1976, does not replace any of those other books; it complements them.

The other main goal of this book is to present historic photographs. We had thousands of pictures to choose from, some well known and some probably only seen by archivists and researchers. With so many historic photographs at our disposal, we could have filled 10 books. Therefore, this short book is not intended to be comprehensive in any way. Our objective is to show some of the popular photographs once again in a new book as well as to present many more photographs possibly never seen by the general public. Although it is not a comprehensive book, a brief history is first needed to make it a well-rounded book.

Beginning about two million years ago, glaciers continually advanced and retreated across what is now eastern North Dakota. As they moved, the glaciers deposited thick layers of sediment. The last glacier began retreating from the area about 12,000 years ago. As it melted, it created a vast glacial lake, Lake Agassiz. More than 9,000 years ago, Lake Agassiz shrank and disappeared, revealing the Red River and also the rich soil that nurtured prairie grasslands for centuries. Farmers breaking ground in the late 19th century turned over the virgin prairie and exposed that fertile soil once again, and the Red River Valley became an agricultural paradise.

Archeological evidence indicates that as long as 9,000 years ago, Paleo-Indian nations occupied and traversed this area. They lived as hunter-gathers, hunted big game, and as far back as 2,000 years ago even practiced semisedentary agriculture. By the time white Europeans arrived and began settling the area in the 19th century, many different Native American nations had called this area home or passed through it while foraging, including Assiniboine, Cheyenne, Blackfeet, Crow, Dakota, Mandan, Hidatsa, Arikara, and Chippewa.

In 1803, the Louisiana Purchase doubled the territory of the United States, but the Red River Valley was not included in the acquisition. The United States obtained the land from Great Britain in the Treaty of 1818. The treaty also created the current border with Canada at the 49th parallel from Lake of the Woods to the Rocky Mountains.

The many conflicts between the United States and Plains Indian nations during the 19th century generally did not involve Cass County. However, two military forts were built not far outside Cass County. Fort Abercrombie on the Red River to the south was established in 1858, and to the southwest, Fort Ransom was built in 1867. Declining bison herds, disease, constant war, and increased pressure from white settlers, among other things, caused Native American nations to cede their land. Most of the land that is Cass County was ceded to the United States government in an 1864 treaty with the Red Lake and Pembina Chippewa. The rest of the land was acquired by a subsequent treaty with the Sisseton and Wahpeton Dakota in 1872.

North Dakota has been a part of many different territories throughout its history. Some of the land that is North Dakota was part of Missouri Territory in 1818, Michigan Territory in 1834, Wisconsin Territory in 1836, Iowa Territory in 1838, Minnesota Territory in 1849, Nebraska Territory in 1854, and finally Dakota Territory in 1861. North Dakota officially became a state on November 2, 1889. There are 53 counties in the state.

Dakota Territory was created in 1861 and consisted of the present-day states of North Dakota and South Dakota. It also contained most of what is now Montana until 1864 and Wyoming. In 1868, Dakota Territory was reduced to include what is now North Dakota and South Dakota with the territorial capital established in Yankton.

In 1871, the Northern Pacific Railroad crossed into Dakota Territory at Centralia. The next year, the town name was changed to Fargo after William G. Fargo, a director and financial backer of the railroad and a partner in the Wells-Fargo Express Company. Cass County was established in 1873, and Fargo was chosen as the county seat. Cass County is named for George Washington Cass, president of the Northern Pacific Railroad at the time and a bonanza farm owner. The City of Fargo was organized in 1875, and the city's first election was held on April 5, 1875. Six aldermen were elected, and George Egbert was chosen as the first mayor. By 1880, the population of Fargo was 2,693.

Legislators from Dakota Territory had requested Congress many times to divide the territory. Nearly every year a petition was sent to Congress and residents hoped for admission as two states. On November 2, 1889, Pres. Benjamin Harrison approved the admission of North Dakota to the United States. When the State of North Dakota was created in 1889, the population of Cass County was already approaching 20,000.

The history of Cass County cannot be told without examining the bonanza farm phenomenon. Cass County was not settled by rugged pioneers and immigrants who conquered the wilderness and carved out a civilization that made them Americans, as Frederick Jackson Turner theorized in his frontier thesis. Similarly, Cass County was never a safety valve for disgruntled Eastern immigrants, nor was it a bastion of Jeffersonian democracy filled with yeomen farmers. Bonanza farms led the way in agriculture and settlement of Cass County. Bonanza farms were massive commercial farms that averaged between 3,000 and 30,000 acres, and sometimes they were much larger. They were owned by railroad executives who took advantage of the flat, fertile Red River Valley. Bonanza farms transformed the virgin prairie from a diverse ecosystem teeming with a variety of flora and fauna into a monoculture of wheat in a very short time.

The dictionary defines "bonanza" as a source of great and sudden wealth or luck; a spectacular windfall. Gilbert Fite writes in *The Farmers' Frontier*, "The bonanza farm represented in agriculture many of the same characteristics and patterns found in the business world—large scale, and sometimes corporate organization, absentee ownership, professional management, mechanization, and specialized production—all of which were being applied to the industrial sector of the economy in the late nineteenth century." Bonanza farms were also directly linked to the railroad.

The Northern Pacific Railway Company was chartered in 1864 by the United States Congress as the first northern transcontinental railroad. It was granted some 45 million acres of land in exchange for building rail transportation through undeveloped territory. In Dakota Territory alone, the charter provided for a land grant of 11 million acres, roughly one-fourth the area of North Dakota. The land grant entitled the Northern Pacific Railway to 40 sections of land for every mile of railroad built; the railroad was to receive the odd-numbered sections. The first real successes of the company did not come until financier Jay Cooke got involved in 1870.

Initial accomplishments of the Northern Pacific Railway were short lived. The financial panic of 1873 caused thousands of businesses to collapse and the national unemployment rate to soar. The recession was damaging for many people and businesses across the country, but it was actually one of the reasons for the establishment of bonanza farming in the Red River Valley. From 1873 to 1875, the Northern Pacific Railway made a concerted effort to get its bondholders to convert their bonds into land, thus keeping the railway solvent. More than 1 million acres were disposed of this way with half of the land going to only 40 different people. It was this method of land acquisition that allowed the enormous bonanza farms to get started.

The crop that made bonanza farming so popular and profitable was hard spring wheat. This type of wheat is ideal for making bread. It can be consistently produced to a high quality in the Red River Valley. The development of the Minnesota Patent Process for milling hard red wheat was the other development that led to the bonanza farm phenomenon. The bonanza farms of the valley kept a steady supply of wheat flowing into Minneapolis, making it the milling capital of the world.

James B. Power was most responsible for the advent of bonanza farming in Dakota Territory. He believed that the best way to promote the area and settle the land was to dispose of railroad land to people who would establish large-scale commercial farms, which in turn would bring business to the railroad. The first bonanza farm was created in 1874 when Power convinced George Washington Cass, president of the Northern Pacific Railway, and Benjamin P. Cheney, a director of the railroad, to purchase land. The Cass-Cheney farm, as it was known, became the first bonanza farm. Cass and Cheney hired Oliver Dalrymple, a successful Minnesota wheat farmer, to manage their new farmland.

Dalrymple came to Minnesota Territory in 1856 to practice law. He farmed in Minnesota very successfully until 1874, but he lost his farming profits by speculating in the grain trade. Cass had come to know Dalrymple as a good farmer who used advanced farming techniques. Dalrymple's contract with Cass provided for gradual acquisition of the land he managed. Exercising this option, Dalrymple expanded his holdings to about 100,000 acres in the late 1890s with as much as 65,000 acres under cultivation. Pres. Rutherford B. Hayes even visited Dalrymple's bonanza farm near Casselton, North Dakota, on September 6, 1887.

Another successful bonanza farm was the Amenia and Sharon Land Company, which was incorporated in 1875. There were originally 40 stockholders, living in Amenia, New York, and Sharon, Connecticut, who pooled together their resources to make an initial purchase of nearly 28,000 acres of land. The largest stockholder was Eben W. Chaffee, who went to Dakota Territory to select land about 20 miles west of Fargo. The Amenia and Sharon Company built a depot and grain elevator on the Northern Pacific Railway, which eventually became the town of Amenia. At its height, the company held more than 58,000 acres with 42,000 under cultivation. Chaffee, who was just as powerful as Dalrymple but less well known, operated the farm until his death in 1893.

In 1878, the Cass farm managed by Dalrymple had a net profit in excess of $57,000. In 2006 dollars that is just a few thousand dollars short of a $1 million profit. A large profit, swiftly and in the short term, defined these corporate farms. Bonanza farms started to decline in number and size, however, when wheat prices dropped. As a result of overproduction of wheat at home and abroad, rising labor costs, and a change in weather patterns, bonanza farms were no longer able to maximize profitability. Farm owners began to sell off land to immigrants who operated much smaller and more diversified farms. Bonanza farms succeeded for a short time but in the end could not compete with diversified family farms.

Not all farms were bonanza farms. In fact, one of the unique aspects of bonanza farms was that there were never more than 100 of them. Most of the farms in Cass County, like the rest of the state, were small farms. For example, in 1870, there were 1,720 farms in all of Dakota Territory, with an average size of 176 acres. By 1910, there were more than 74,000 farms in North Dakota with an average size of 382 acres.

Gilbert Fite writes about the significance of bonanza farms in *The Farmers' Frontier*, "Bonanza farming in the Red River Valley had an important influence upon agriculture throughout the great unsettled West. It advertised the agricultural resources of the region as perhaps nothing else could have done. The reports of quick and large profits, even if exaggerated, excited the imagination of thousands of restless settlers and stimulated the rapid westward movement of the 1880s. Moreover, it is likely that the highly mechanized operations of large-scale farmers encouraged the more widespread use of machinery among smaller farmers who read about or witnessed first hand the new horse and steam powered equipment. The business that bonanza farming produced in the Red River Valley was highly important because it helped greatly to place the Northern Pacific Railroad on a sounder financial basis. This, in turn, permitted the company to build in western North Dakota and on to the Pacific Coast, where it played a significant role in the agricultural settlement all the way to Puget Sound. Finally, bonanza farming helped to present the West as a large, rich, expansive region only waiting to be exploited by the settlement of hundreds of thousands of additional farmers. It was both part of, and a stimulant to, the Great Dakota Boom."

In 1888, one Cass County booster wrote, "The United States exceeds any country in the world in the amount of wheat growing; Dakota any state or territory in the Union, and Cass any county in the territory." Early boosters on the Plains exaggerated a lot, but that boast about wheat growing was accurate. North Dakota leads the nation in production of several crops including durum and spring wheat, oats, barley, flaxseed, dry beans and peas, lentils, sunflower, and canola. Cass County leads the state in production of soy beans and is second in the state in spring wheat and corn production.

Despite the continued high agricultural production in Cass County, small towns throughout the county are dying. The United States Census Bureau lists the population of Cass County at 123,138 in 2000. The Fargo-Moorhead Chamber of Commerce estimated the 2005 county population at 128,615. The Fargo-Moorhead Chamber estimated the city of Fargo 2005 population at 91,048. West Fargo is the county's second-largest city, with a 2005 estimated population of 17,581. Subtracting the cities of Fargo and West Fargo, the population of rural Cass County was estimated at 19,986 in 2005. The third-largest city is Casselton, with a 2005 estimated population of 1,891. The combined population of the rest of the small towns averages less than 300.

"Much of the history of North Dakota is explained by its colonial status," writes David Danbom in an essay on North Dakota in the book entitled *Heartland: Comparative Histories of the Midwestern States*. "All Midwestern states endured a colonial phase, in which they were dominated economically, socially, culturally, and politically by outsiders. But in North Dakota, this phase never ended. North Dakota exports raw fossil fuels, unfinished farm products, and young people and imports finished products and capital." The future of rural Cass County is one of continued population decline. The city of Fargo is consistently ranked as one of the best places to live in America because of its medical facilities, education, transportation, and high standard of living, among other things. It does have the distinction of having a very important and unique history with its bonanza farms.

The Northern Pacific Railroad divides Cass County in half east to west, and the Great Northern Railroad bisects the county from the northern border to Casselton before angling to the east. Follow the Great Northern line south and the county is split into quarters. For a more modern division, Interstate 94 now divides the county in half east to west and State Highway 18 divides the county north to south forming four quarters. In order to present the photographs of the county in a somewhat equal proportion, not according to population, we decided to divide the book into four geographical chapters. Moving clockwise, chapter one is northwestern, chapter two is northeastern, chapter three is southeastern, and chapter four is southwestern Cass County.

Each chapter contains a mixture of photographs of people, town, and rural scenes including schools, churches, businesses, railroads, farming, and recreation, among other things. An index at the back of the book is organized by town name only. A bibliography is also included, but it is intended to be more of a list of books for further reading.

Well-known and unknown photographs are featured, and the book contains virtually no information or photographs about the city of Fargo. We excluded Fargo because there is an excellent pictorial history entitled *Fargo, North Dakota, 1870-1940*, by David Danbom and Claire Strom that supplies that history and photographs. The Fargo book is also part of the Images of America series and is still in print.

Please enjoy this latest installment in the history of Cass County, North Dakota.

# *One*

# Northwestern Cass County

In northwestern Cass County, seven towns dot the prairie: Absaraka, Ayr, Buffalo, Erie, Page, Tower City, and Wheatland.

Absaraka, the story goes, was named by a local resident, Mrs. John Hay, who noticed crows flying in the area and decided to call it "Home of the Crows," or in Dakota, "Absaraka." Other anecdotal evidence claims that the town name is a corruption of an early Hidatsa Indian tribe that inhabited the area called the "sparrow hawk people," or "Absaroke." The first white man to own land where Absaraka is located was Chester Thompson. Absaraka had existed since 1881, but Thompson did not have a town site surveyed and platted until 1885. Before that, Thompson offered free lots to anyone who would build a home or business in town. Thompson also donated the lots for a school and church. Absaraka is located on the Great Northern Railway in Empire Township 10 miles northwest of Casselton.

The story of the origin of Ayr is that it was named for Ayr, Scotland, where some early settlers were from. The Park Farm was responsible for donating land that eventually became the town. It was first called Fleming and then Elgin, but since an Elgin already existed on the railway, it was changed to Ayr. F. H. Dickenson was credited with naming the town in 1884. Dickenson managed the elevator alongside the railroad tracks. The first store and school were built in 1884. The population of Ayr has decreased from 107 in 1940 to its current population of 22. Ayr is located about 20 miles northwest of Casselton, and it is credited with being the smallest town in Cass County.

The plat for Buffalo was recorded in Cass County in 1880. It is located about 20 miles west of Casselton. The town was incorporated in 1883, and by that year there were already 36 businesses in town. The first settlers in the area of Buffalo were the H. B. Strand family, who arrived in 1878. Strand was the first postmaster and opened the first business. A Northern Pacific Railroad promotional brochure for Buffalo in 1904 said, "Buffalo, No. Dak. has 600 inhabitants, one hotel, two restaurants, newspaper, graded school, three elevators, three churches, machinery warehouse, one hardware store, two blacksmith shops, four general stores, telephone, and one bank. Produces wheat, oats, flax, and corn." Buffalo had a population high of 261 in 1950 and currently has a population of 209.

In order to get the railroad to build where they wanted, Frank Williams and George Churchill went to the top of a hill, drove a post into the ground, and painted "Erie, D.T." on it—which was the name of their hometown: Erie, Pennsylvania. Their scheme worked because in 1881 the Great Northern Railroad built a line through what became the town of Erie. A combined store and post office was built in 1882, and the school district was formed in 1881. In its early years, Erie had a doctor, dentist, hotel, livery barn, three grocery stores, barbershop, pool hall, butcher shop, millinery shop, drugstore, bank, restaurant, post office, machinery shop, furniture store, lumberyard, shoemaker, harness maker, blacksmith shop, three elevators, railroad depot, and gas stations. Erie was built on the Great Northern Railway about 20 miles northwest of Casselton.

The town of Page is in the northwest corner of Cass County, 60 miles by road from Fargo, making it the town furthest from the county seat. Page is located at the intersection of four townships—Rochester, Page, Rich, and Lake—on the old Great Northern Railroad. Page was founded by George Cook in 1882. It had all the amenities of other small towns in Cass County. In the 1960s, the Brass Rail Saloon and Hotel was moved from the town to the Cass County Historical Society museum, Bonanzaville, in West Fargo. Page had a population high of 482 in 1950 and currently has a population of 225 residents. It is about 35 miles northwest of Casselton.

Charlemagne Tower, a director of the Northern Pacific Railroad from Philadelphia, owned the land on which the town of Tower City was built. In April 1879, George Ellsbury surveyed the land and named the town for Tower. Settlement began in earnest shortly thereafter, and by 1881, Tower City had about 500 residents. In 1883, there were three churches, a new schoolhouse, two hotels, a bank, a public hall, a newspaper, a steam elevator, a bed spring factory, and the Tower City Milling Company. In the 1880s, $15,000 was offered to the state of North Dakota if it would locate the capital in Tower City. The offer was refused because Bismarck offered $100,000 and 160 acres of land for the capitol building. The year 1883 marked the population high for Tower City at about 800. The current population is 252, up from a historic low of 233 in 1990. Tower City is 25 miles west of Casselton and about 16 miles east of Valley City, the seat of Barnes County, on Interstate 94.

In 1872, the Northern Pacific Railroad came through the area west of Casselton and built a station named Second Siding. In 1878, a post office and general store were opened with William Turner as postmaster. Hanna Brown from New York was known as the proprietress of the town because she owned the section of land where the town was located. In 1879, she had the site platted and the name changed to Wheatland after the large wheat fields nearby. It is located six miles west of Casselton.

Roy Faught, pictured here in 1937, operated the general store in Absaraka from 1936 to 1942 when he sold the business to his brother John. The Absaraka Store, as it was known, was built in 1888 by William Staples, the son of a merchant from Minnesota. After moving to Absaraka in the late 1800s, Staples built the town's first elevator, general store, lumberyard, and other businesses in addition to operating a large farm.

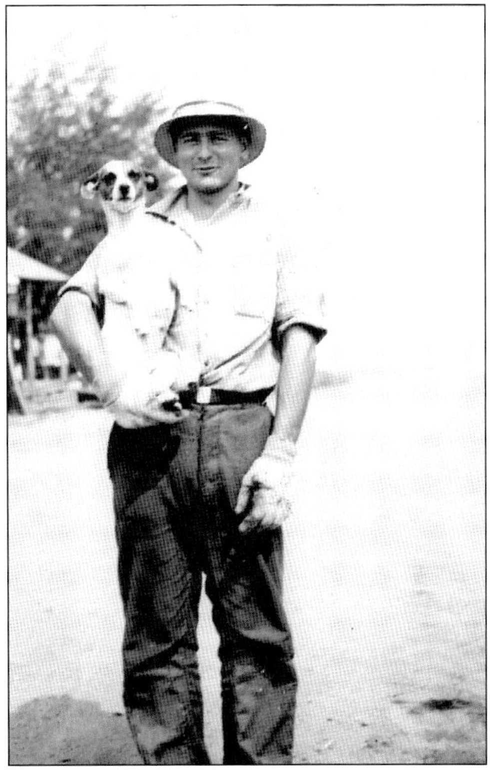

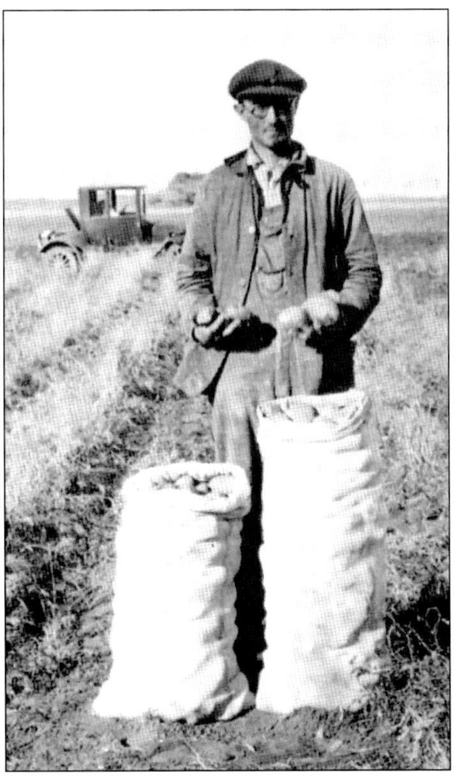

Robert E. Monilaws of Absaraka compares fertilized potatoes on the right side of the picture to unfertilized potatoes on the left side of the picture around 1924. By fertilizing the fields, farmers gained 31 bushels of potatoes per acre. Monilaws continued farming the land his parents homesteaded in 1879 near Absaraka.

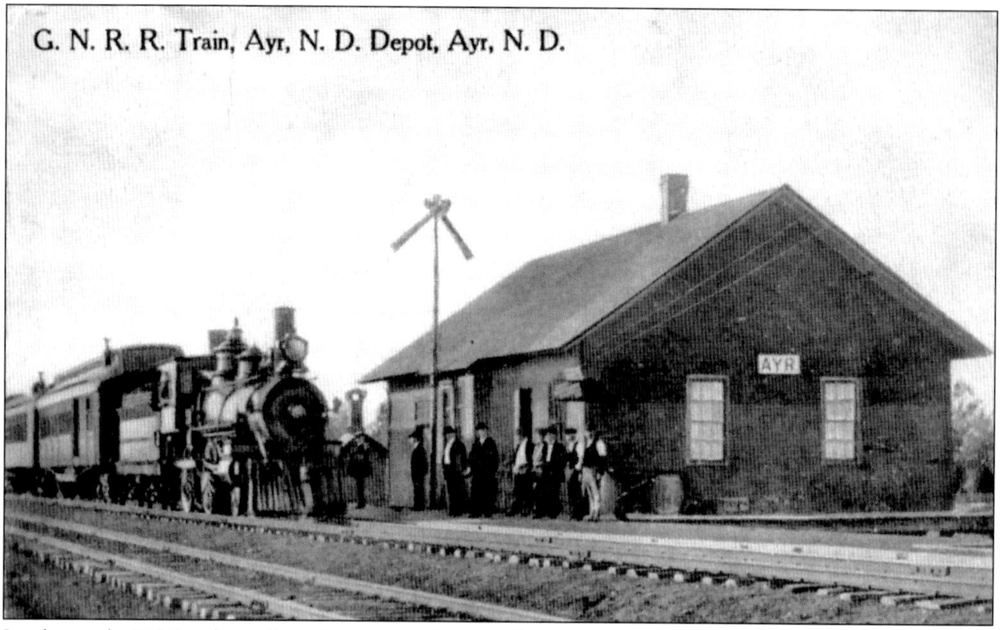


In the early 1880s, the railroad continued expanding westward across the county. In 1882, the Great Northern Railroad reached what later became the town of Ayr. Grain from local farms was hauled by teams of mules to neighboring towns before the Park Farm Elevator and the Cargill Elevator were built next to the depot in Ayr. The land for the original town site was donated by the Park Farm.

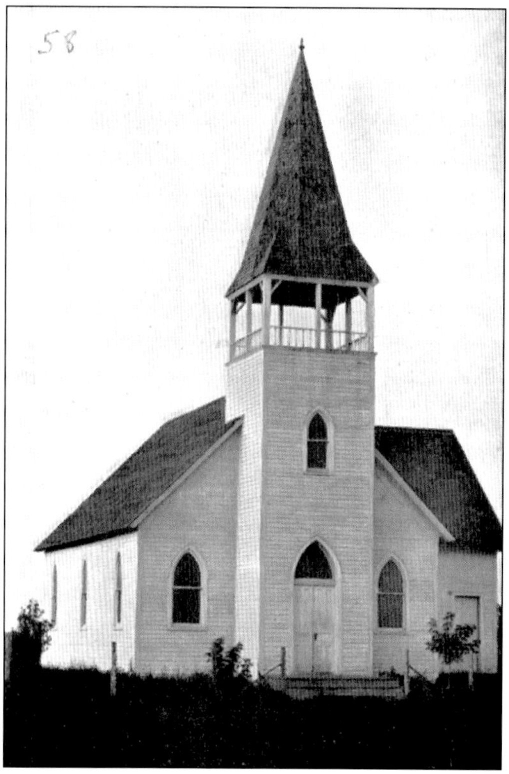

The Ayr Presbyterian Church was organized in 1883 by men originally from Scotland who worked on the Park Farm. The congregation began planning a church building in 1901. It was completed by 1904, after land for the church was donated by a local resident. This photograph of the church was probably taken a few years after it was erected.

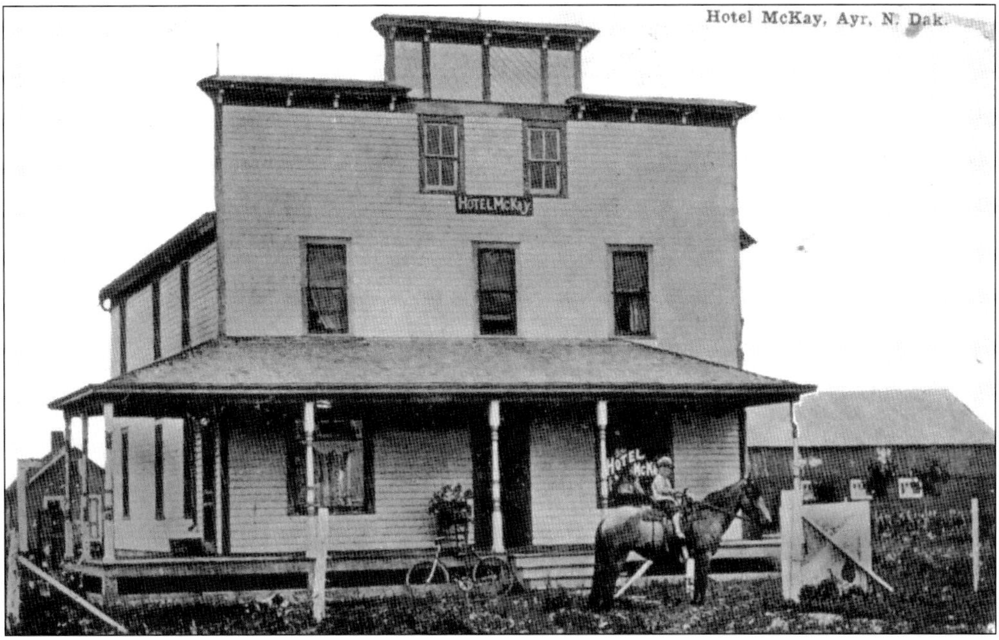


Many small towns along the railroad had hotels where men working for the railroad company could spend the night and get a bite to eat. Bars were often located in the lobby of hotels before North Dakota became a "dry state" on July 1, 1890. Prohibition was not repealed in North Dakota until 1932. The Hotel McKay is seen here during the 1890s.

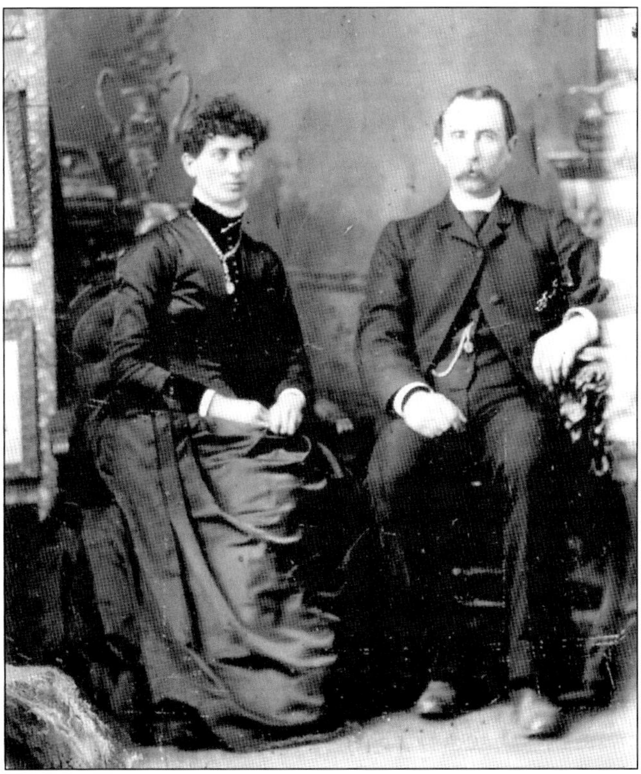

John Beattie and his wife, Margaret Ellen Thompson Beattie, sit for a portrait after their wedding in 1889. John was born in Scotland in 1859. His family moved to Ontario, Canada, before homesteading near Ayr in 1881. Many of the early settlers of Ayr were immigrants from Scotland. Originally named Fleming and then Elgin, the town was renamed Ayr in 1884 after a city of the same name in Scotland.

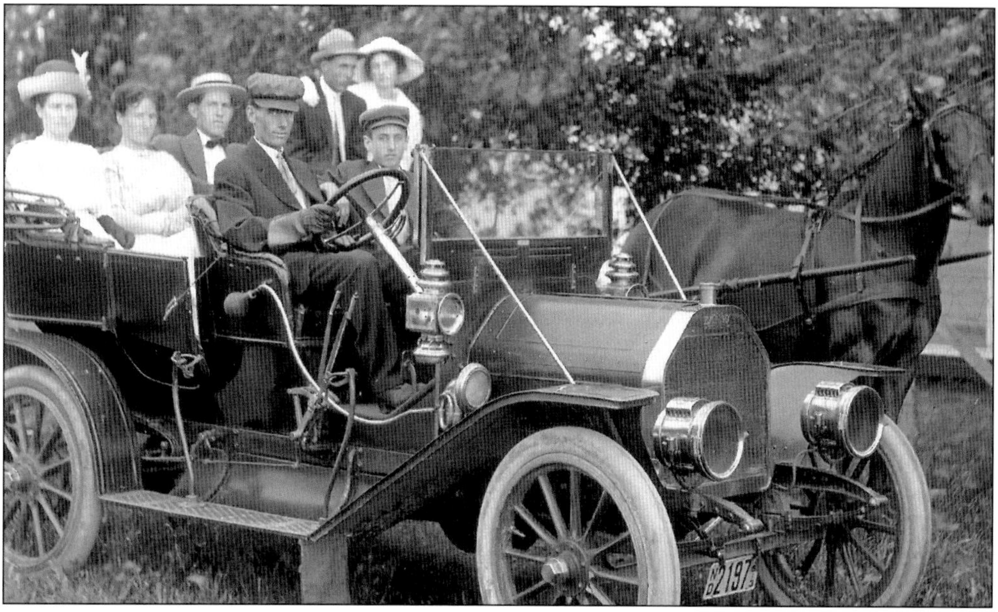

The early 1900s saw a revolution in transportation as horse-drawn vehicles were phased out in favor of automobiles and internal combustion engines. In this 1913 photograph from Ayr, a family sits in their E-M-F 30 automobile in front of a horse and buggy. Many early automobile companies, such as E-M-F, were short lived. E-M-F was notorious for building poorly crafted vehicles before being bought by the Studebaker Company.

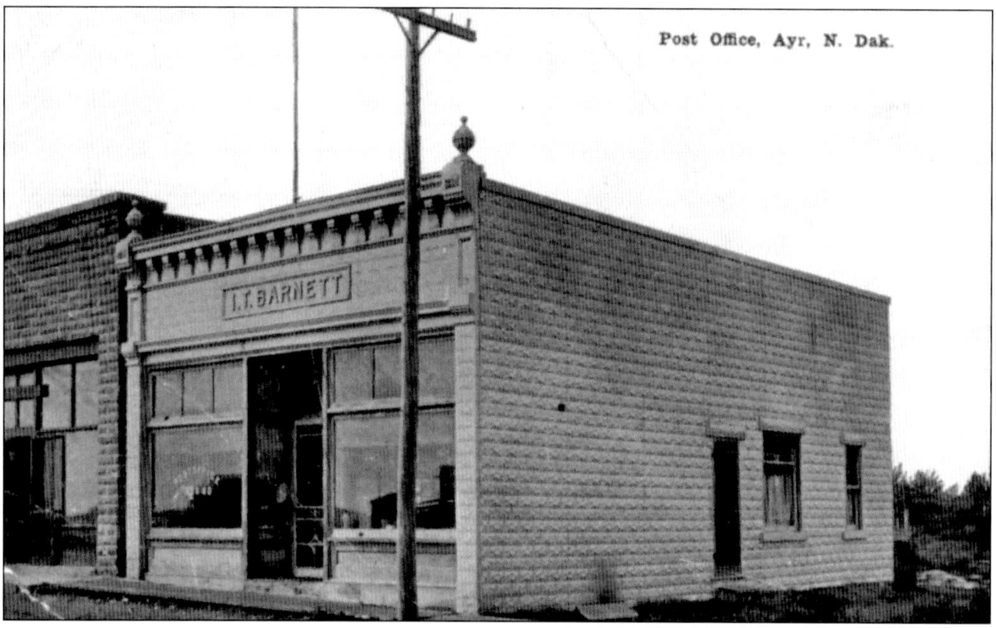


I. T. Barnett came to Dakota Territory in 1879 and married Eliza Boston in 1883. They moved to Ayr in 1890 where he built and operated a restaurant and boardinghouse. The building burned down but was rebuilt using stone. Barnett became postmaster in 1907 and operated the post office out of his commercial building. He continued as postmaster until his death in 1940.

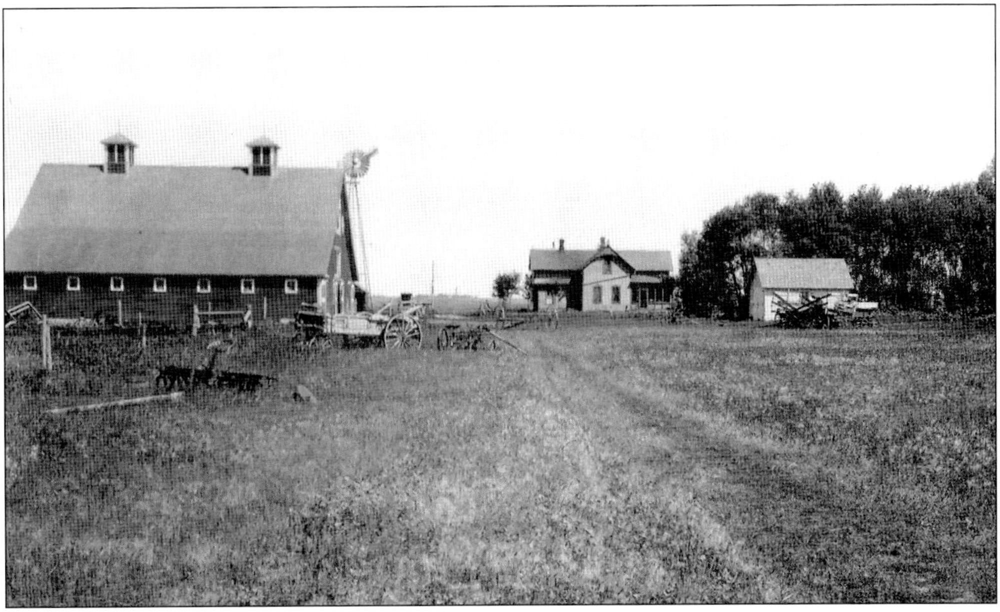

Andrew Jensen and Henry Brown return home from a fishing trip with a pole full of fish. Both men homesteaded near Buffalo and became merchants. Jensen left his home in Denmark and moved to Iowa where, in 1876, he married Ingebord, who was also from Denmark. Three years later, the couple moved to the Red River Valley where they homesteaded. In 1898, Jensen left the farm to seek his fortune in the Klondike gold rush, making several trips between North Dakota and Alaska. The family continued to profit from the mining interests even after Jensen returned to North Dakota. Five of the Jensen's children graduated from North Dakota Agricultural College, two graduated from Valley City Teachers College, and one graduated from the University of North Dakota. The Jensens' farm is pictured above, around 1900.

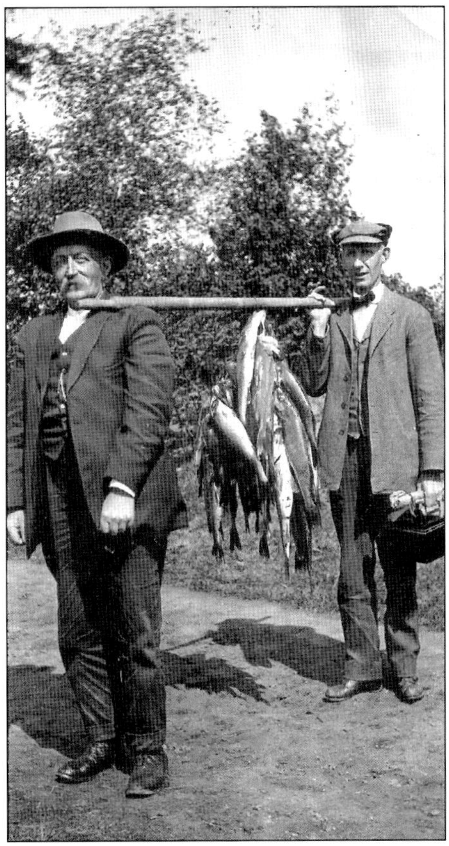

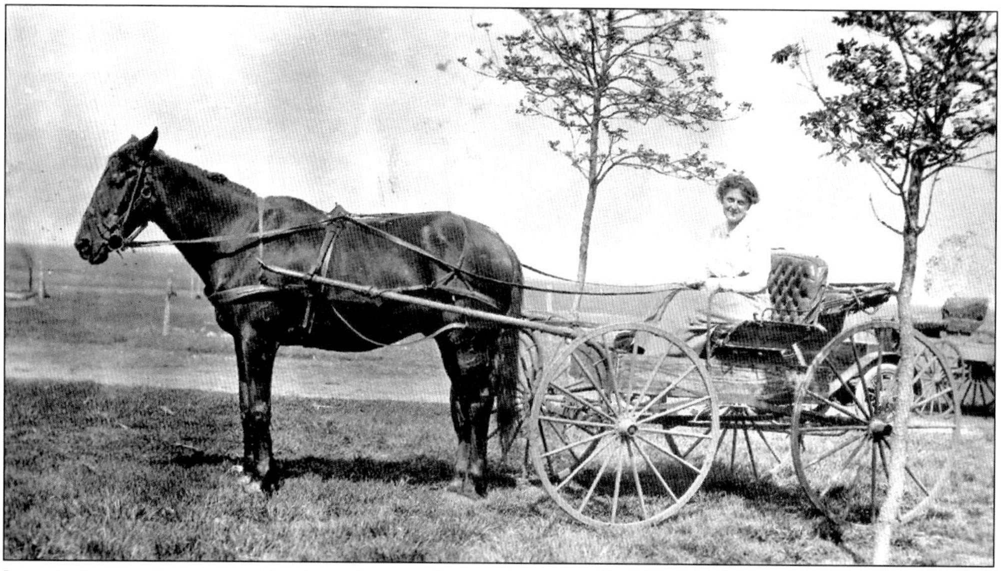

Jennie Jensen-Petersen rides in a buggy that is being pulled by her horse named Dexter near Buffalo, North Dakota, around 1910. Before automobiles became common, the best and fastest way to travel in Cass County was by using a horse and buggy. Even after automobiles were introduced, many continued riding in horse-drawn buggies because heavy gas-powered automobiles often became stuck in the region's muddy roads.

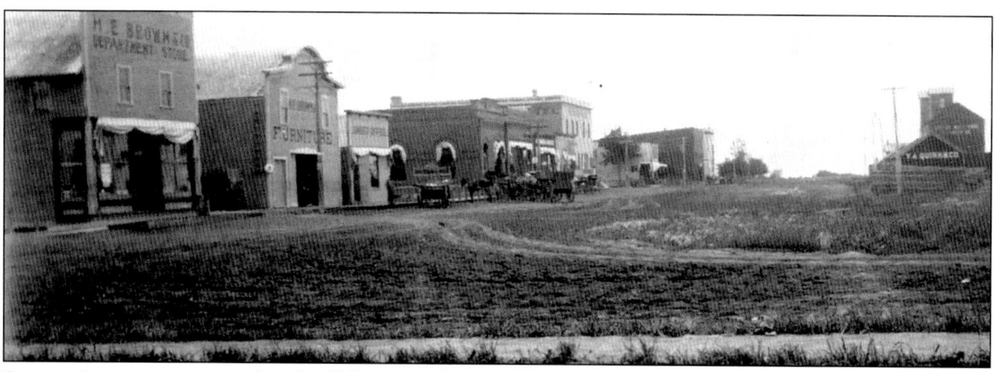

Strong Avenue is pictured in Buffalo around 1890. The building on the left is the H. E. Brown and Company department store, followed by the H. E. Brown Furniture store and the lumber office. On the right of the photograph is T. A Quirk and Company. A grain elevator is in the background.

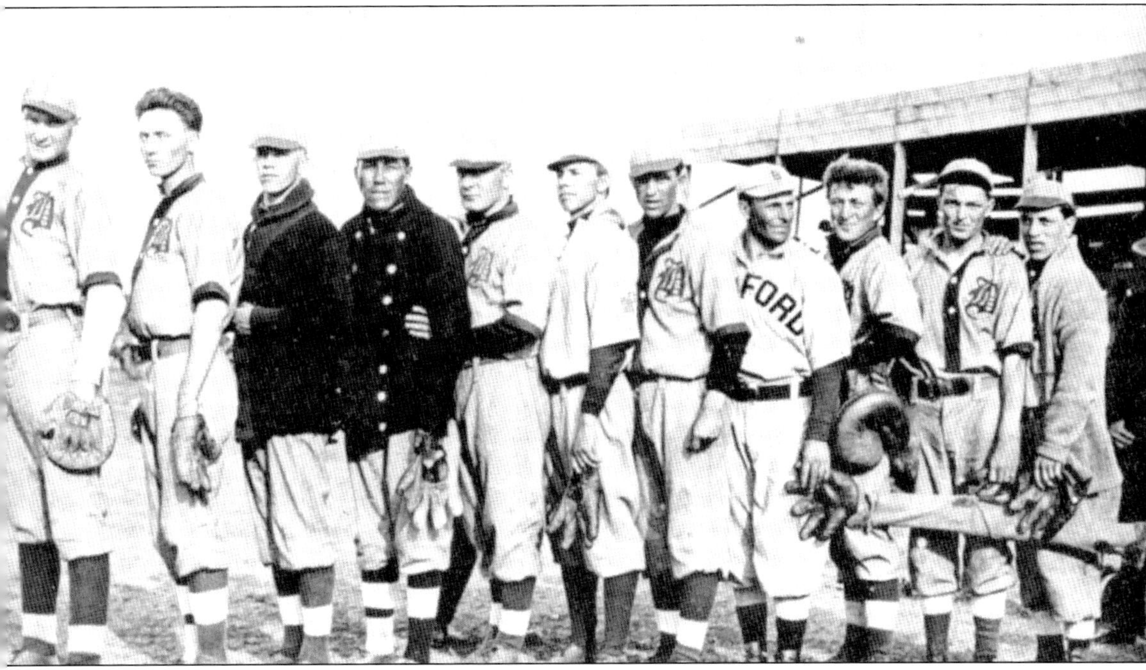

The Buffalo baseball team poses for a photograph in July 1913; that same month they defeated the team from Tower City who reportedly hired paid professionals for the game. Harry Christensen, fifth from the left, fought in World War I. He also owned and operated the Buffalo Light and Telephone Company before selling the business to Otter Tail Power Company and Northwest Bell Telephone Company in 1929. Christensen's wife, Myra, taught English and Latin at the high school in Buffalo from 1914 to 1920. Second from the right is Lewie Easton, who bought the U-R Next Barber Shop in Buffalo from W. J. Frederick in 1909, which he operated until his death in 1966. Easton also served as the town's mayor for a time.

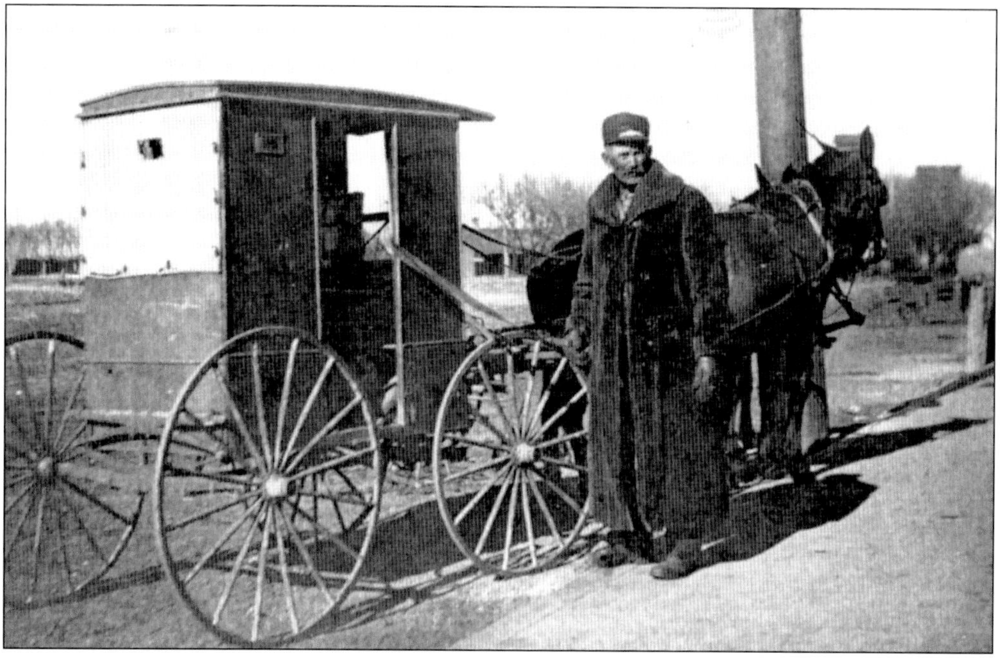

Peter Masterson poses with his mail wagon in 1903. Masterson was appointed Buffalo's first mail carrier earlier that year. During the winter, Masterson used a horse-drawn sleigh instead of the wagon. Buffalo had two mail routes: one north, one south. Mail was delivered to the north one day and to the south the next day, six days a week.

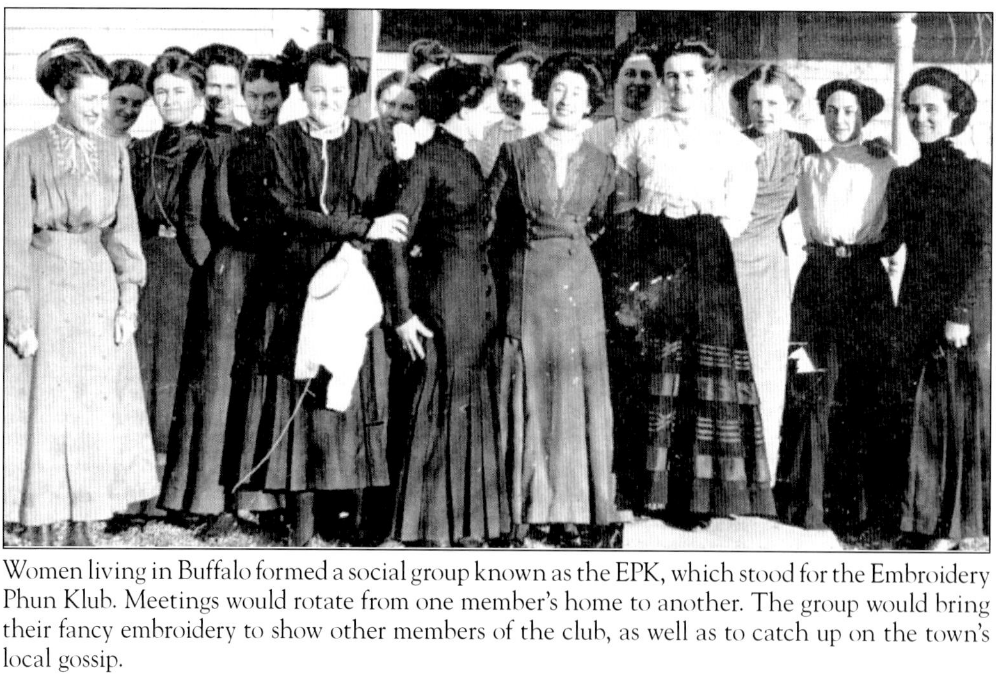

Women living in Buffalo formed a social group known as the EPK, which stood for the Embroidery Phun Klub. Meetings would rotate from one member's home to another. The group would bring their fancy embroidery to show other members of the club, as well as to catch up on the town's local gossip.

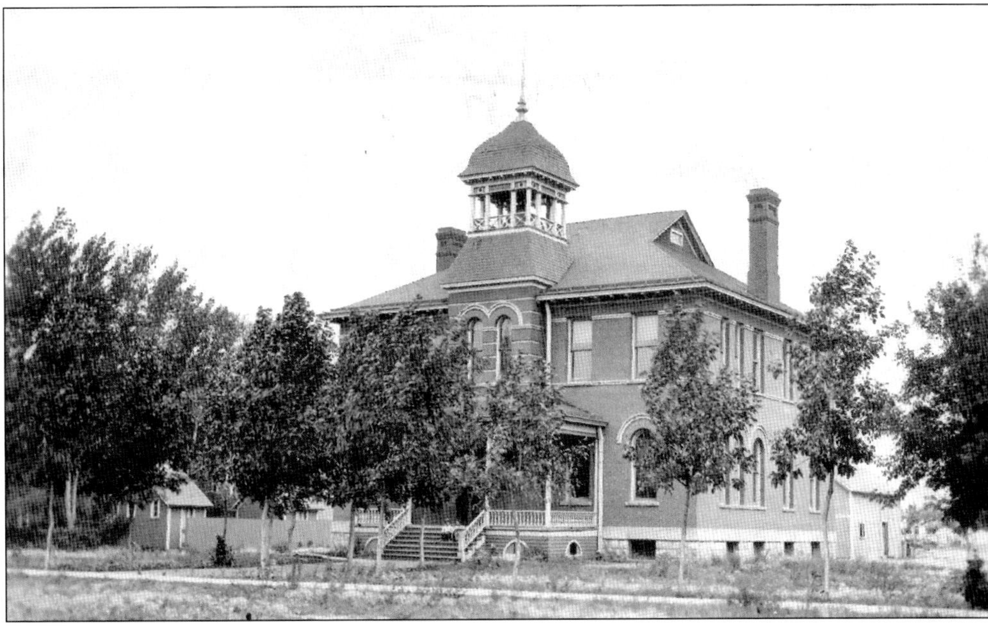

Buffalo's first school opened in 1880. The building was also used as a church until a new school was built seven years later and the old building was sold to Buffalo Township to be used as the township hall. The town's second school building burned but was rebuilt using brick at a cost of $12,000 in 1902. This c. 1910 photograph is of the sturdier school building.

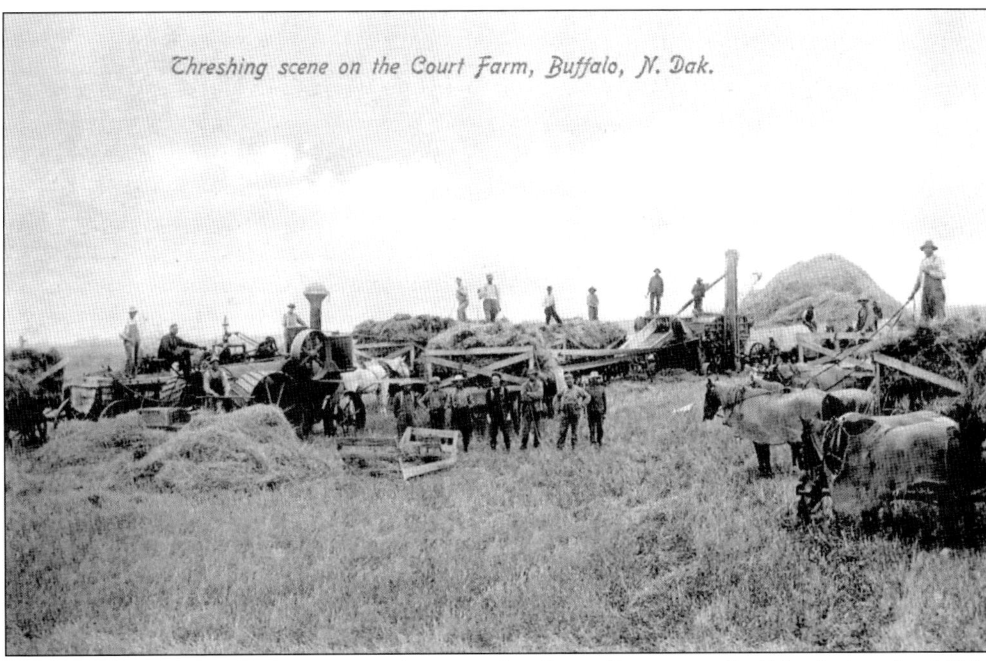


A threshing crew works to process wheat on the Court Farm near Buffalo during the 1890s. Horse power and steam power were used to harvest and thresh wheat on farms across the county during this time. In this case, a steam tractor drives a belt that operates a threshing machine. Farmers toss wheat into the machine to be processed.

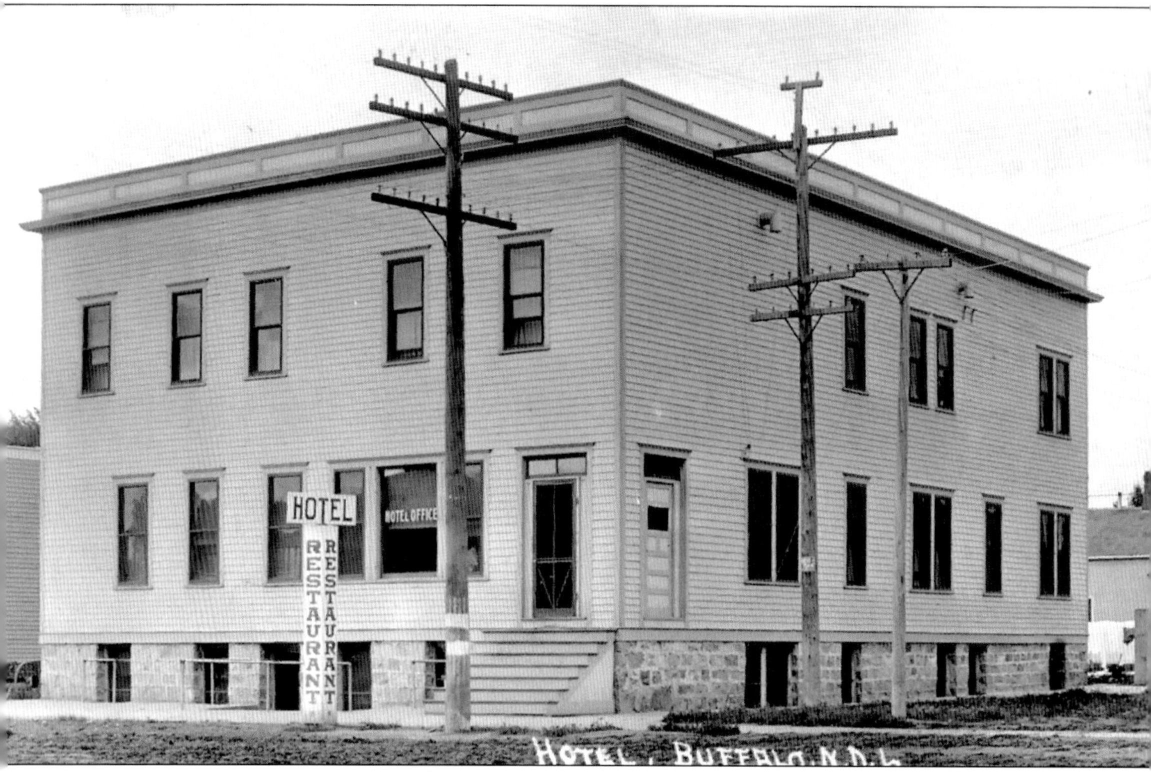


In 1902, M. L. Vinson, a single woman at the time, purchased a lot in Buffalo where Nels Kringler operated a blacksmith shop that burned down two years earlier. Vinson's plan was to build a hotel and have her father, John Vinson, run the establishment. The hotel was built then sold only six years later. Over the following years, the hotel was remodeled and sold various times. The building was dismantled in 1972. While in operation, the hotel contained a dining room and ballroom that held many community functions. The first floor was often rented out as a restaurant and also held a post office at one time. After later attempts at remodeling the building, rooms were rented out as apartments. It is reported that several of the town's teachers lived at the hotel during this time. Toward the end of its life, the building was used as an apartment building for senior citizens. The Buffalo Hotel is pictured here with a restaurant in the main level during the 1920s.

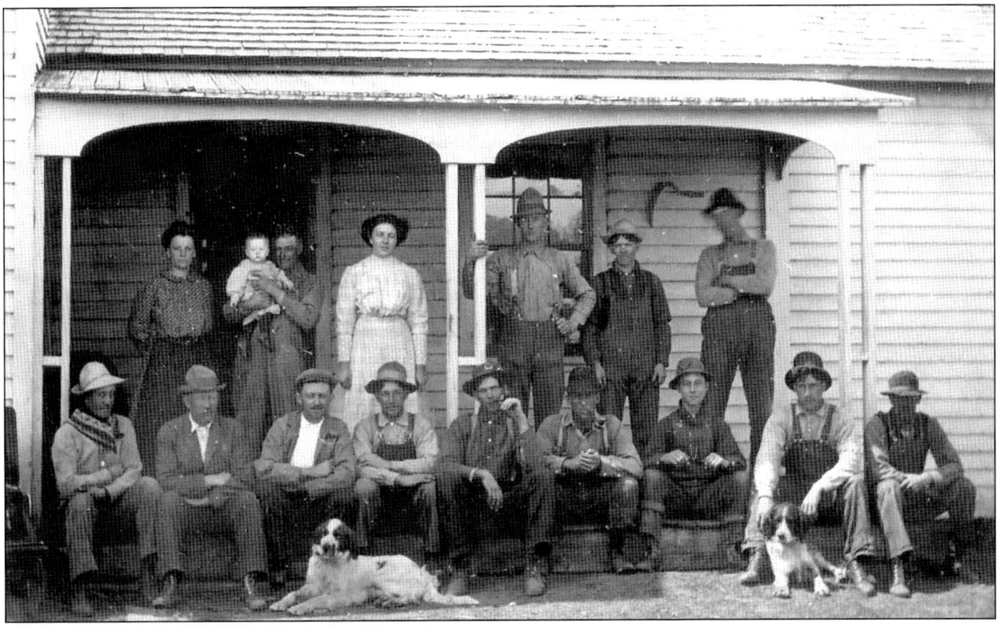

Farm workers stand on the porch of their living quarters near Buffalo, around 1911. This postcard photograph is addressed to R. J. Fields of Saint Paul, Minnesota. The writer is wondering if Fields will be coming to Buffalo in the fall to help operate the threshing machine. Most threshing rigs were powered by steam engine tractors, which could explode if not operated properly.

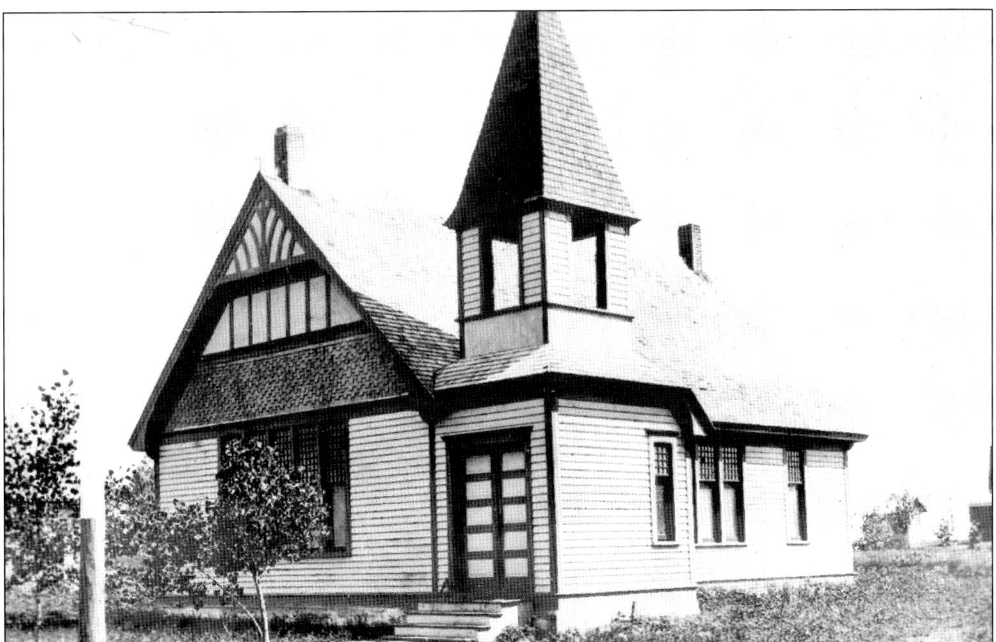

Originally organized in 1889, the church had to be reestablished in 1892 because its records had been lost. Reverend Featherstone became the church's first official pastor in 1892. A small church building was erected around 1902. This photograph of the First Presbyterian Church of Erie was probably taken shortly after the building's construction.

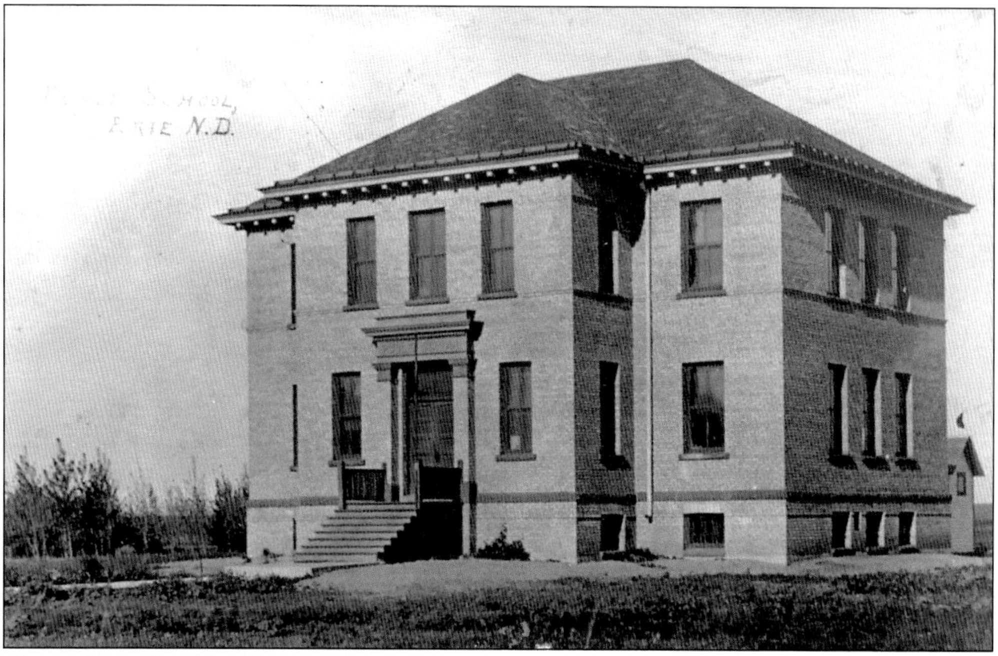

This public school building in Erie, built around 1900, was used until 1967 when the school closed. Students from the Erie school were then sent to Page, Hunter, and Arthur. Many small towns in Cass County have been faced with closing their doors or consolidating due to a reduction in rural populations.

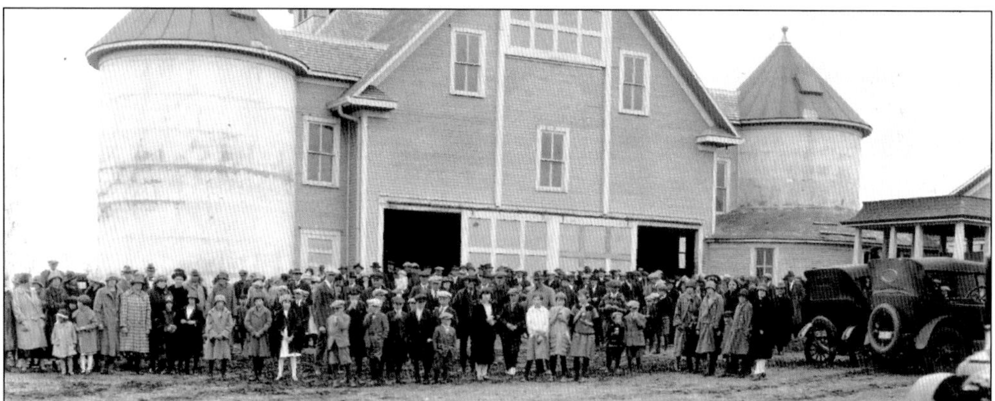

A large group of children and adults is gathered in front of a barn on the Harley family farm for a photograph between 1910 and 1920. What appears to be the porch of the farmhouse can be seen on the right of the photograph behind parked automobiles. The massive barn, in most of the background, was probably used in a dairy cow operation.

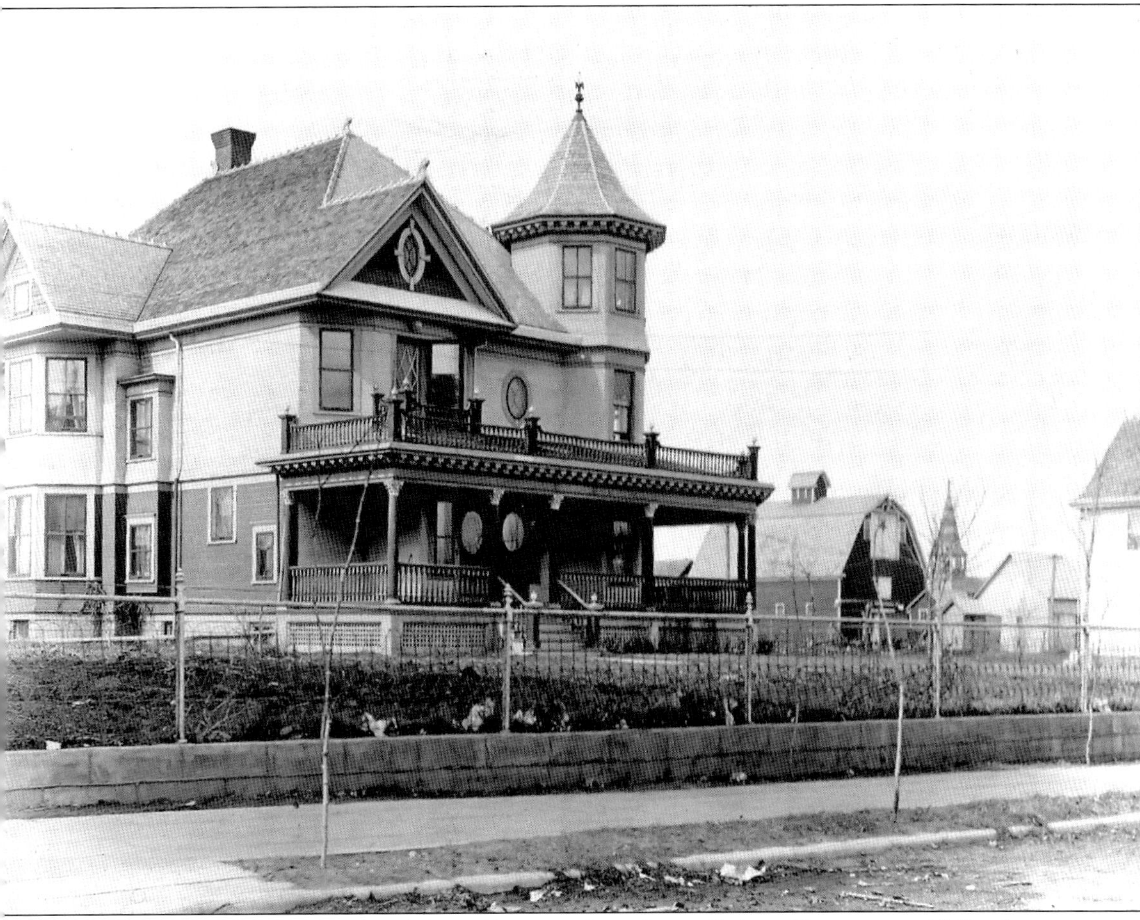

William James Thompson moved from Ontario, Canada, to Dakota Territory in 1879, where he began farming. He married Isabel Beattie, a Scottish immigrant from Ayr, North Dakota, in 1882. The couple moved to Page seven years later. Thompson continued farming while he built a two-story brick building in Page that housed apartments, a general store, and the Farmers State Bank. The luxurious home pictured was built in 1914 on Main Street in Page by Thompson and was completely furnished by Marshall Fields of Chicago, according to information written on the back of the photograph. The family lived in the home for four years before moving to Fargo. While in Fargo, Thompson built and owned several drugstores, meat markets, icehouses, and other businesses. Despite Thompson's interests in Fargo, he continued to own and operate an extensive wheat farm.

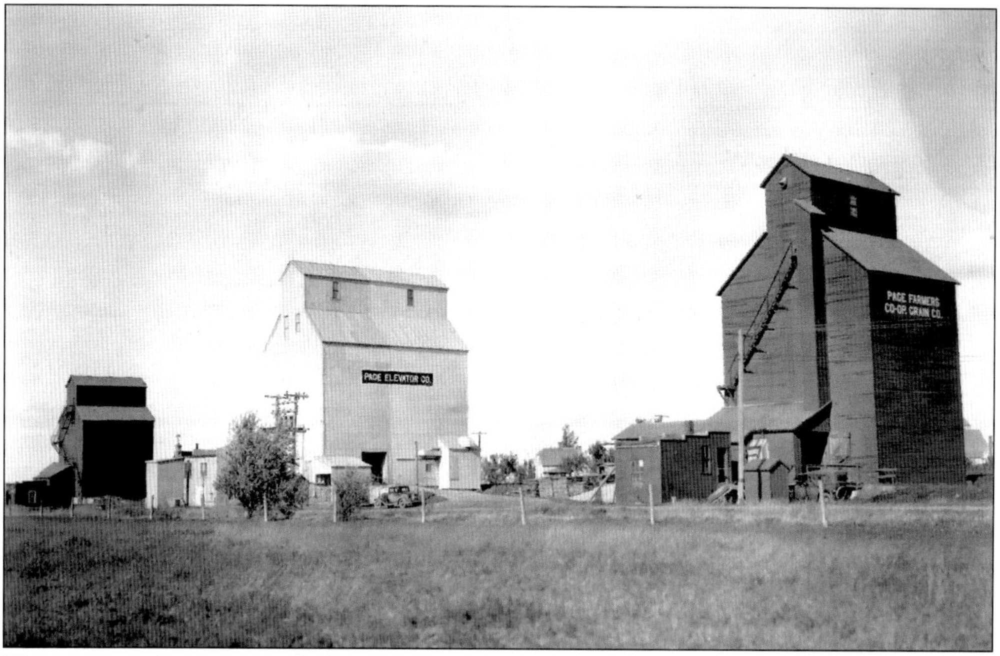


Three grain elevators stand alongside the Great Northern Railroad line running through Page during the 1920s. The first elevator was built in Page by the Cargill Company during the mid-1880s after reports that 50,000 bushels of wheat were shipped from the town in 1883. By the early 1900s, six grain elevators were operating in Page.

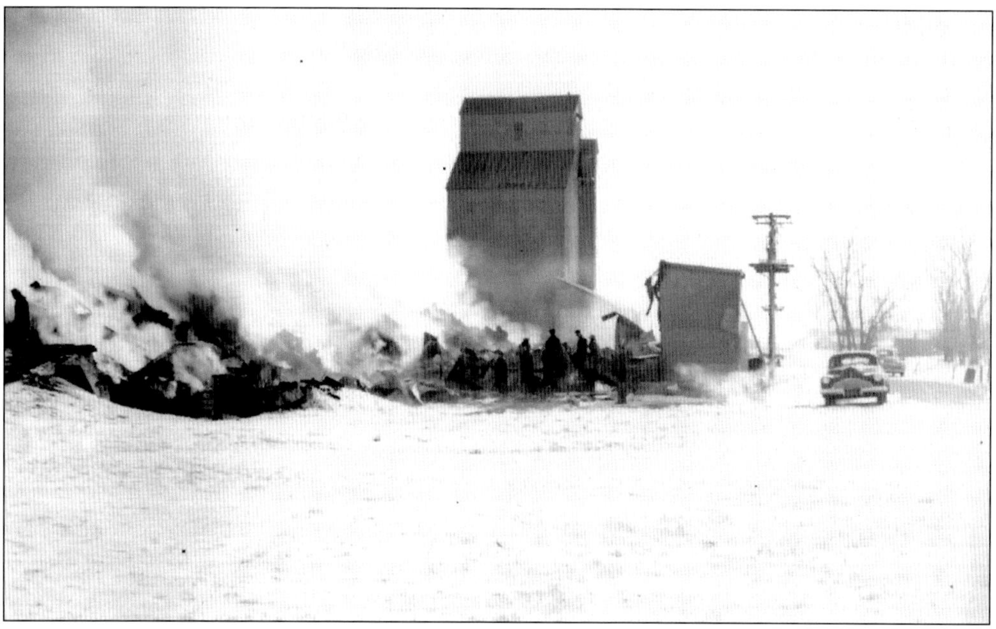

The Page Elevator smolders after burning down in February 1946. The building began burning and was fueled by high winds that carried sparks all the way to the other side of town. Buildings next to the elevator caught fire several times, but the flames were extinguished by the local fire department. Despite efforts to save the grain inside, nothing could be salvaged.

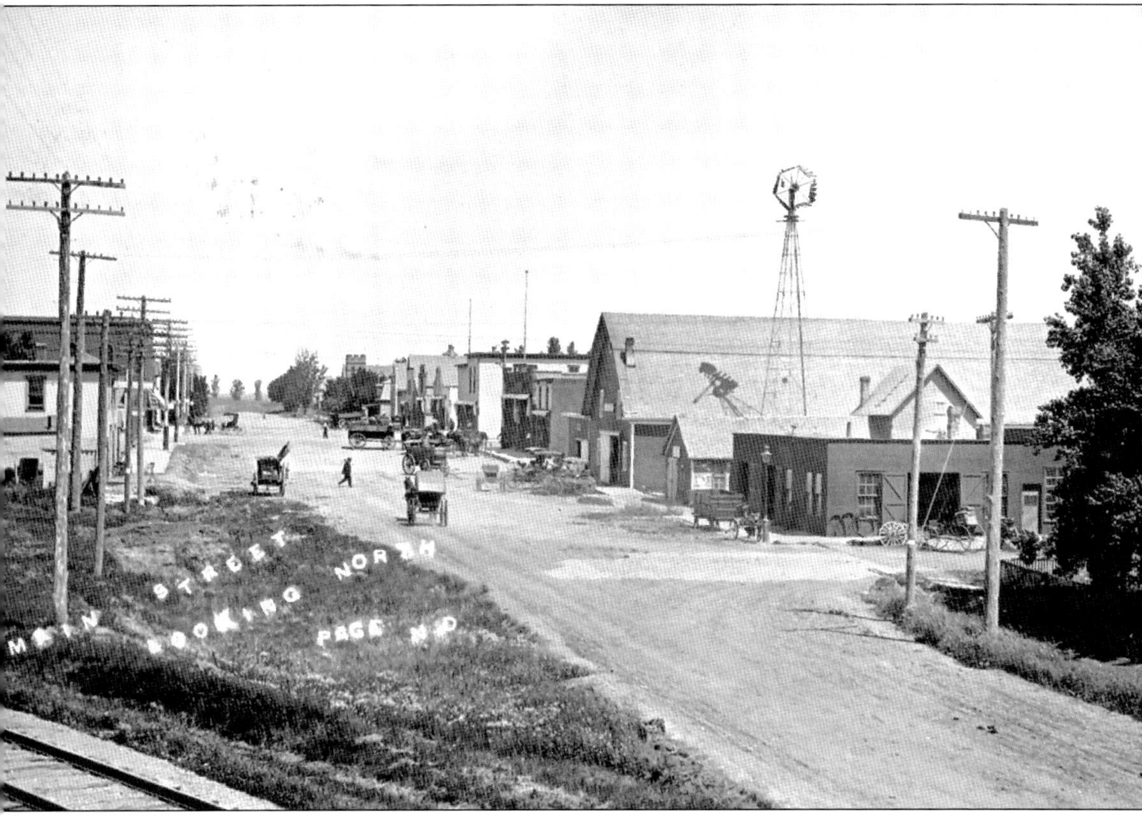


This is Page's Main Street looking north from the Great Northern Railroad tracks around 1911. The first building on the left is the Brass Rail Saloon and Hotel. The business was run under Bert "Jappe" Trenneman. Rooms were available upstairs from the saloon. The hotel was near the Great Northern Railroad, and workers from the line would come into town late at night for a room. They could walk upstairs and stay for the night, then pay in the morning once the saloon had opened. Each room had ropes hanging next to the window as a fire escape. Water for the bathroom was brought up and down the stairs each morning. After the hotel was closed, the building was operated as a museum in the town of Page for a short time. The building was eventually moved to the grounds of the Cass County Historical Society.

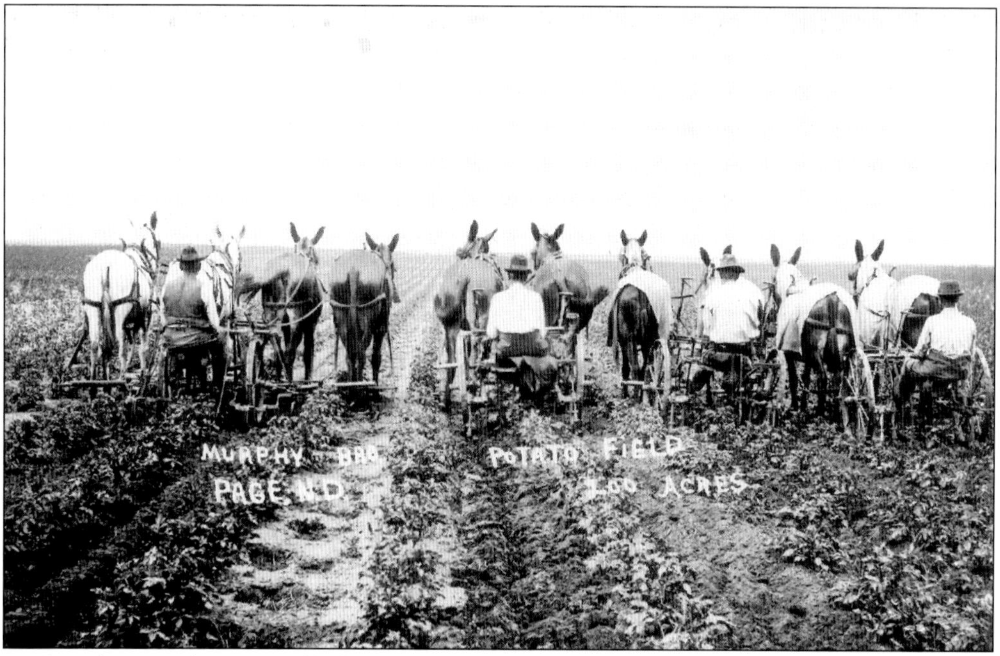


In this photograph, men pull plows on the Murphy Brothers' farm around 1910–1920. The Murphy Brothers grew over 200 acres of potatoes on their farm near Page. Most farmers in the Red River Valley planted grain crops. When the soil became depleted of nutrients, some began planting potatoes and sugar beets instead.

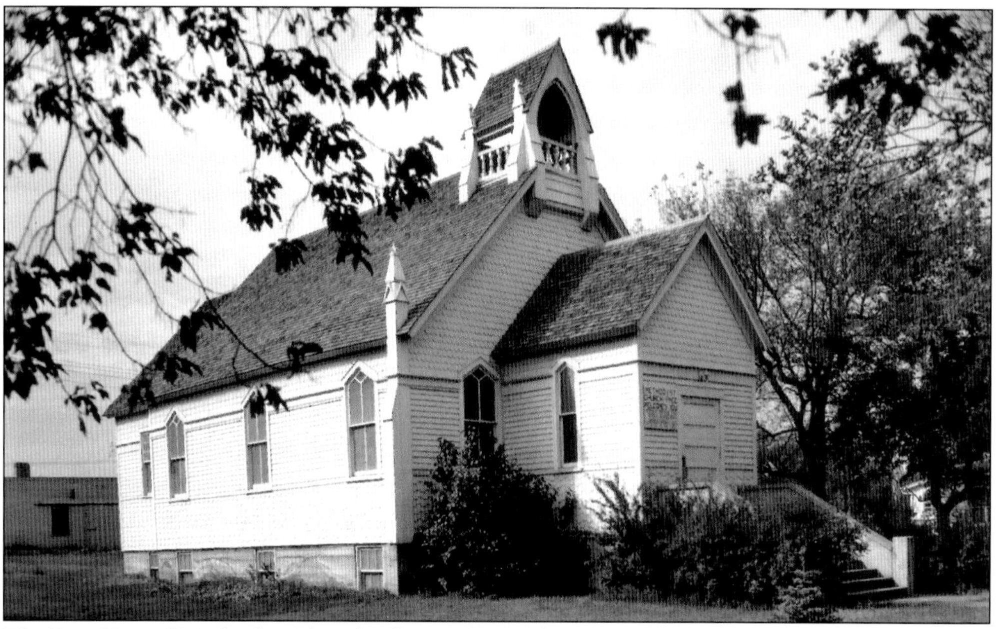

The First United Methodist Church of Page, shown during the 1950s, was built in the mid-1890s. It was not the first church organized in the community, but it is the oldest building still standing in the city of Page as of the late 1970s. The building was moved after the construction of a foundation. The church bell was taken down in the 1970s and now marks where the church originally stood.

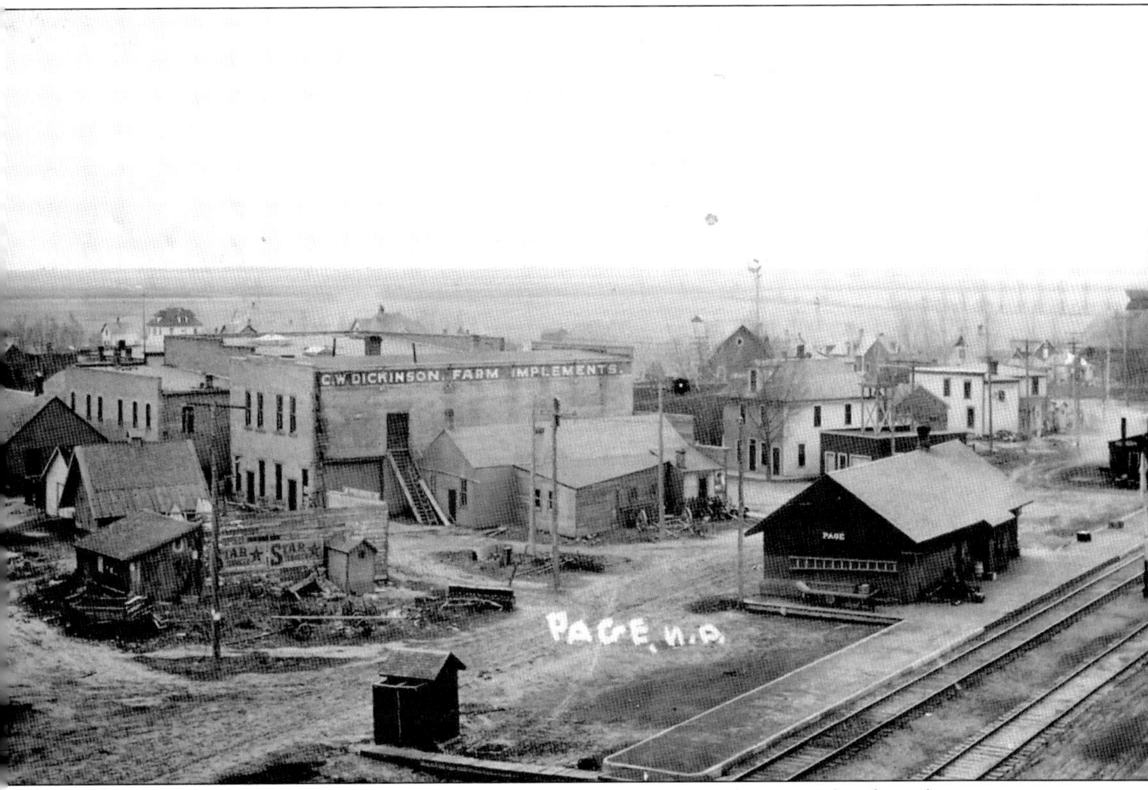


The train depot in Page was completed in 1883. G. G. Hartley was the first depot agent. Reportedly, the Great Northern Railroad could not find anyone who wanted the job of depot agent in the town of Page. James J. Hill, president of Great Northern Railroad, personally asked Hartley to serve as an agent for the depot that was to be built in Page. Hartley, who farmed land near town, agreed under the condition that he would be able to choose the design of the depot for the town. Hill agreed, and several plans were presented for Hartley's approval. He chose the most expensive design. The depot was used until the mid-1970s. It was purchased by a local resident and moved to be used as a warehouse and shop. The C. W. Dickinson Farm Implement building can be seen in the background of this c. 1912 photograph. Dickinson's Implement sold a total of 16 Deering binders in 1901, mostly to new farmers in the area.

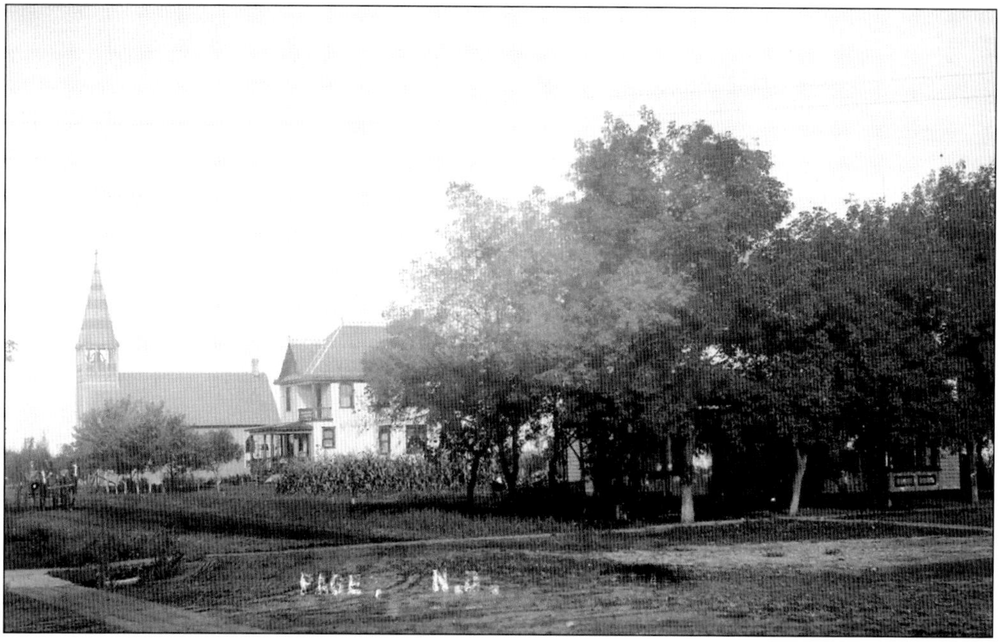


The original St. James Catholic Church in Page is pictured in the background of this photograph from the late 1890s or early 1900s. Construction for the church began in 1893. In 1916, a tornado ripped through Page moving the church eight feet from its foundation. The building was sold or torn down to make room for a new church built later that year.

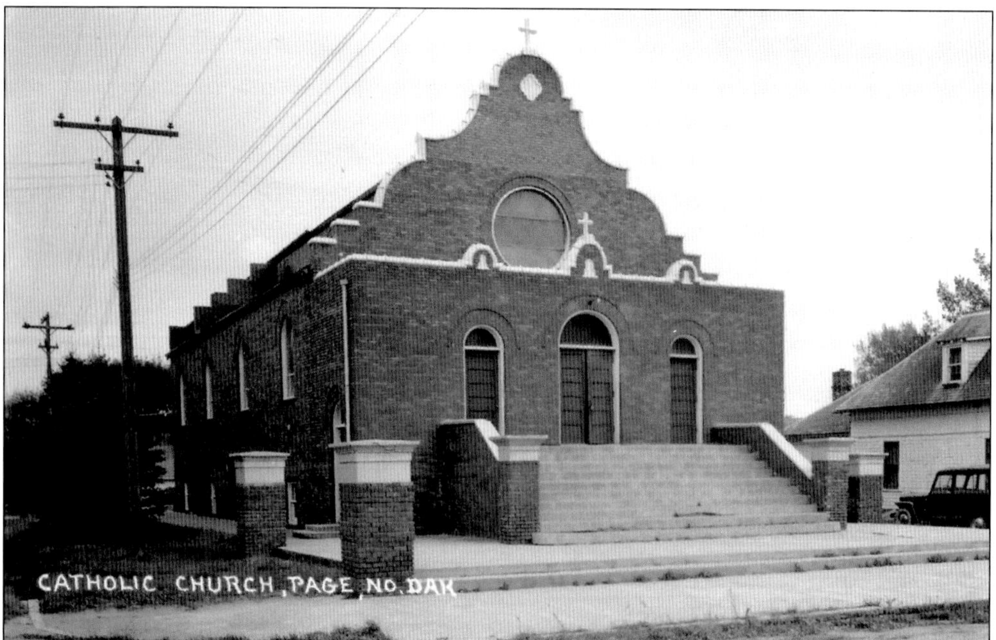


Before Page had a resident priest and sanctuary, couples from the community would often catch the train to Casselton early in the morning or late at night, get married, and return home on the next train. Fr. Charles Fay became the parish's first resident priest in 1914. This photograph of St. James Catholic Church was taken between 1950 and 1954.

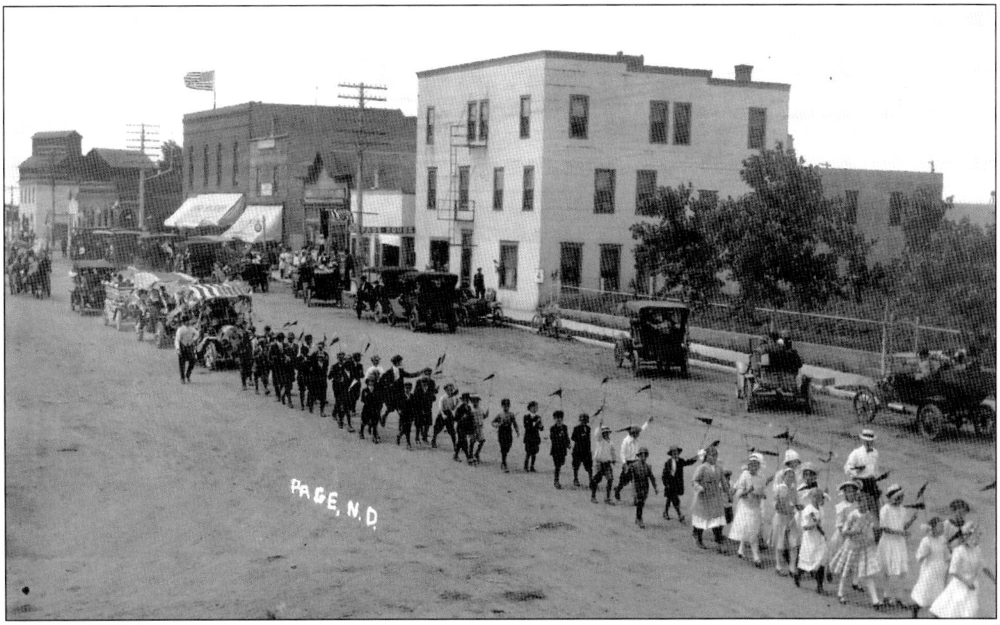


A parade marches down Main Street in Page on June 30, 1913. The parade was part of Gala Days Mid-Summer Festival. The celebration included a band concert, parade, baseball game, horse and motorcycle races, tug of war, a greased pig grabbing contest, and a grand ball dance. Many towns throughout the county held annual community celebrations that usually included different events throughout the day or weekend.

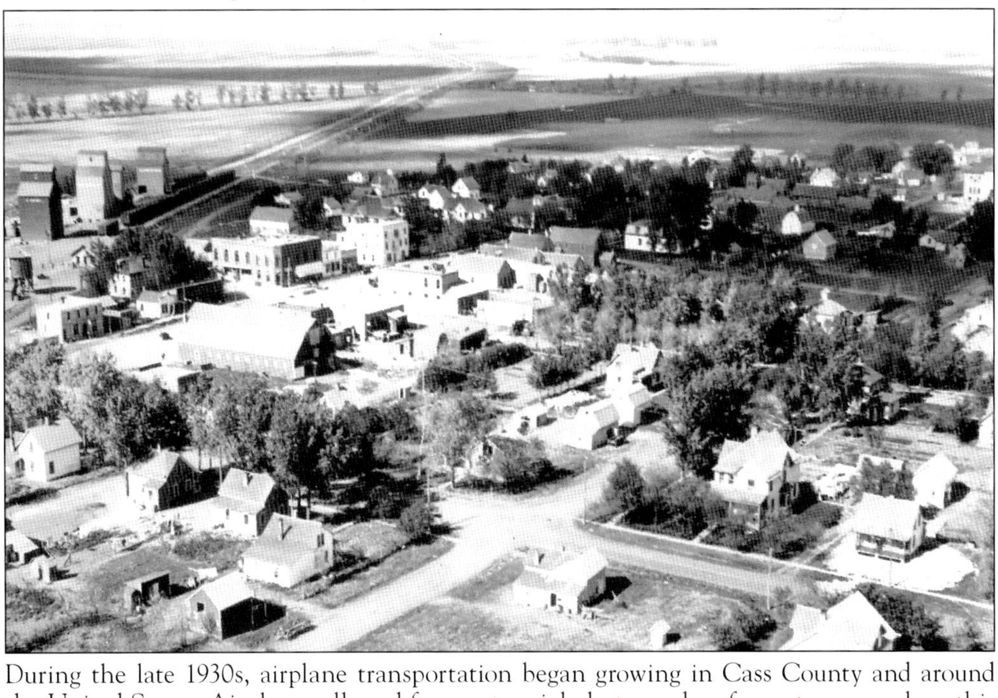

During the late 1930s, airplane transportation began growing in Cass County and around the United States. Airplanes allowed for great aerial photography of area towns, such as this photograph of Page from the 1930s. Some of the town's grain elevators can be seen in the upper left corner as the Great Northern Railroad stretches off to the Northeast.

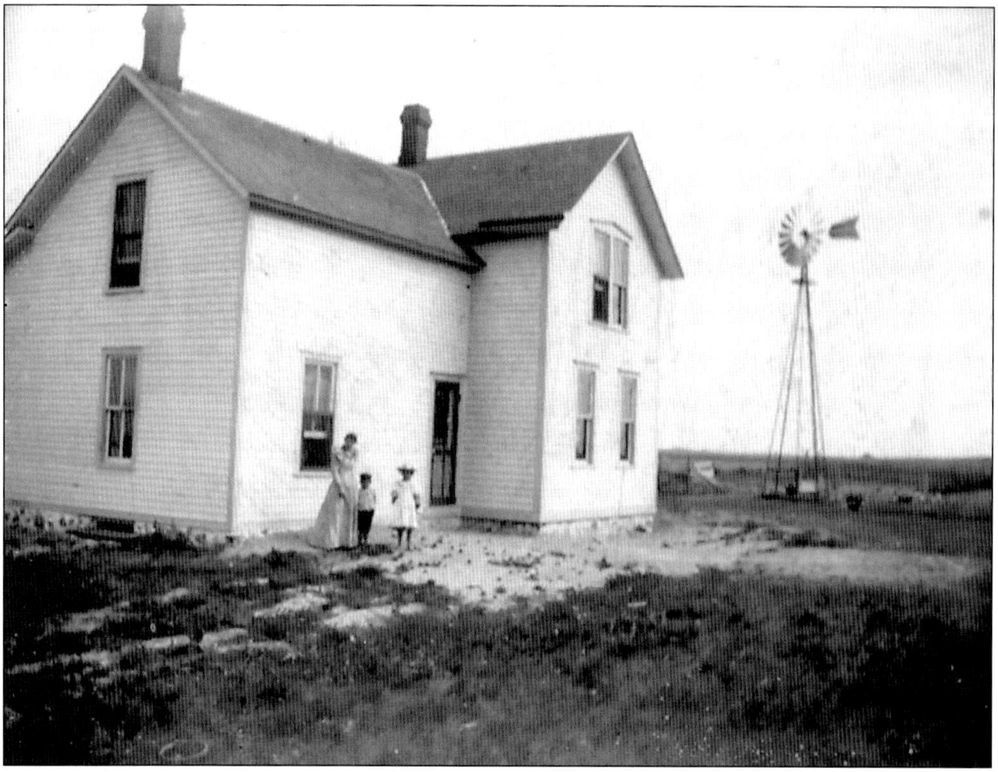

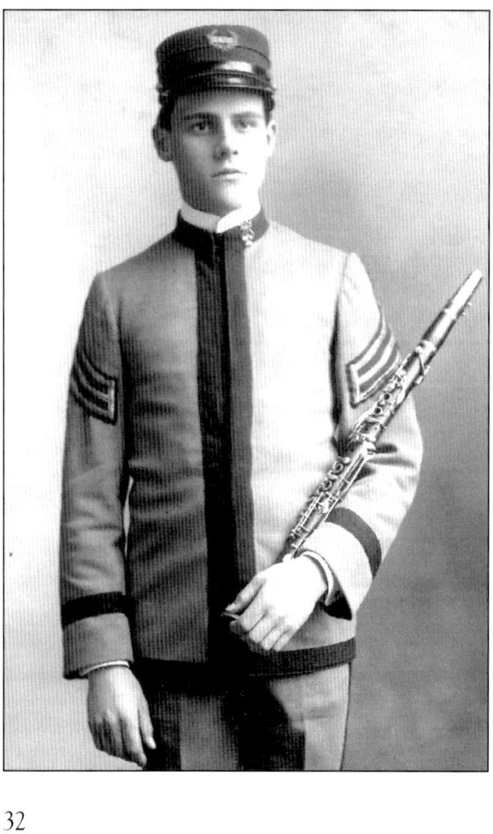

The lower photograph shows Charles H. Clark of Tower City posing in his marching band uniform with a clarinet between 1905 and 1910. Many young men and women, like Charles, came from throughout Cass County to attend classes at the North Dakota Agricultural College in Fargo, now North Dakota State University. The college specialized in the science of improving agricultural commodities and livestock. Students would often take the knowledge learned at the school to help make their family's farm more profitable. The Clark family farm, pictured above, was two or three miles north of Tower City. The house burned down in 1903, shortly before Charles began college, but was rebuilt on the same foundation.

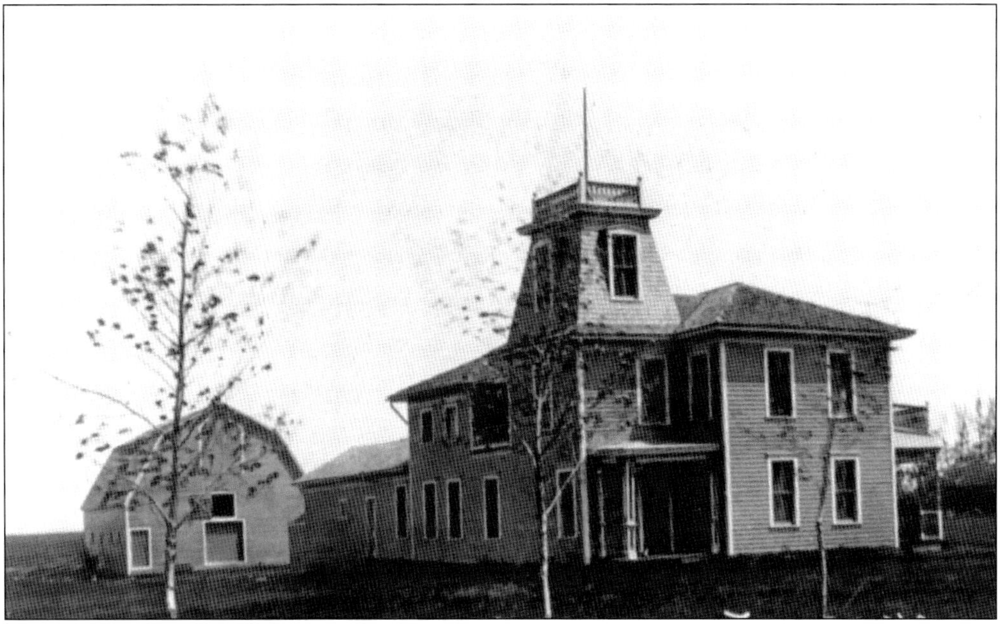

George Ellsbury died in 1900. His farmhouse near Tower City is pictured here around 1910. Ellsbury participated in Henry Hastings Sibley's expedition in Dakota Territory in 1863 after the Sioux Uprising. Ellsbury also fought against the South as a soldier for the Union army during the Civil War. He returned to Dakota Territory where he worked as a farmer and an artist in Tower City.

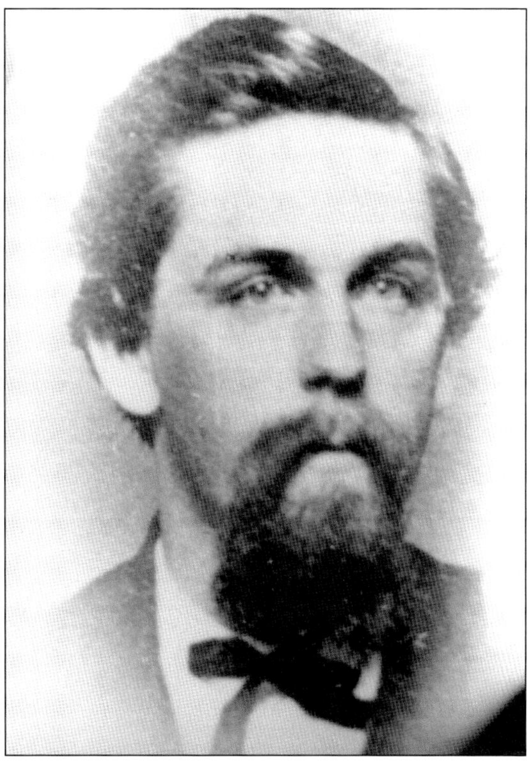

Ellsbury (right) moved from Minnesota to Dakota Territory in 1879. Charlesmagne Tower, who was a prominent businessman and director of the Northern Pacific Railroad, owned land along the railroad in Cass County. Ellsbury surveyed the land one block on either side of the railroad, platting a town that he named after the owner, creating Tower City.

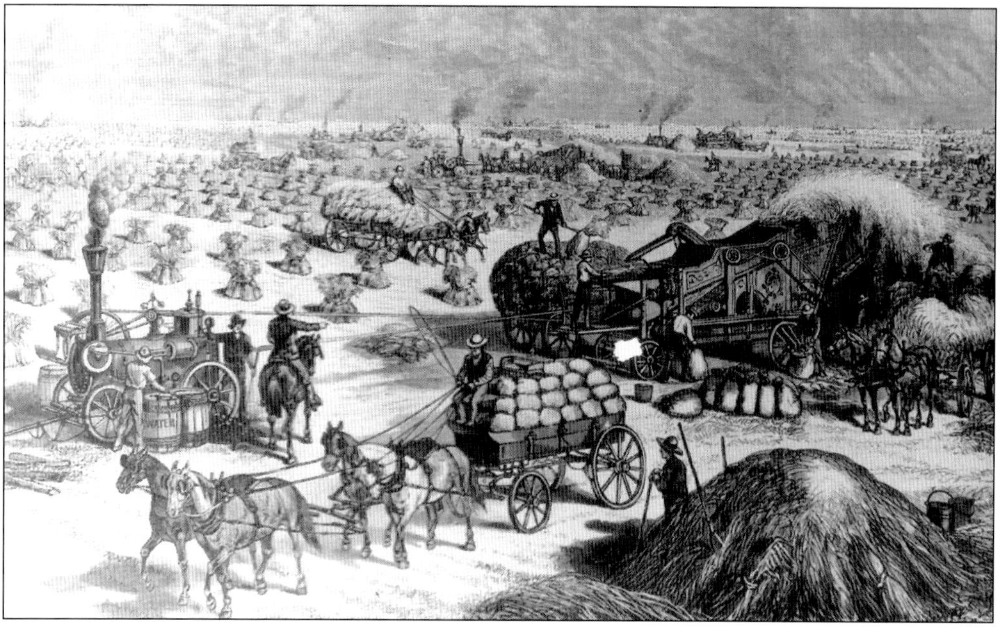

This illustration of steam threshing on the Dalrymple Farm in Cass County was drawn by George Ellsbury, who lived in Tower City. Ellsbury was a well-known magazine illustrator who became famous for his drawings of battles between the United States Army and Native Americans as well as Civil War battles. Later Ellsbury created many aerial-view map drawings of cities and farm scenes that helped sell the West to potential settlers.

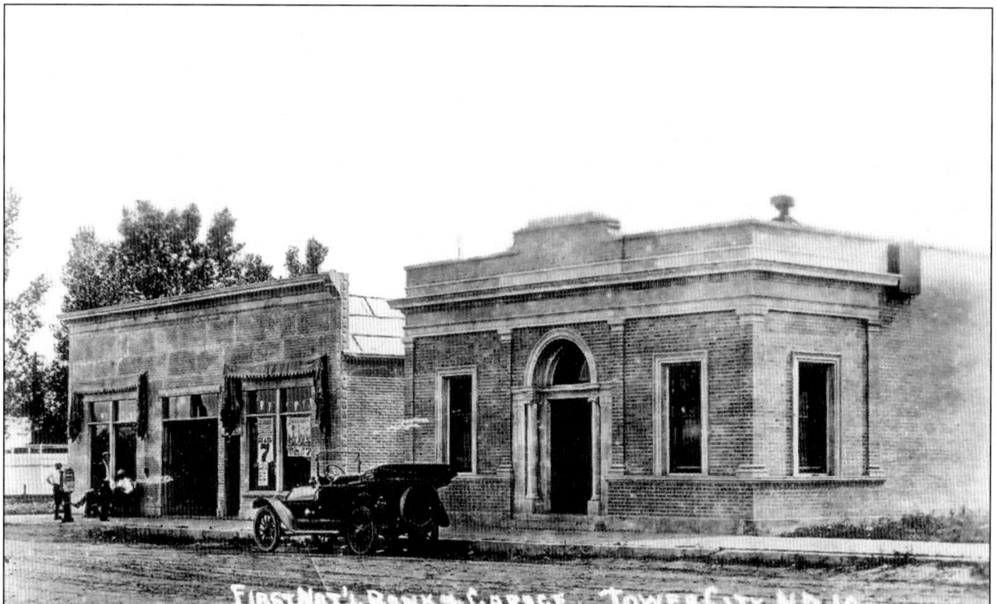


Shown in this *c.* 1910 photograph are the First National Bank and town garage in Tower City. Notice the brick used to construct the buildings. Much of the brick used in the town's buildings was produced by L. Messenger, who operated a brick kiln on his farm one-half mile south of town.

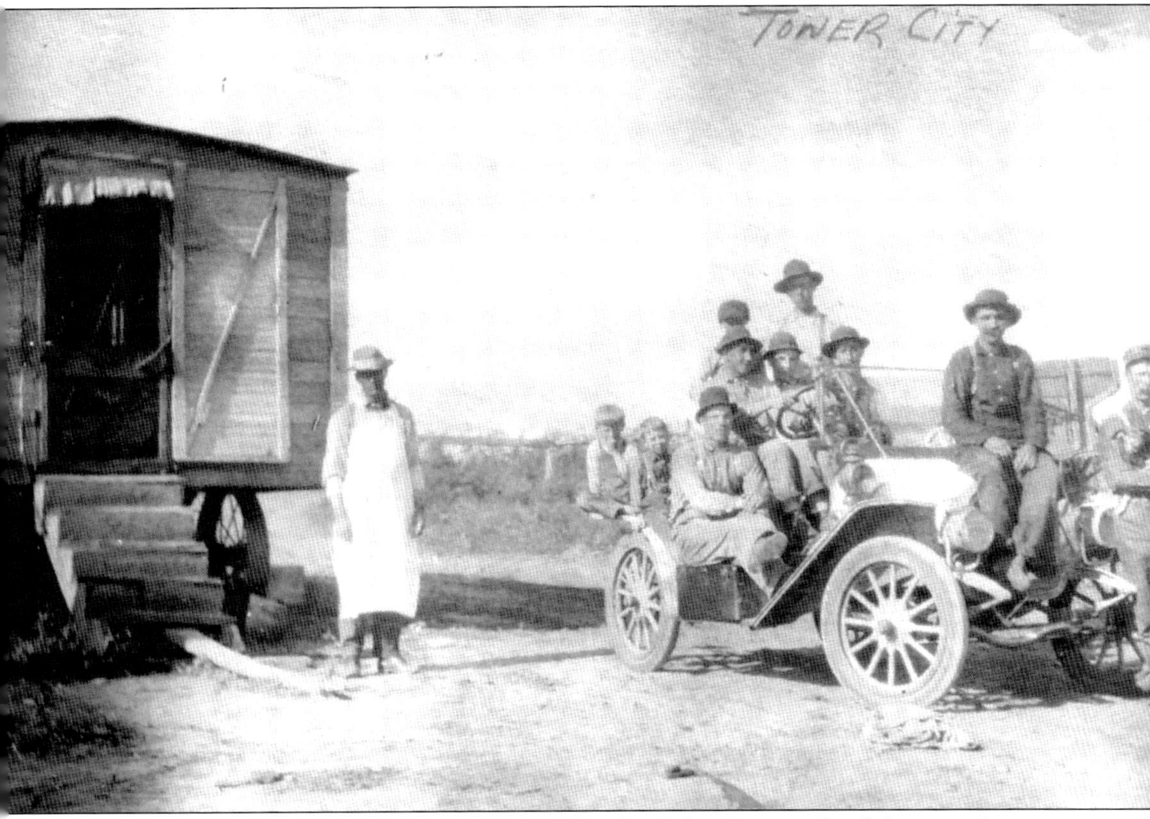


A cook stands in front of a "cook car" on the left side of the photograph while men relax on an automobile near Tower City around 1917. Bonanza farms that existed during the later part of the 19th century had enormous crews of men to work the horses and machinery needed to complete the harvest. Women usually worked in cook cars that contained a cook stove and supplies needed to feed the work crews. The cars were large wagons with steel wheels that would be pulled by a team of horses or steam tractor. The wagons followed the work crews in the field, preparing the days' four or five meals for approximately 30 men per wagon. Cooks began work around 4:00 in the morning and usually did not end until about 11:00 at night. Meals consisted of meat, potatoes, beans, bread, dried fruit, cookies or cake, and always plenty of coffee. Leftover food was used to make sandwiches and stews for the next meal.

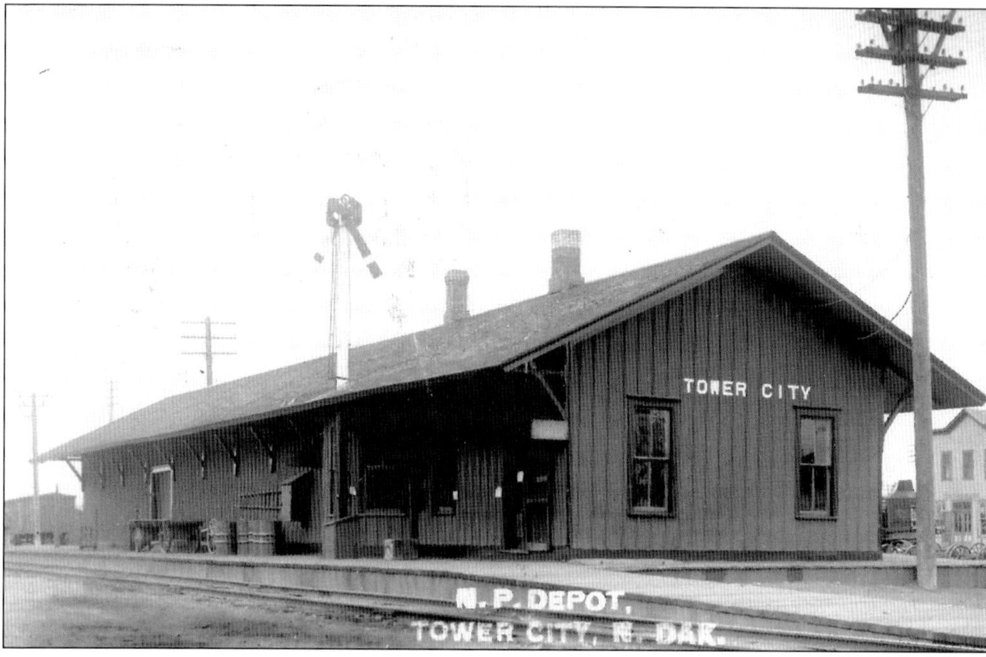


The Northern Pacific Railroad built tracks through what later became Tower City in 1873. The town was founded in 1879, but there was no depot for trains to stop. Instead, the train stopped at a coulee less than one mile from town, known as Spring Tank, until a depot was built one year later. The Tower City depot is pictured here around 1912.

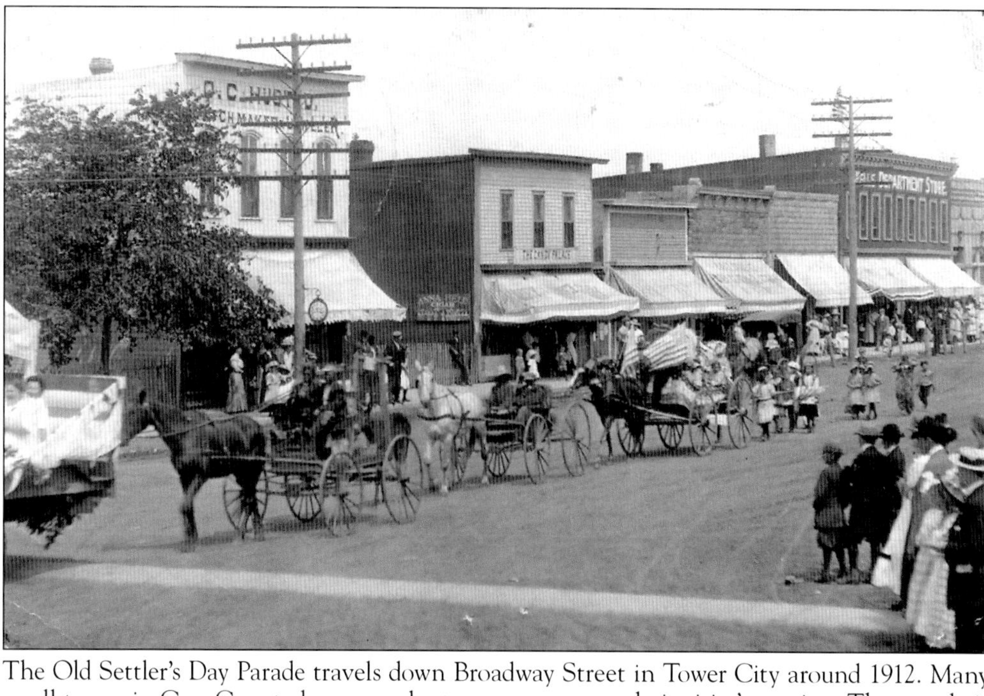

The Old Settler's Day Parade travels down Broadway Street in Tower City around 1912. Many small towns in Cass County have parades to commemorate their cities' creation. The parade is often accompanied with a street fair or dance that involves people from the entire community and the surrounding area.

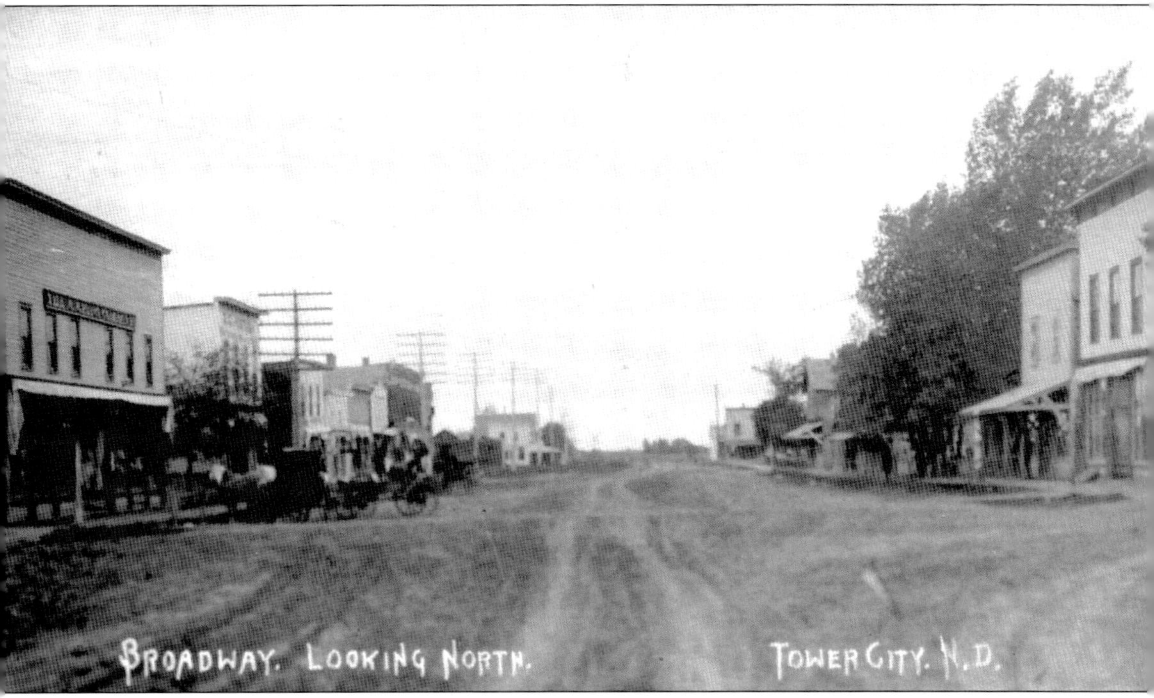


A plan to build another railroad through Tower City was developed in 1883. The Dakota and Great Southern Railroad was to run south to Sioux Falls and continue to St. Louis, Missouri. North branches were also planned, one to connect Grand Forks with Tower City and another to the northwest that would run through Canada. George Ellsbury was elected president of the railroad, but stock never sold and the railroad did not materialize. In 1886, a group of Baptists began working on creating a college in Tower City, to be known as Tower University. An endowment of $100,000 was to be given to the town for the college. Work began on the future college site, but the money was never given. Construction on the site stopped, and the city offered the town's school building for the university's use. Stock was sold to operate the college's two departments. The university closed after only two years of operation. This photograph of Tower City shows the town's business district along Broadway Street around 1908.

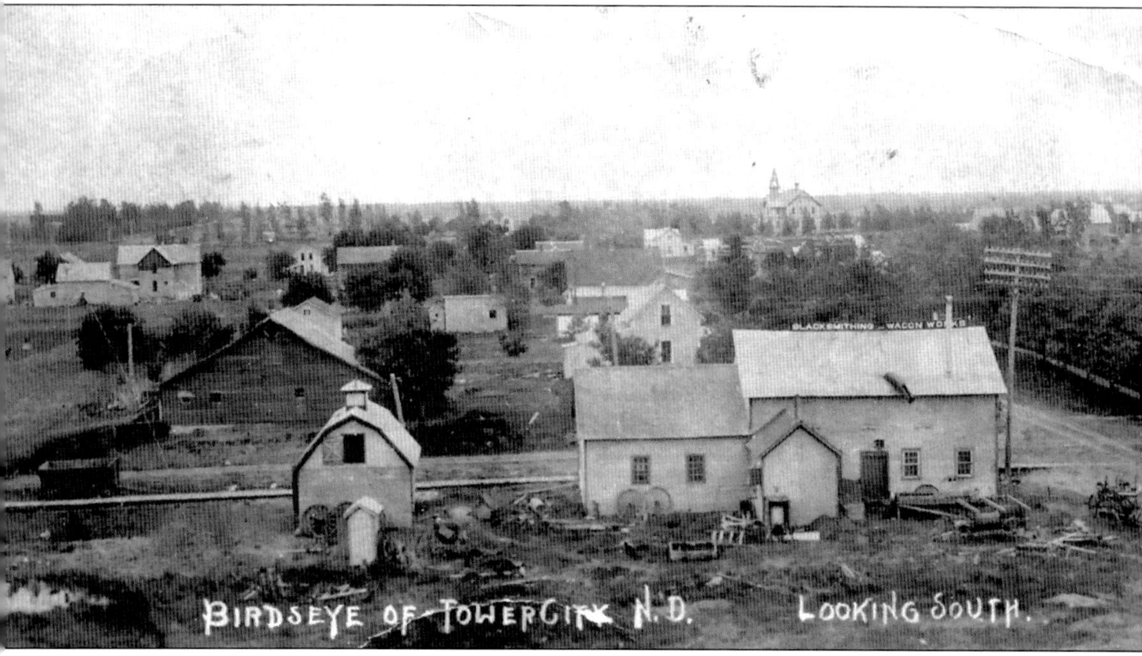


Toward the end of the 19th century, Tower City began maneuvering to become a premier city in the eastern Dakotas. When Dakota Territory was being split into North and South Dakota, Tower City offered $15,000 to the state if it built the new capitol in town. Bismarck offered $100,000 in addition to 160 acres of land, and the Tower City proposal was refused. After this defeat, Tower City began developing a plan to reorganize Cass and Barnes Counties, forming a new county where it would be the county seat. Valley City, the county seat of Barnes County, got word of the plan and sent representatives to Bismarck to kill the idea. The ambitious founders and promoters of Tower City were never able to secure a major advancement for the town. This photograph shows a view of Tower City from the top of a grain elevator around 1908. The town's second school building can be seen in the distance. The school was built in 1883 and burned down in 1910.

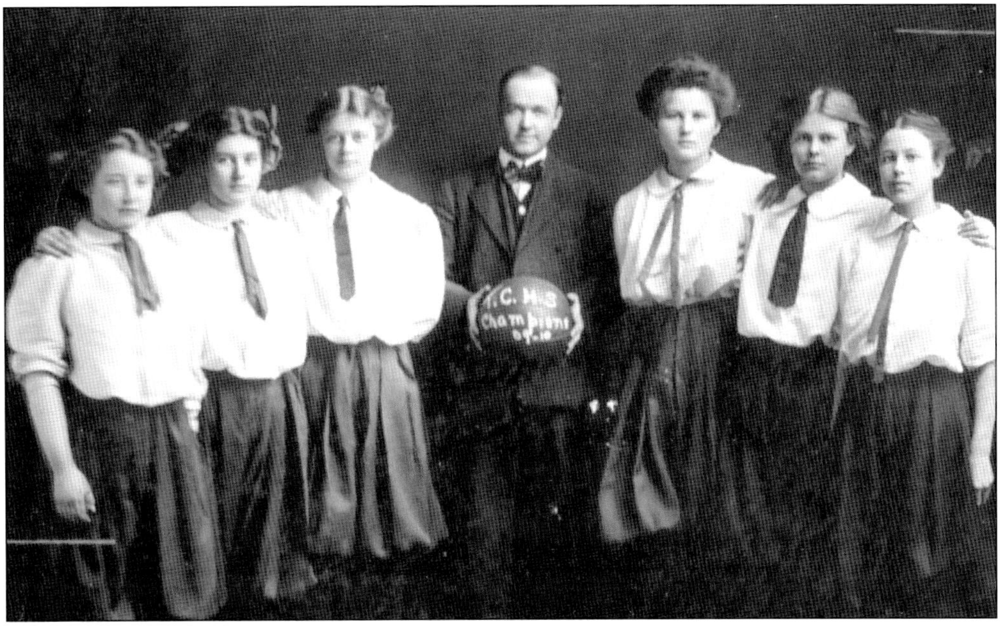

This photograph shows the 1910 girls' basketball team from Tower City High School. Pictured are, from left to right, Albertha Kiff, Myrtle Kiff, Louise Roethke, coach R. B. Murphy, Mary Boehm, Edna Roethke, and Beulah Buswell. Murphy became the school's superintendent in the fall of 1902. He coached both boys' and girls' basketball teams. His girls' team was undefeated from 1905 to 1909.

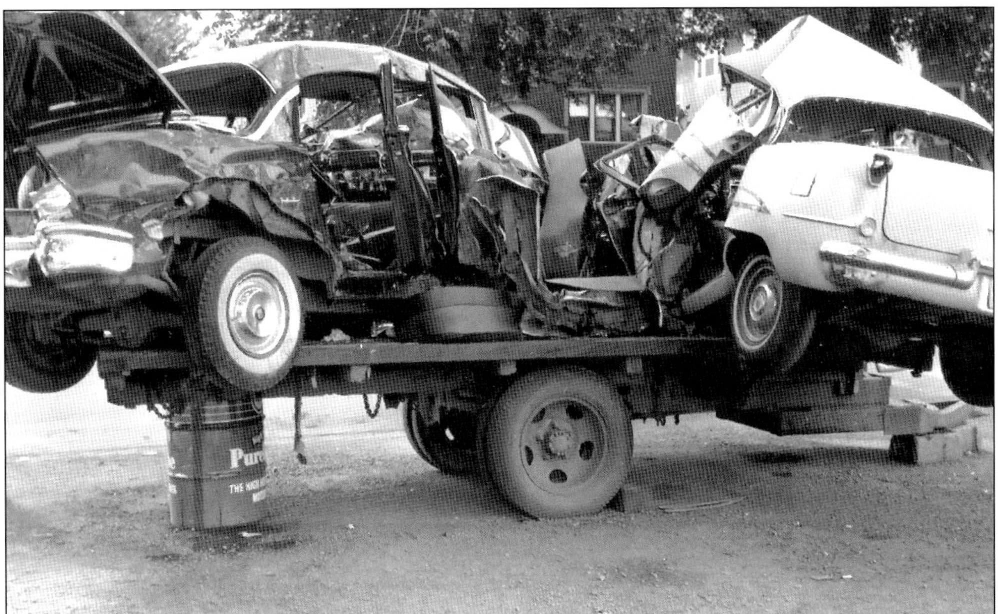

A trailer is displayed in Fargo on August 27, 1956, with two cars that collided in Tower City earlier that year. With the advent of smoother roads and faster cars, accidents like this one were common. Narrow dirt roads and two-lane highways sometimes led to head-on collisions that could cost a person his life.

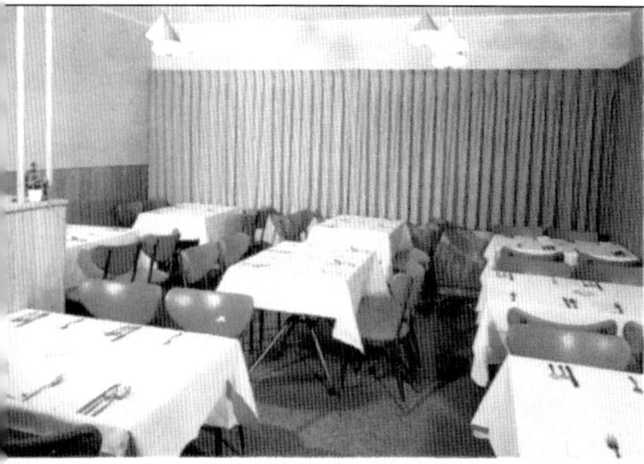

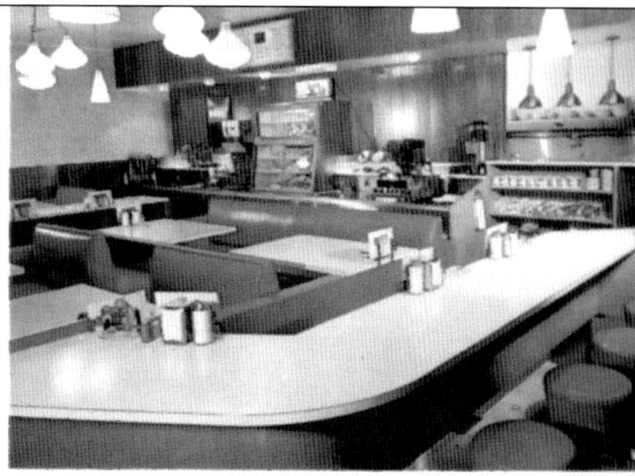

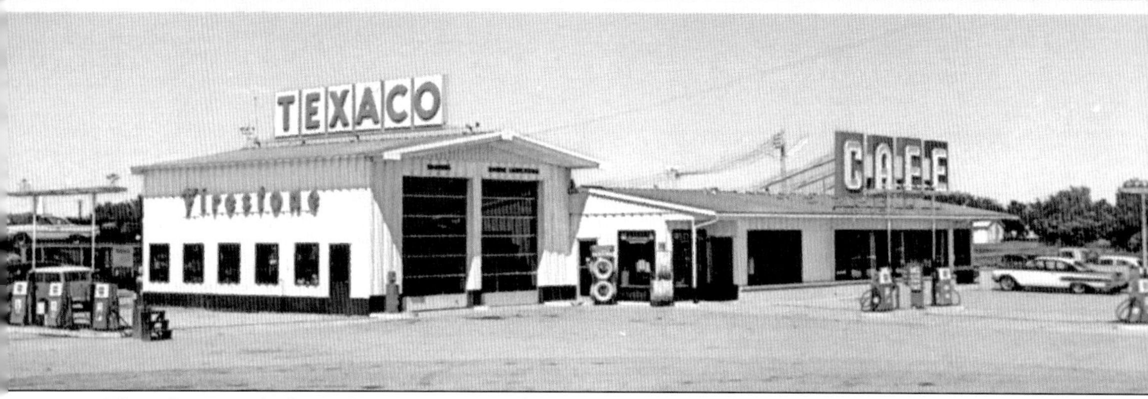


This photograph shows Tower Texaco, otherwise known as the Tower City Truck Stop during the 1960s. The back of this postcard advertised the Texaco station as "the Northwest's newest and finest truck stop. U.S. Interstate 94, forty miles west of Fargo. 24-hour service, air-conditioned bunk rooms, and Tower View Cafe. Texaco products, Firestone tires, and ample parking. A place to remember." The station became a popular stop along the newly constructed Interstate 94. The reputation of the gas station's restaurant, the Tower View Café, grew as word spread about its delicious pies. The truck stop and café opened in November 1960 under the management of Willard Richman, Bill Richman, and Norman Anderson. Interstate 94 opened in North Dakota during the 1960s. It followed much of the same route as old Highway 10 and stretches from Montana, through Cass County, all the way to Canada, just across the border from Michigan. Cass County is the junction between Interstate 94 and Interstate 29, which runs from Canada to Mexico.

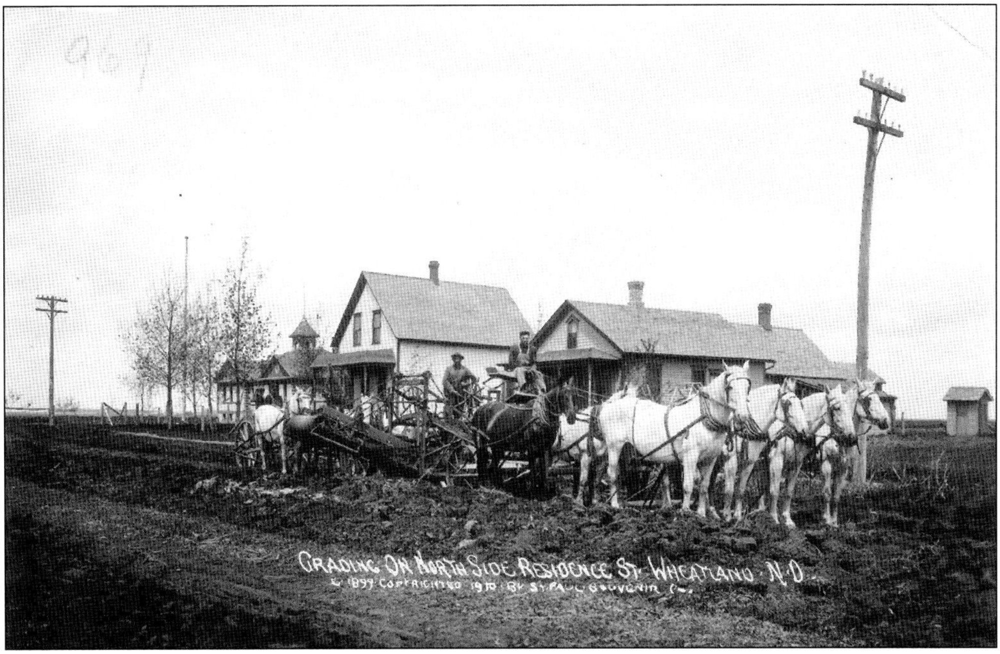


In this photograph, Walt Edward and Fred Kingsley drive a team of horses pulling a road grader on the north side of Residence Street in Wheatland around 1910. In the spring, roads became so muddy they were nearly unusable. Grading a road helped resurface the dirt and smooth out grooves that were made by the large, thin wheels of buggies and early automobiles.

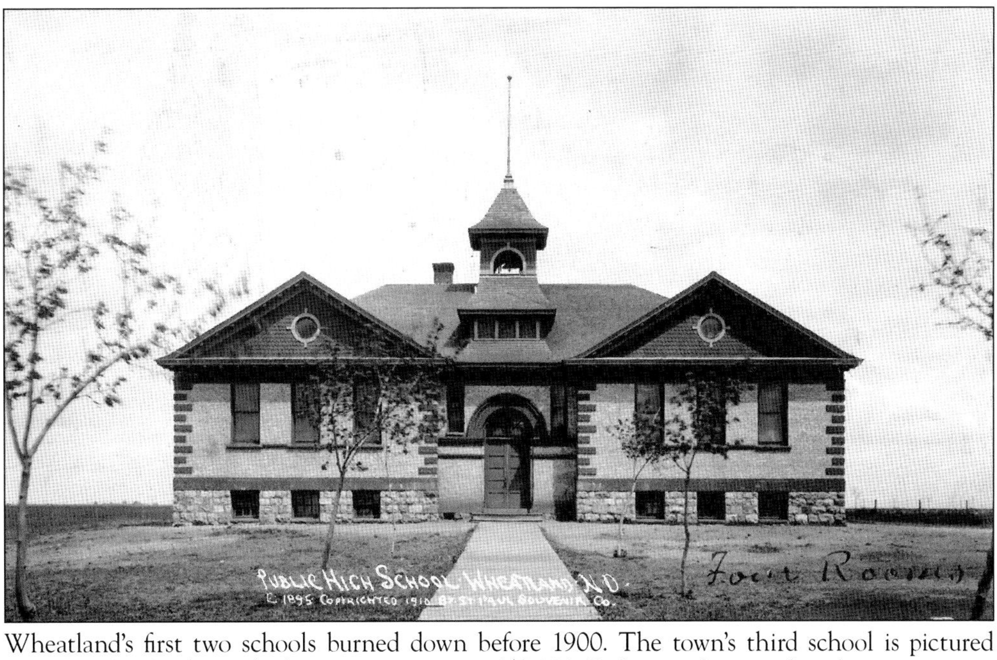


Wheatland's first two schools burned down before 1900. The town's third school is pictured here shortly after being built in 1901 at a cost of $7,800. Before modern modes of transportation became popular, Wheatland's high school basketball team used a horse-drawn sleigh that was pulled through the snow to reach other towns for games.

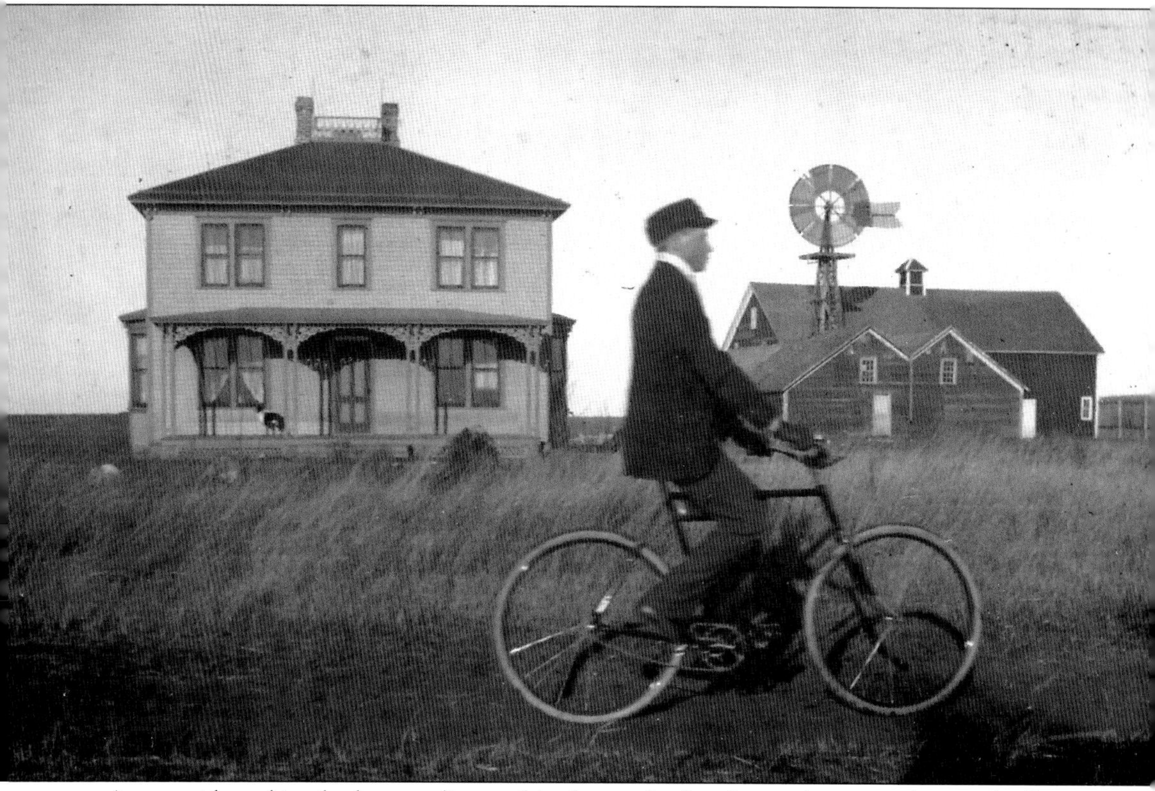

A man rides a bicycle down a dirt road in front of a farmhouse, barns, and a windmill near Wheatland during the late 1890s or early 1900s. Bicycles became extremely popular toward the end of the 19th century in the Red River Valley. Besides being a popular form of entertainment, recreation, and transportation, many communities began sponsoring bicycle races and competitions with monetary prizes for the winners. Before automobiles became commonplace, bicycles were an easy and cheap form of transportation for those who did not use a horse and buggy. Cities such as Fargo began passing laws regarding bicycles and riders. Accidents between bicyclists and pedestrians became more common. Once people began buying automobiles, bicycles became more of a novelty than a common mode of transportation. Eventually bicycles were reserved mostly for recreation by adults and toys for children.

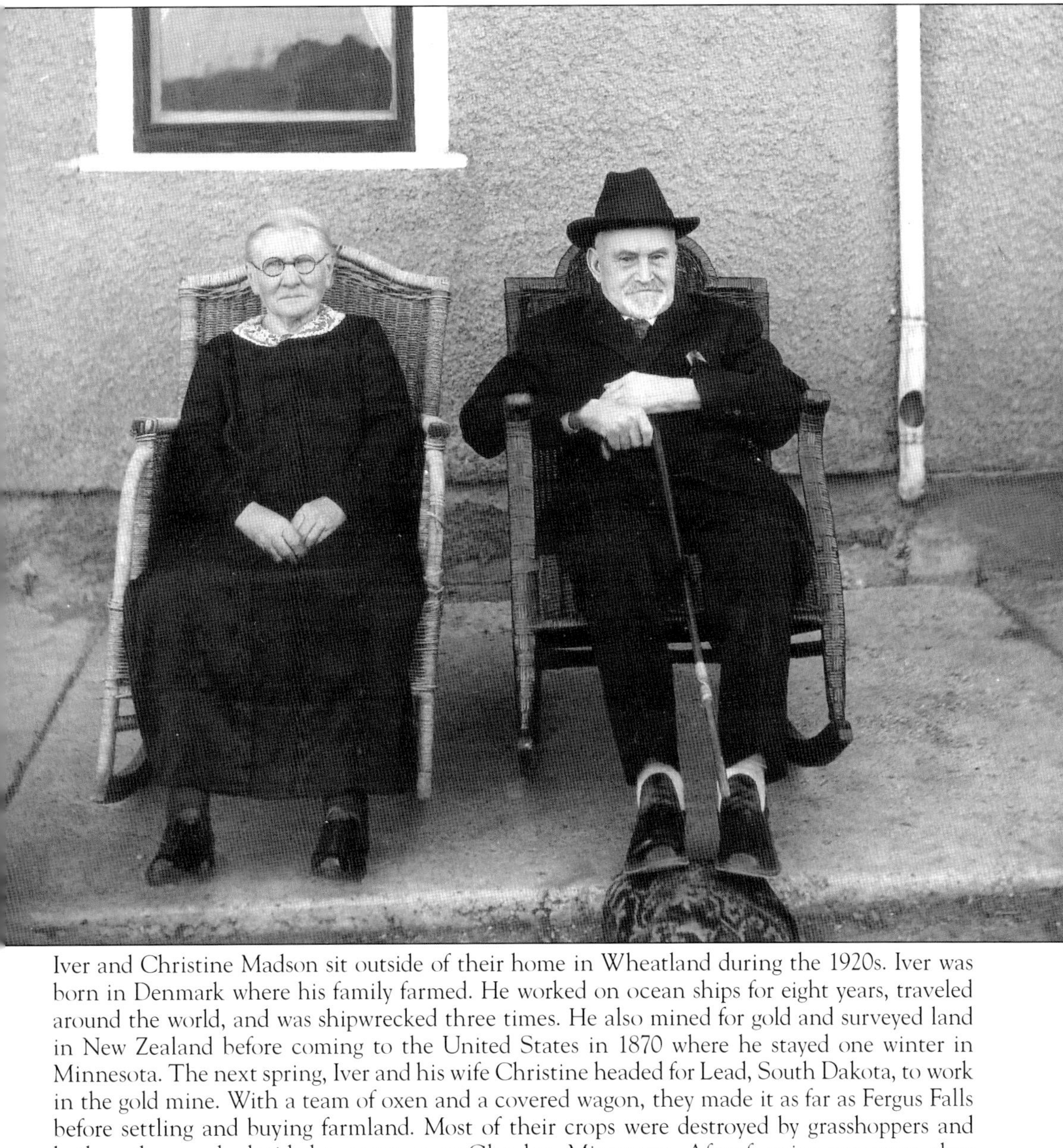

Iver and Christine Madson sit outside of their home in Wheatland during the 1920s. Iver was born in Denmark where his family farmed. He worked on ocean ships for eight years, traveled around the world, and was shipwrecked three times. He also mined for gold and surveyed land in New Zealand before coming to the United States in 1870 where he stayed one winter in Minnesota. The next spring, Iver and his wife Christine headed for Lead, South Dakota, to work in the gold mine. With a team of oxen and a covered wagon, they made it as far as Fergus Falls before settling and buying farmland. Most of their crops were destroyed by grasshoppers and hail, so the couple decided to move on to Glyndon, Minnesota. After farming two years, they homesteaded in Wheatland Township. The Madsons became successful farmers, and in 1878, they built the first two-story home in the area. It was known as the "light house" because people could see the light through the upstairs window for miles.

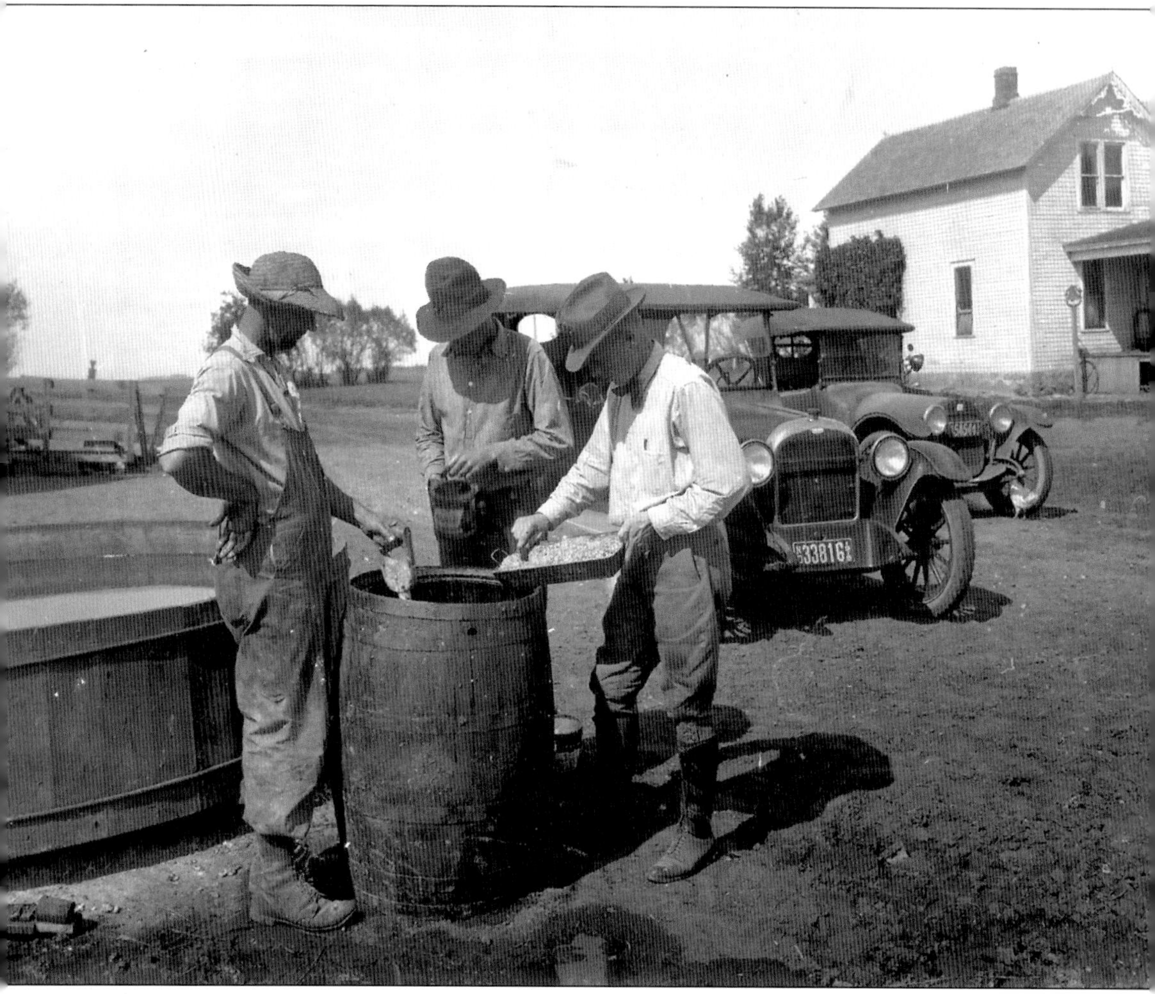

This photograph shows men filling a barrel of oats with poison near Wheatland during the 1920s. Area farmers spread poison over their fields as a method of pest control. Throughout the late 1800s and early 1900s, farmers continually fought plagues of insects. During the 1870s, many settlers' farms were constantly inundated with grasshoppers that swarmed Dakota Territory and Minnesota. Some farmers were forced to give up working the land and return to the East or move to other places. According to some accounts, the grasshoppers were so thick that they turned the sky dark during the day. Once the insects had devoured all the fields in an area, they would search for anything consumable, sometimes eating parts of settlers' homes before moving on. The grasshoppers came back several years in a row during the late 19th century. The insects accompanied a drought that swept the region at the time making conditions even harder for early settlers.

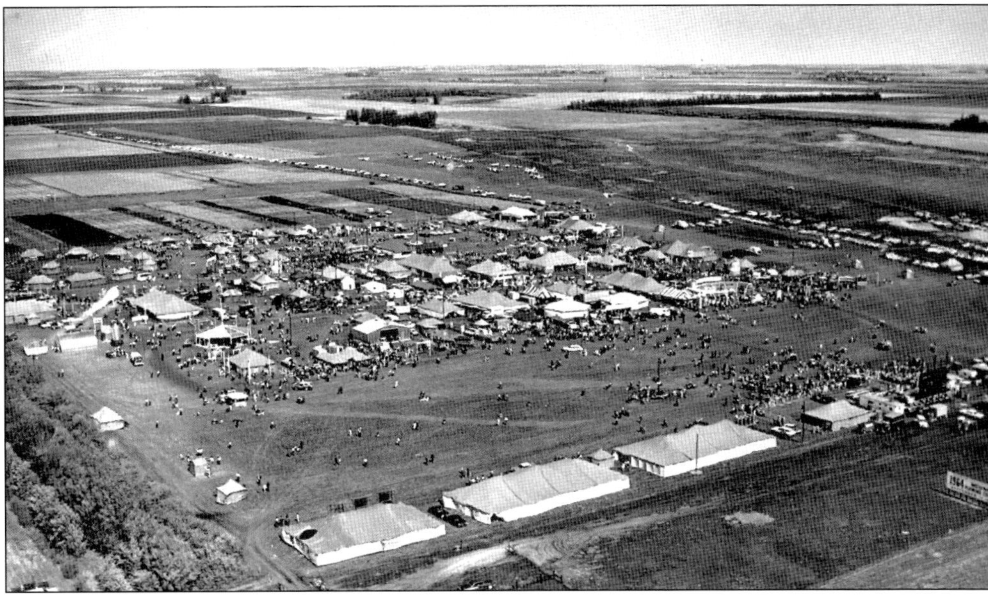

Many organizations worked together to turn the State Plowing Contest of 1964 into a national competition known as the National Plowing Contest and Soil Conservation Field Days. The farm of Elmer and Ramona Fraase near Wheatland was chosen to host the event. Three acres of trees were planted as an example of windbreaks. Fraase planted 300 acres of alfalfa to be used as an airplane runway and parking lot during the event. The aerial photograph above shows the "tent city" that was filled with farm displays and exhibits. Power lines and light poles were erected as well as a 250-foot radio tower. Interstate 94 was still under construction, but permission was obtained from the government to open the road during the event, connecting the plow contest with the city of Fargo.

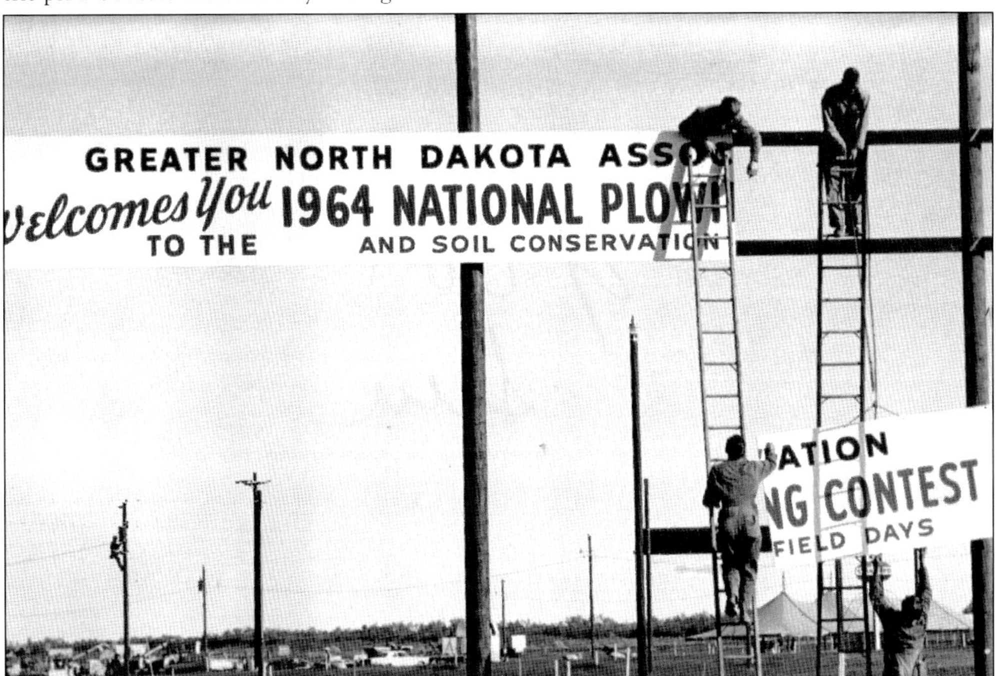

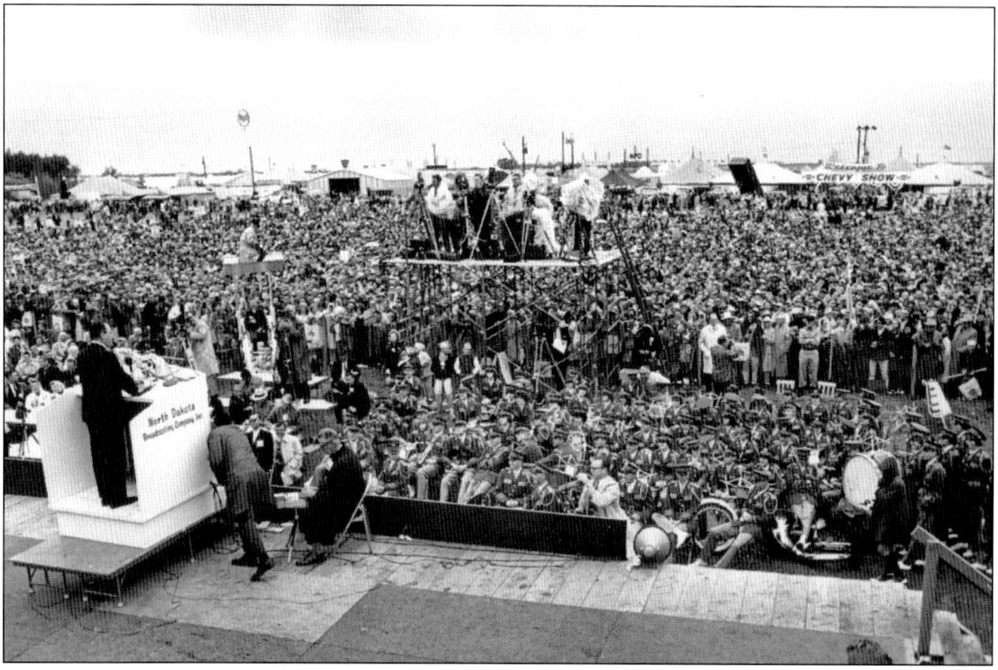


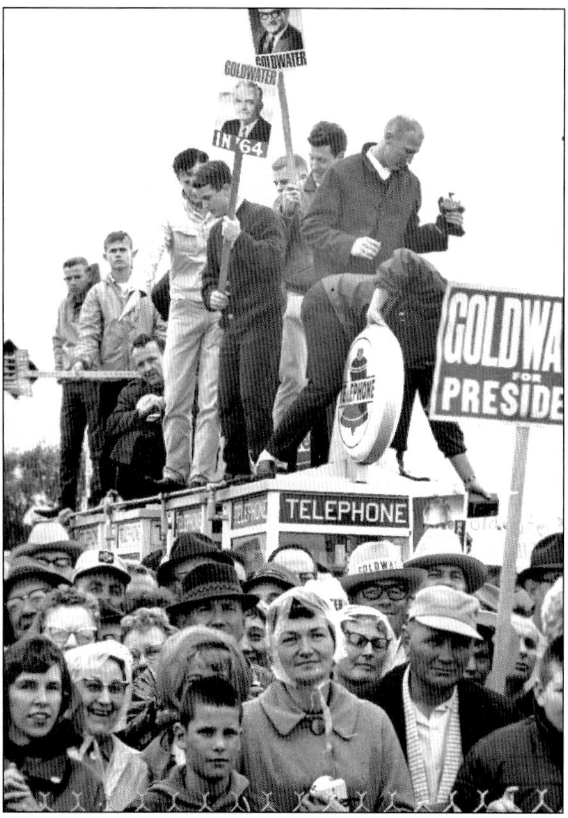


On the last day of the plow contest, politicians came to speak while the crowds were gathered for the event. Minnesota senator and vice-presidential candidate Hubert H. Humphrey (above, standing on the podium) spoke in the morning to a large crowd. He was joined by North Dakota's governor Bill Guy and other local Democrats. An interparty lunch, which was served by local Democrat and Republican ladies organizations, was served in the home of the Fraase family for the visiting political dignitaries. Republican presidential candidate Barry Goldwater also gave a speech to a large crowd later that afternoon. Goldwater supporters fought to get a view of the senator by climbing to the top of telephone booths during his speech in the picture below.

# *Two*

# NORTHEASTERN CASS COUNTY

Chapter 2 focuses on the towns in the northeastern quarter of Cass County: Amenia, Argusville, Arthur, Casselton, Fargo, Gardner, Grandin, Harwood, Hunter, Mapleton, and Prosper.

Like every town in Cass County, Amenia lies along a railway. Like several other towns in the county, it sprung from a bonanza farm. In August 1879, the railway that became the Great Northern made its way through the area of what was to become the town of Amenia. The town began developing in 1881 around the elevator, and a depot and general store soon followed—a process of development that repeated itself throughout the plains. The town was named by an investor in the Amenia and Sharon Land Company, Thomas Young from Amenia, New York. Amenia did not incorporate as a town until a special election was held in 1927. Amenia is about seven miles directly north of Casselton, and the population is currently 89.

Argusville, about 15 miles north and west of Fargo, was first settled in 1880 and platted in 1881 as a station for the Great Northern Railroad. Frank Aldrich, who did the town platting, named it after the *Fargo Argus*, the first daily newspaper in North Dakota. Some of the earliest settlers came from Wisconsin. By 1891, the settlement had a general store that also served as a dance hall. By 1900, Argusville had the typical services common for small towns. The town officially incorporated in May 1921 and currently has a population of 147.

The town of Arthur began its history as Rosedale. The town name was changed to Arthur in 1881 in honor of the 21st president of the United States, Chester A. Arthur. By that year, John Brandenburg had established a general store and lumberyard. The school district was formed in 1882, and Arthur Township was organized two years later. Arthur did not become an incorporated town until 1921. Arthur is about 14 miles directly north of Casselton, and unlike most small towns in Cass County, it currently has a stable population of 402. The former Arthur Town Hall is now part of the Bonanzaville museum of the Cass County Historical Society.

The town of Casselton lies almost exactly in the geographical center of Cass County. Its history goes back to the first bonanza farm in the Red River Valley, the Cass-Cheney Farm. Goose Creek was the first name given to the young settlement, but both Cass and Cheney disapproved of the name. The name was changed to Swan Creek, but not for long. Two residents, Mike Smith and Emil Priewe, suggested the name be changed to honor George Cass. The name became Casseltown and was later changed to its current spelling of Casselton. As a result of being the center of a giant bonanza farm and being one of the first towns to be settled, Casselton had a head start over the rest of rural Cass County. In addition to being the location of the first bonanza farm, Casselton is also famous statewide because it had the good fortune of being the hometown of three former North Dakota governors: Andrew Burke, William Langer, and George Sinner. With a current and growing population of 1,855, Casselton is the third-largest town in the county, behind Fargo and West Fargo. Since the 1970s, Casselton has become a bedroom community for people commuting 25 miles to the Fargo-Moorhead metro area.

Fargo's history begins with the arrival of the Northern Pacific Railroad in 1871. Originally called Centralia, the name was changed to honor William Fargo, a founder of the Wells-Fargo Express. Fargo was incorporated in 1875 and is the seat of Cass County. In 2005, the estimated population was 91,048. For more information on Fargo, see *Fargo, North Dakota, 1870-1940*, by David Danbom and Claire Strom.

Charles Dayton and his wife, Elizabeth, set out in 1880 to claim a homestead they had filed for in Dakota Territory. Their 155.3 acres later became the town site for Gardner. Dayton later sold a strip of land to the Great Northern Railroad, and the railroad built a station in 1881. It was named for an extensive land owner in the area, Stephen Gardner. The town site was platted in 1882 but did not incorporate until 1929. Gardner reached its population peak of 136 in 1950 and has since declined to its current population of 80. Gardner is about 20 miles north and west of Fargo along the railroad.

Similar to Gardner, Grandin was a station on the Great Northern Railroad. Almond White and Solomon Comstock purchased and platted the town site, which they registered in 1881. John Anderson was the first settler who opened a blacksmith shop. He named the town for J. L. and W. J. Grandin, brothers and owners of the town site who were from Pennsylvania. The Grandin brothers owned one of the most famous bonanza farms with land holdings of about 82,000 acres. They built a steamboat to haul their grain south on the Red River to elevators in Fargo. The town of Grandin, about 30 miles north and west of Fargo, was incorporated in 1926 and has a current population of 181.

In 1881, White, Comstock, and A. J. Harwood purchased the land that was to become the town of Harwood. The town was platted, a Great Northern Railroad station was built, and the town was named for Harwood. Some of the first settlers came from Illinois. C. G. Bradley opened the first general store and was the first postmaster. Harwood, only 3.5 miles north of Fargo, has become a bedroom community whose population has doubled since the 1970s to its current high of 607.

Hunter was originally named Delano when the Northern Pacific Railroad built a station there in 1880. The town site was platted by Newton Hubbard and William Kindred. In 1881, the post office was moved two miles south and the town name was changed to Hunter after John Hunter, who was an extensive landholder in the area. Hunter is about 20 miles directly north of Casselton and has a current population of 326.

Mapleton was originally called Maple River by settlers in the 1870s because it lies on the river of the same name. Mary Bishop had a log cabin in the area, and Northern Pacific Railroad surveyors claimed that hers was the only human habitation that they found between the Red River and the Missouri River. The railroad made Mapleton a station in 1872, a plat was filed in 1876, and the town incorporated in 1884. Mapleton is five miles directly west of West Fargo and also has become a bedroom community for Fargo-Moorhead. Its population has also doubled since the 1970s to its current high of 606.

A Great Northern station was built along the tracks and became the town of Prosper in 1911. Legend has it that railroad officials named the town for the prosperous farmland that surrounded the station. In 1926, a post office was established and Henry Hanson became postmaster. Prosper is located about 20 miles northwest of Fargo.

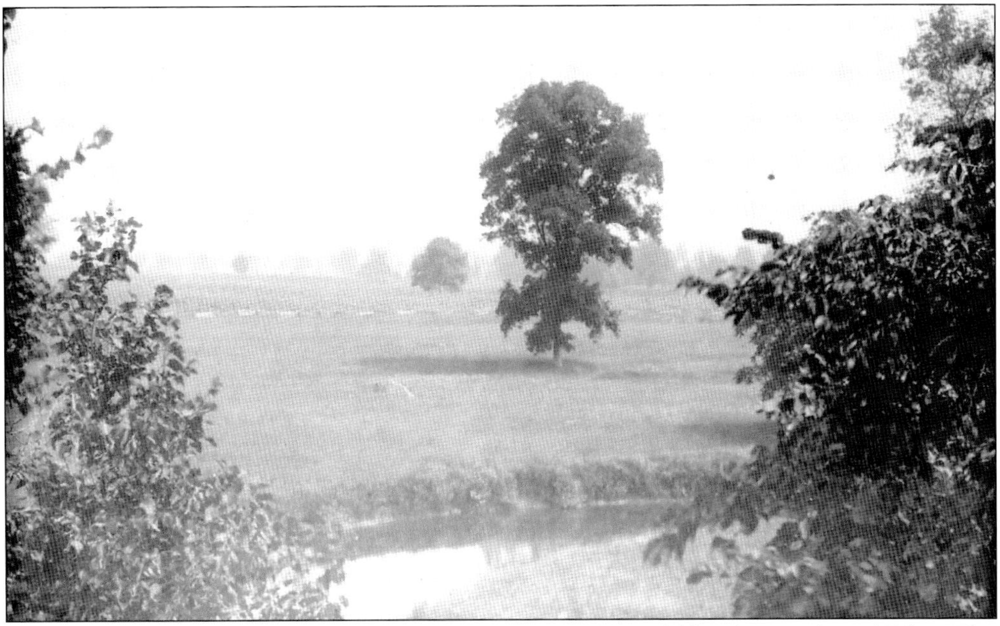

For many immigrants and homesteaders, Cass County looked like the Garden of Eden. The county boasted rich soil, a growing economy, and a hopeful future. People from the East were attracted by land speculation, and immigrants from Europe were attracted to the potential for growing crops and a new beginning in the United States. The land shown in this photograph was owned by the Amenia and Sharon Land Company.

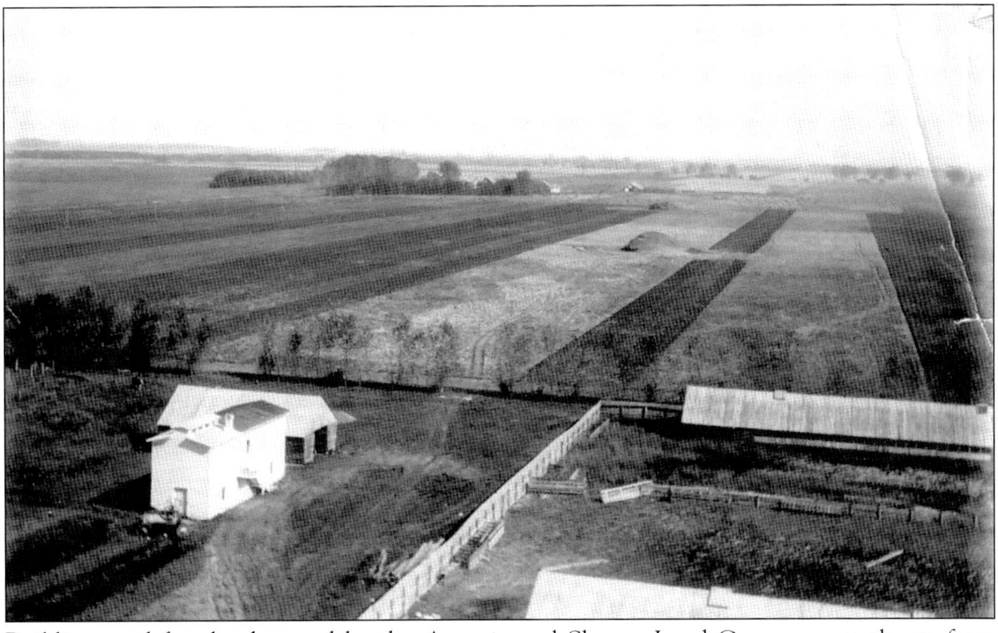

Buildings and farmland owned by the Amenia and Sharon Land Company are shown from atop one of its grain elevators during the 1890s. The Amenia and Sharon Land Company experimented with different strains of wheat, flax, corn, oats, barley, clover, and grasses to determine what crops grew the best in the Red River Valley. The seeds were tested on the company's farm before being sold to area farmers.

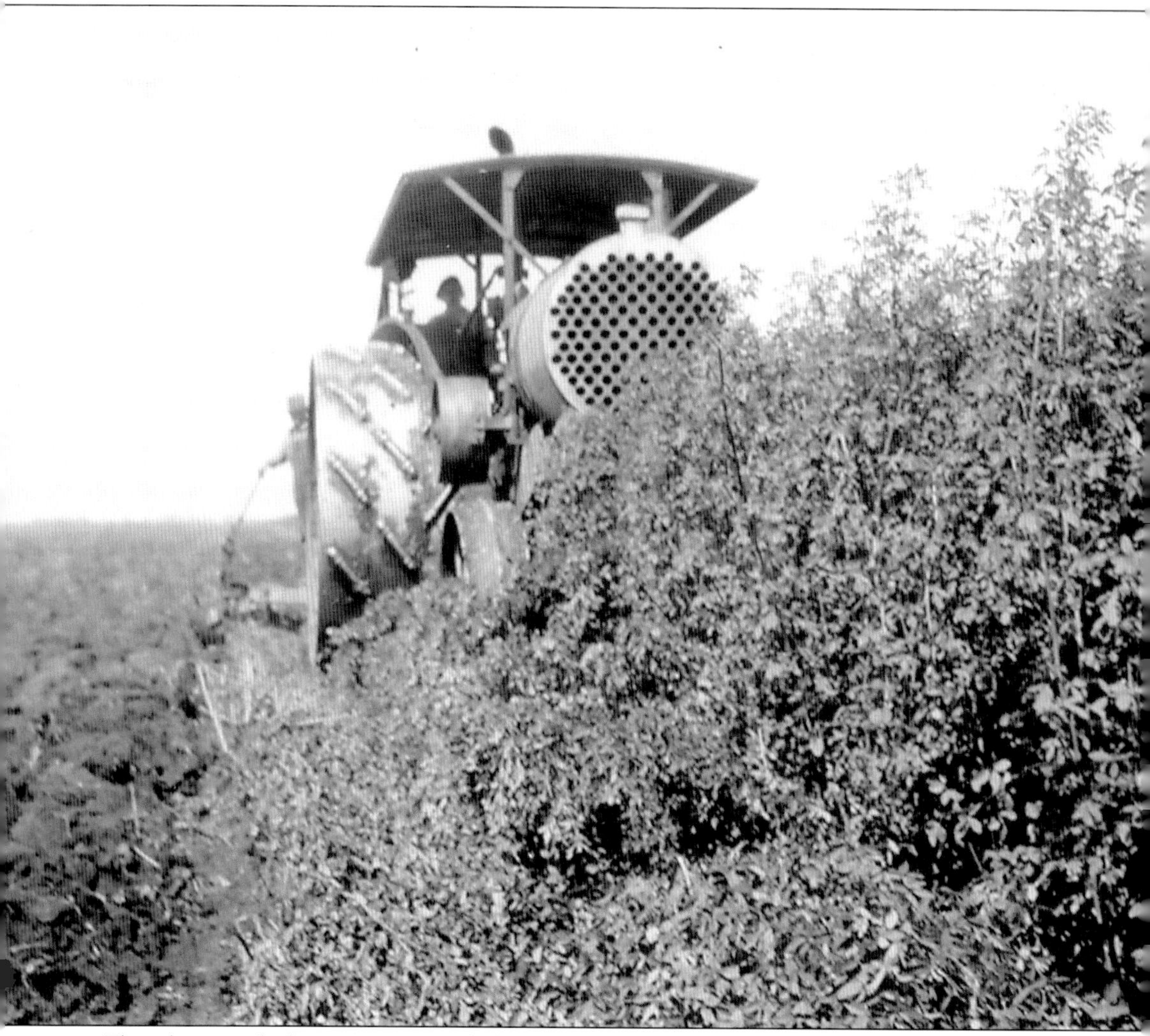

This photograph shows Amenia and Sharon Land Company farmers harvesting sweet clover for seed using a steam tractor around 1900. The company began experimenting growing wheat with clover or grass to produce higher yields of grain crops. Clover was known to rejuvenate soil that was overfarmed. Various grasses and clover would draw nitrogen from the air and deposit it in the soil. Wheat and other grain crops consume nitrogen in the soil. Crops that deposit nitrogen would be rotated with crops that use the nitrogen. The Amenia and Sharon Land Company not only experimented with rotating grain crops with clover and grasses but also conducted tests growing clover at the same time as wheat. When the grain crop matured, the heads of the wheat would grow above the level of clover and could be harvested. The company sold many varieties of clover and grasses as well as grain crop seed. Eventually, clover was replaced by other grasses, such as alfalfa, for use as a rotational crop.

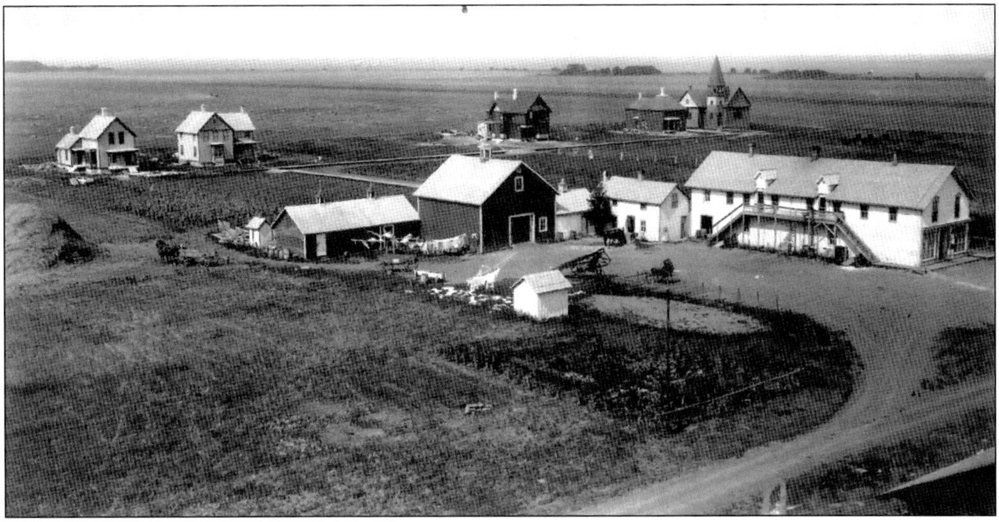

The Amenia and Sharon Land Company began building structures for its workers to sleep, eat, and live while working for the company. This is an aerial view, probably taken from one of the company's grain elevators, of the town's store and offices. Amenia's church and the Chaffee home can be seen in the background.

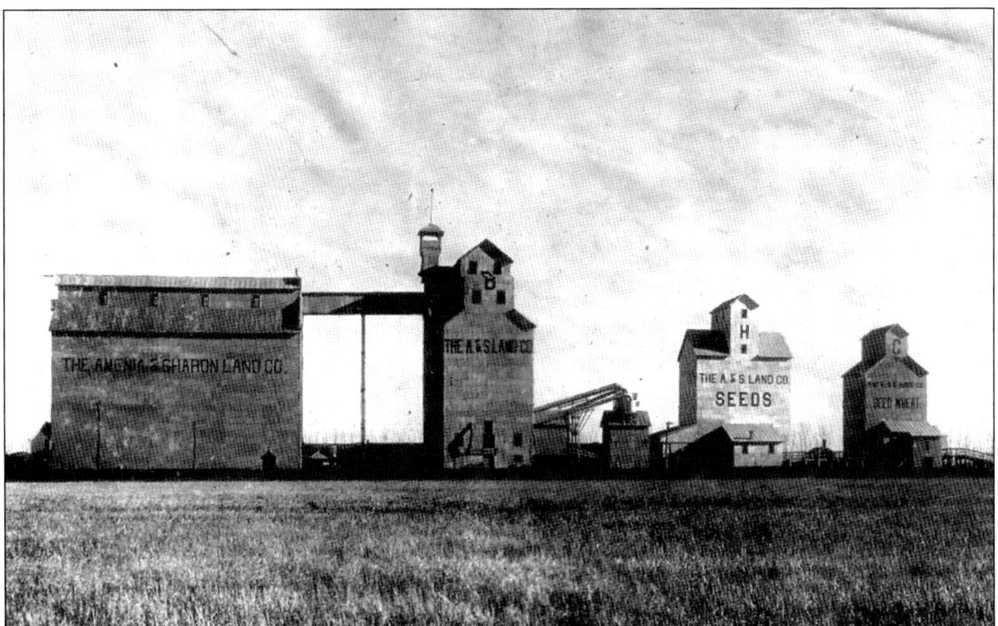


This postcard reads, "The largest grain elevators in the Dakotas – Amenia, ND." The elevators pictured were said to hold 200,000, 50,000, and 30,000 bushels of grain or seed. At the time, there were a total of seven elevators on the Amenia and Sharon Land Company farm; four of the elevators were used exclusively to hold seed.

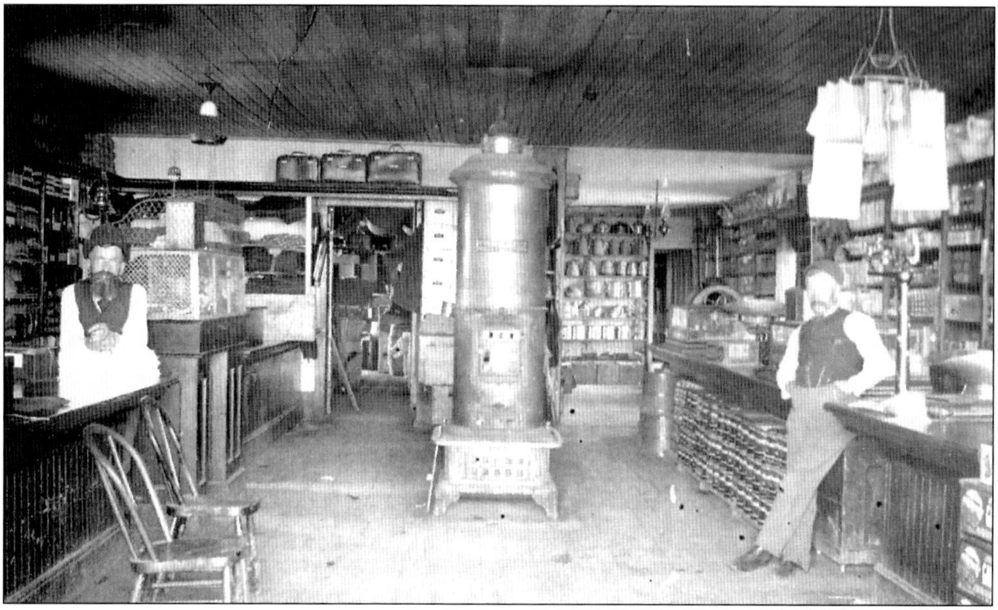

Amenia's general store interior is shown here during the 1890s. The post office counter is in the left front row of the picture. Eben Whitney Chaffee's first office was behind the door on the right side of the picture. The man standing on the left is Nels Mossberg of Wilmar, Minnesota. The man on the right is F. B. Simmons of Hunter, North Dakota.

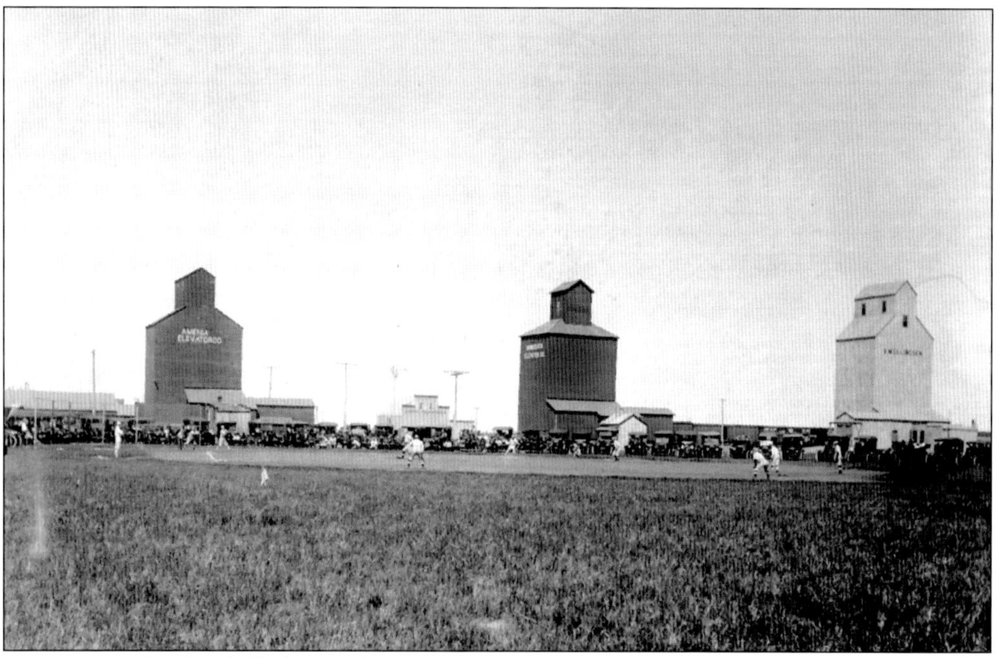

Cars surround a baseball diamond near downtown Amenia during a game around the early 1920s. Grain elevators from the Amenia Elevator Company, Minnekota Elevator Company, and K. Mellingsen shadow over in the background. The field's home plate is in front of the Amenia Elevator on the left.

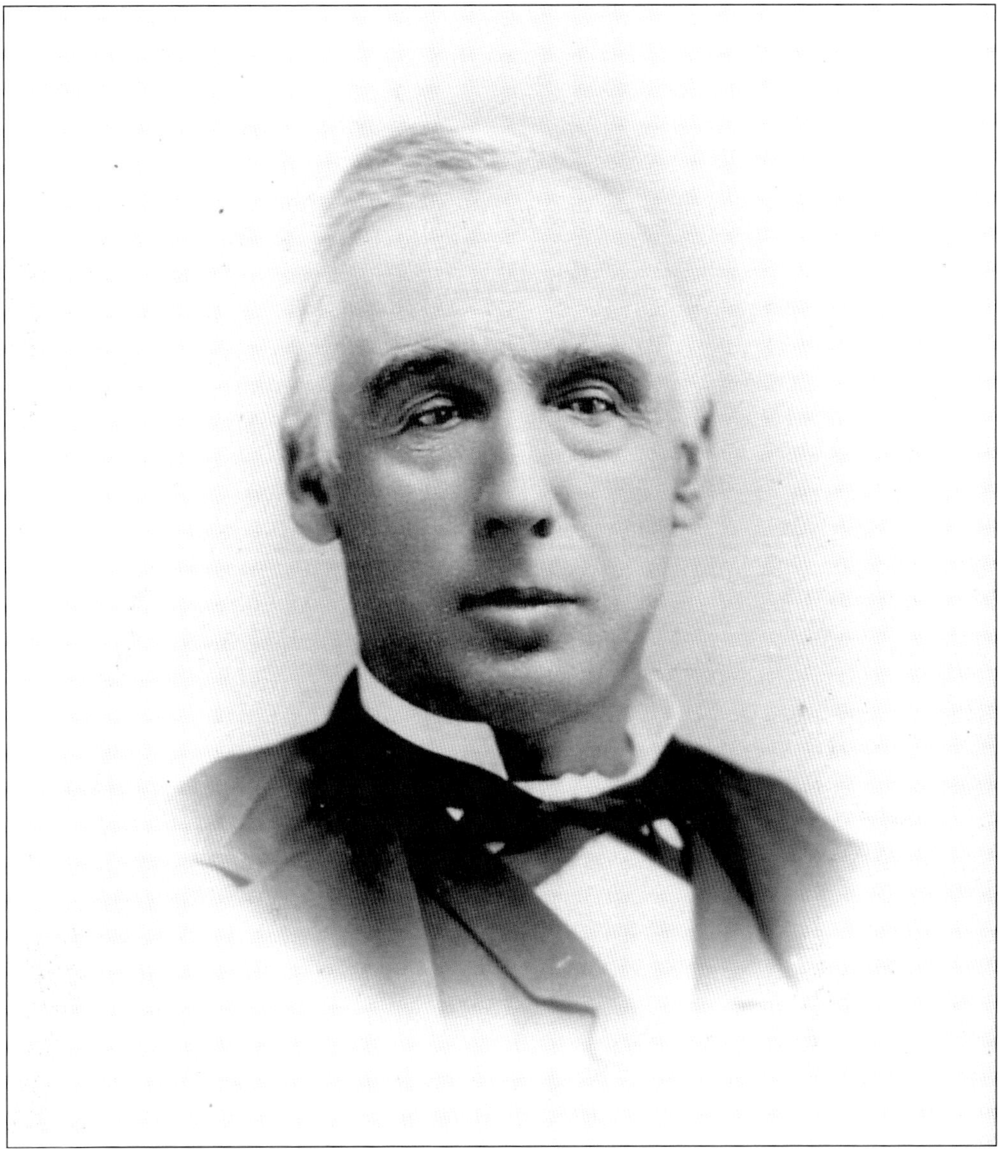

Eben Whitney Chaffee was born in Sharon, Connecticut, in 1824. His family came to North America and began farming in New England near Plymouth Colony in 1635. Chaffee grew up farming his family's land and became a well-respected member of the community. Along with his friends and neighbors, Chaffee invested money in the Northern Pacific Railroad as it began expanding west across the continent. Once investors' bonds matured, the railroad offered bondholders large tracts of land the government had given the Northern Pacific Railroad in exchange for building a railroad across the western United States. Chaffee and his neighbors agreed to the proposition and formed the Amenia and Sharon Land Company in 1875. The name was chosen because most of the investors included in the corporation lived in Sharon, Connecticut, and Amenia, New York. Chaffee was chosen as director of the corporation and traveled to Dakota Territory to select the company's land and run its operations. Land was chosen in the center of Cass County, and a massive farm operation began.

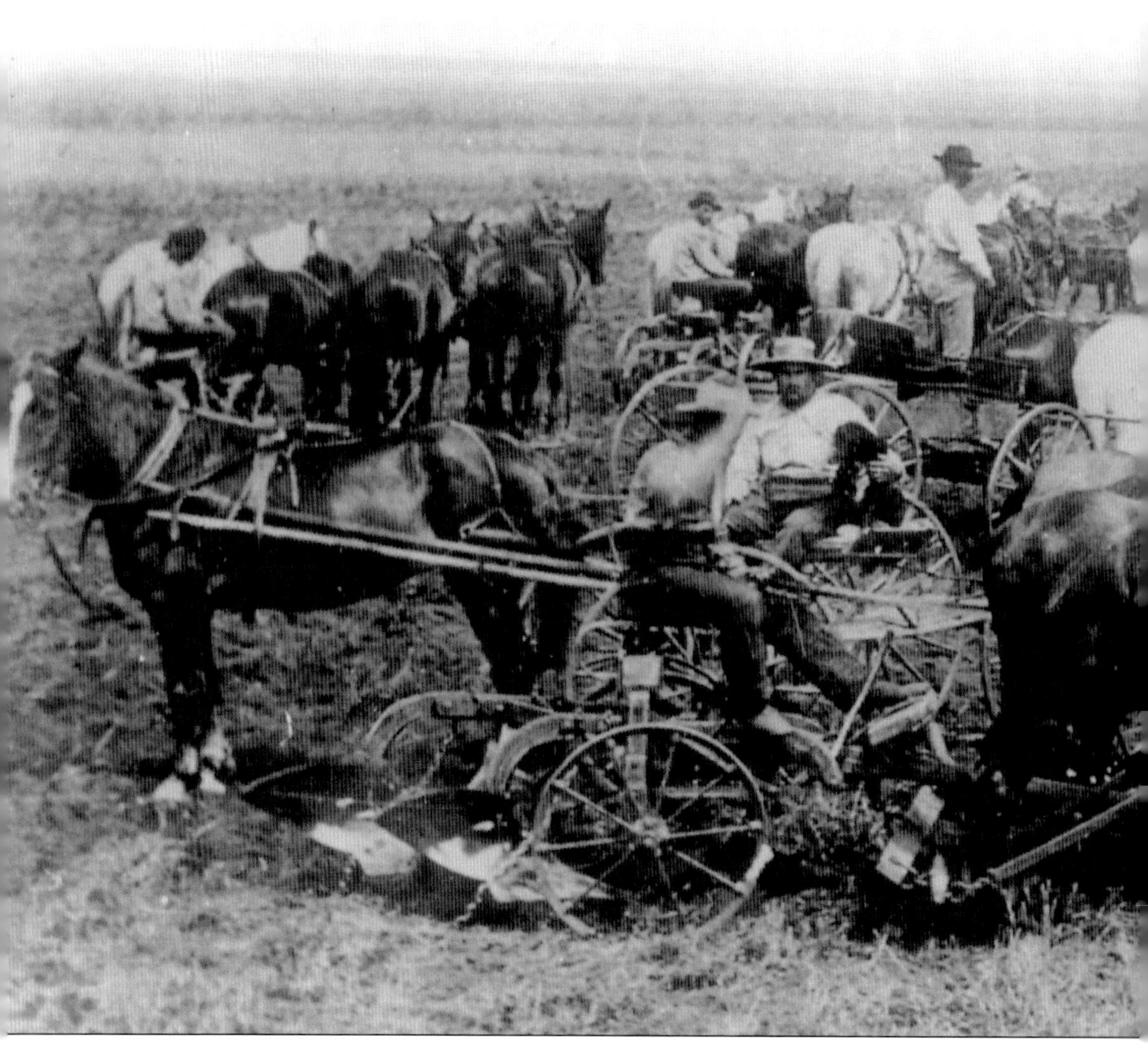

Mules pull plows through the soil of the Chaffee bonanza farm owned by the Amenia and Sharon Land Company. This photograph, taken in 1888 by John R. Hamlin in Rush River Township, was exhibited at the Chicago World's Fair in 1893 and chosen at the 1898 Trans-Mississippi Exposition in Omaha, Nebraska, to be used for a United States postage stamp. Rumor has it the stamp was to be printed using multiple colors and be valued at $2. However, because of budget

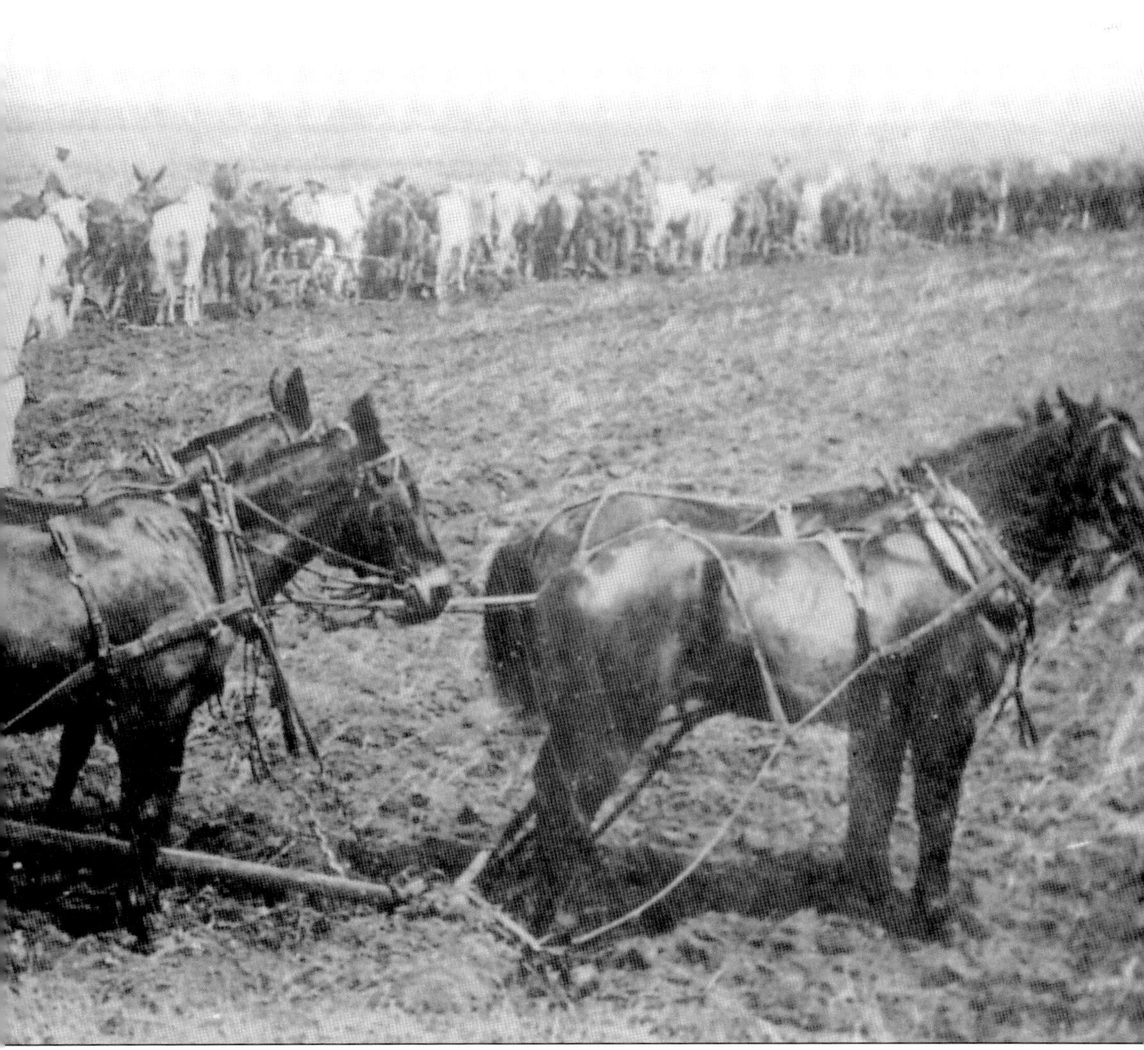

cuts due in part to the Spanish-American War, the stamp was only printed in black and red. It was released with a 2¢ denomination and was entitled, "Farming in the West." From left to right, the men in the middle front of the photograph are identified as Ed Nybakken, field boss Elihu Barber, and foreman Sam White.

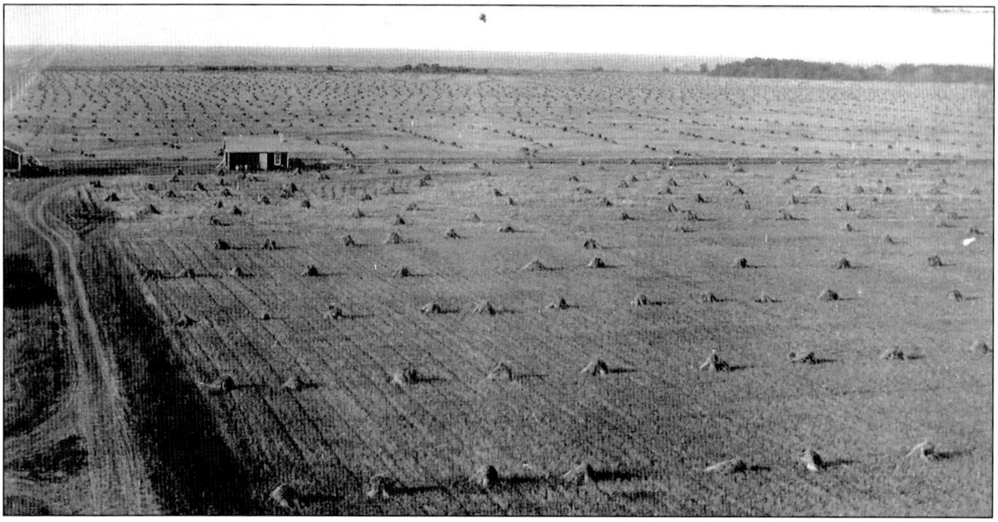

This photograph from the 1880s or 1890s shows a farm belonging to the Amenia and Sharon Land Company near the town of Amenia. The Rush River can be seen in the background behind the grove of trees. The building in the middle of the photograph is a blacksmith shop. The Amenia and Sharon Land Company farmed over 40,000 acres of land.

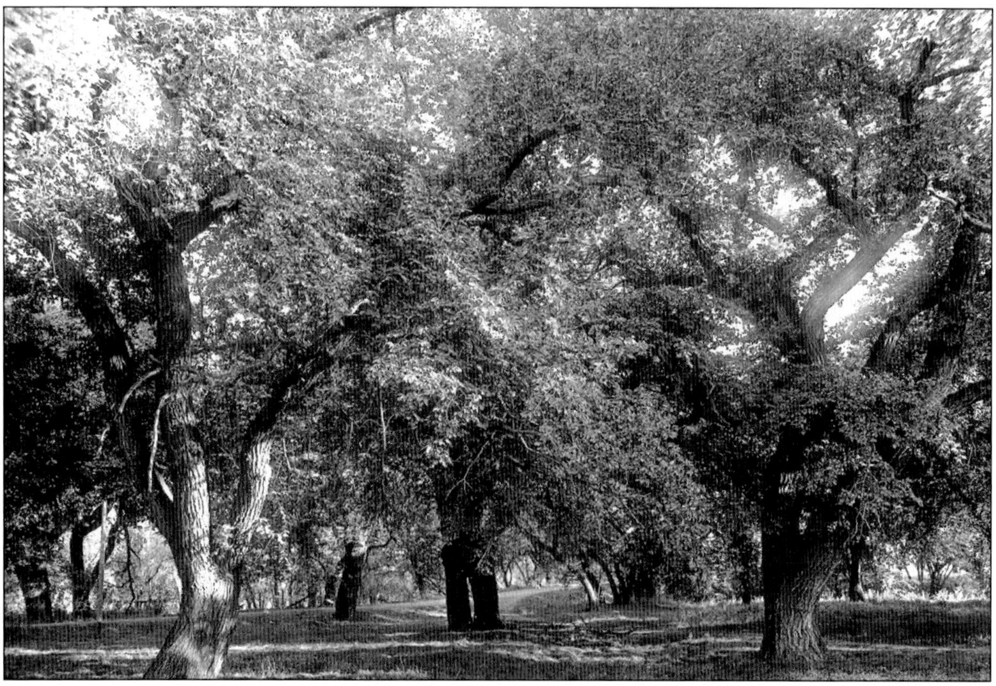

At an early age, W. W. Brown was employed by the Amenia and Sharon Land Company and eventually became manager of its grain elevators. He purchased a 960-acre farm along the Rush River just west of Amenia, known as the Elms. The farm had a lush grove of trees along the river that quickly became a gathering place for people in central Cass County.

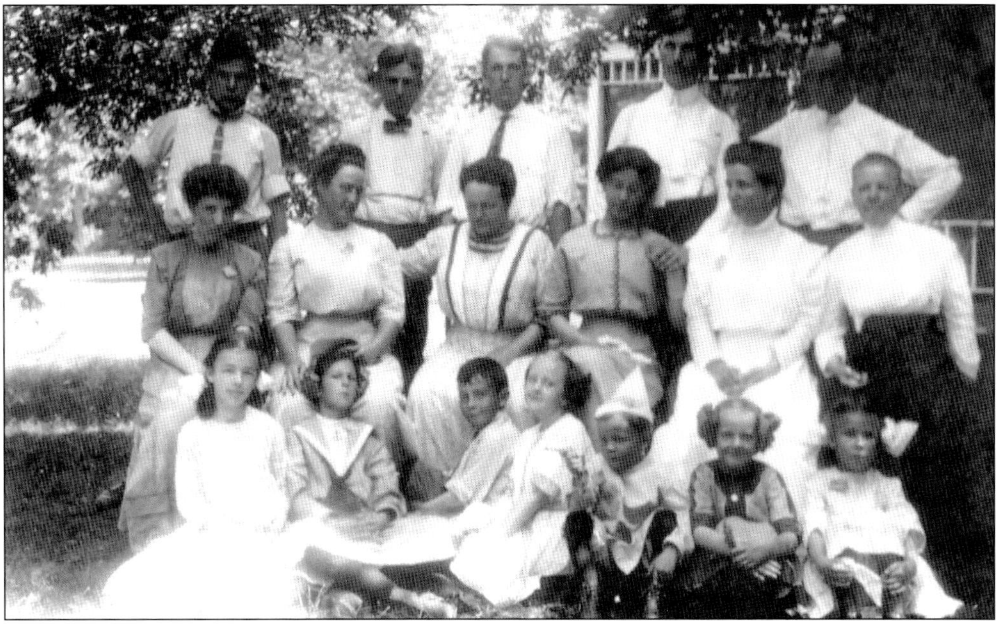

The Chaffee and Reed families pose for a portrait on July 4, 1911. Herbert Fuller Chaffee, son of Eben Whitney Chaffee, took over the Amenia and Sharon Land Company in 1892. His sister Florence married John Horace Reed, who was also involved in the company. After Florence's death in 1884, John took the rest of his family to Dakota Territory where they helped operate the company.

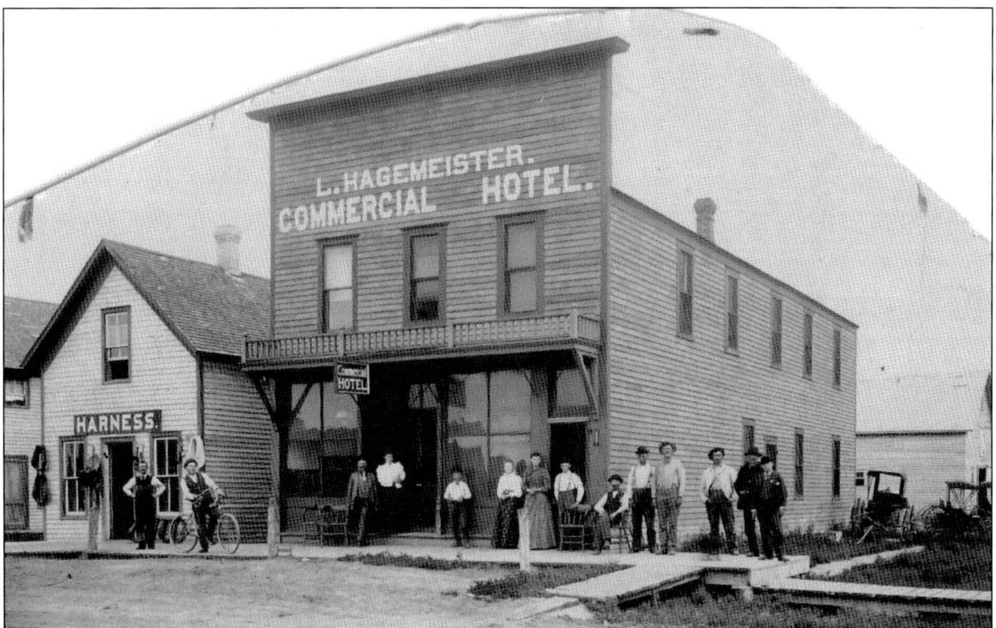


Settlement began in Argusville in 1880. By 1881, the Great Northern Railroad had platted a town site and named it Argusville after the *Fargo Argus*, which was the first daily newspaper in the area. The L. Hagemeister Commercial Hotel and the town's harness shop are shown in this 1890s photograph. Notice the boardwalk sidewalk.

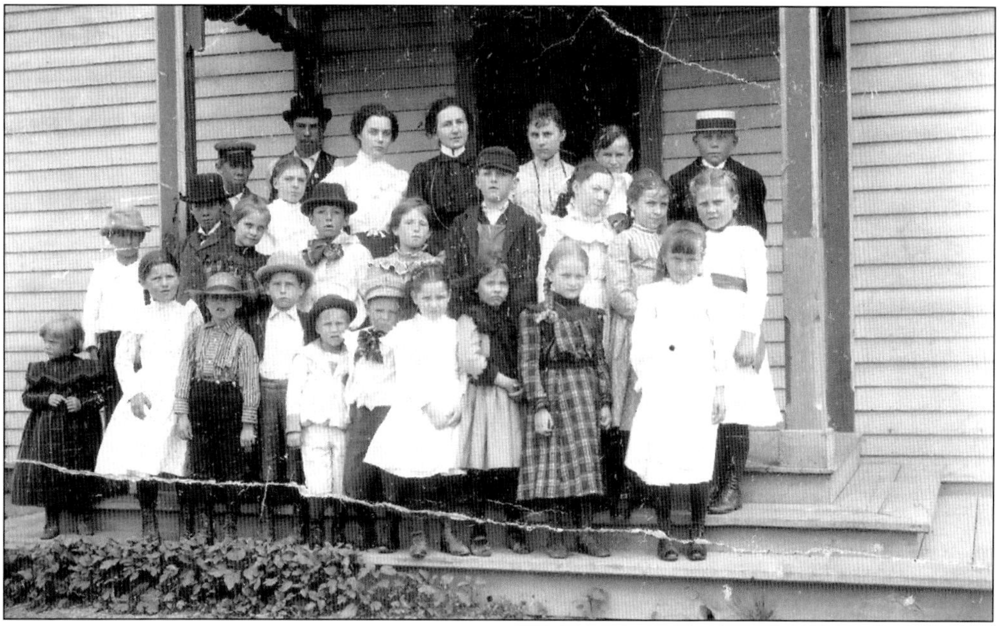

Olive Bogue Bettschen stands with her students on the steps of the Arthur School in 1902. Bettschen had taught 42 students by that year, according to one source. Built in 1882, the school had only one room and was quickly becoming too small. The building was sold to the German Lutheran Church in 1905 after a new school had been constructed.

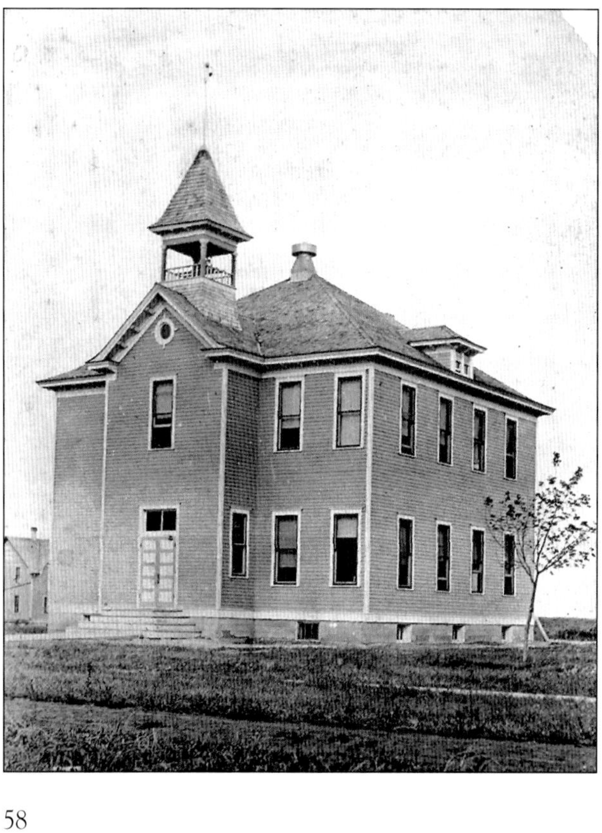

Arthur's second school building is pictured here, around 1911. The new school was another single-story building except it offered two classrooms and a basement. A second story was added in 1911. During this time, school often ended before Christmas and did not resume until the weather became warmer in March. In 1932, the school burned down but was rebuilt soon after.

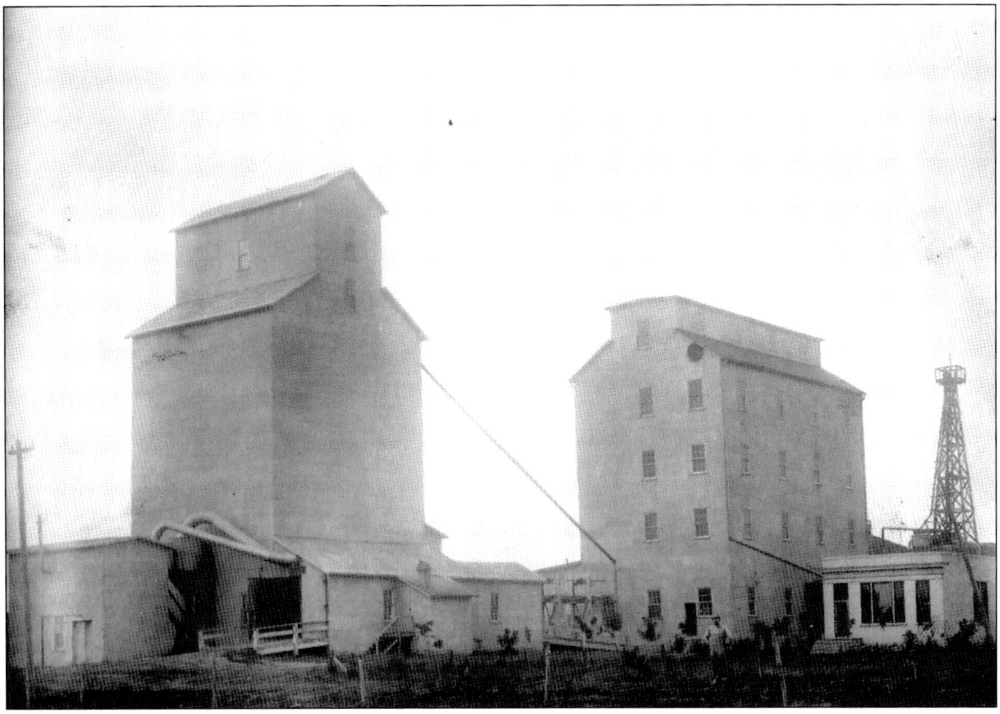

John Miller began his life in Dakota Territory as a bonanza farmer in Richland County south of Cass County. After becoming North Dakota's first governor, Miller returned to his farm and began operating the John Miller Land Company with an office in Amenia. There he became associated with the Chaffee farm and the Amenia and Sharon Land Company. The Chaffee-Miller Milling Company was incorporated in 1906 with John Miller as president. The company managed grain warehouses in addition to manufacturing and selling flour and other grain products. The c. 1910 photograph above is of Chaffee-Miller Milling Company elevators in Casselton. Below is an advertisement for Nodak Flour that was produced by the milling company.

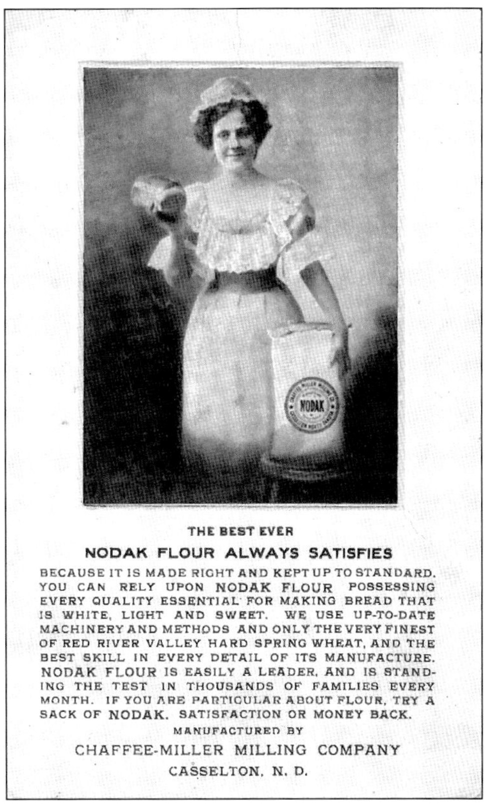

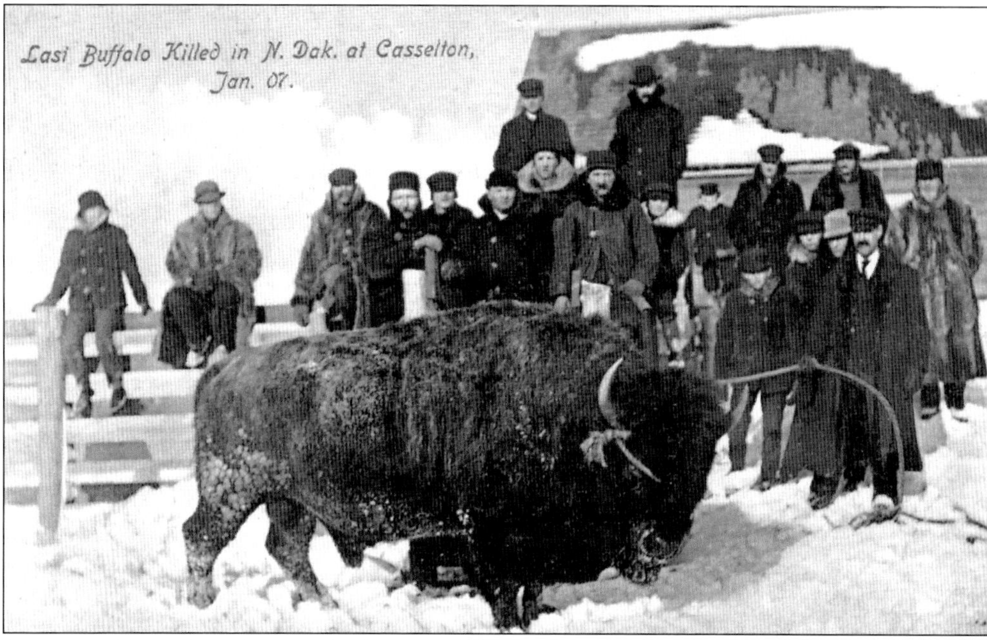


A postcard from Casselton reads, "Last buffalo killed in N.Dak., Jan. 1907." Bison, or buffalo, roamed the prairie of the central plains in North America for centuries. Native Americans relied on bison for food and shelter up until the late 19th century. Once close to extinction, bison are now being raised as commercial livestock.

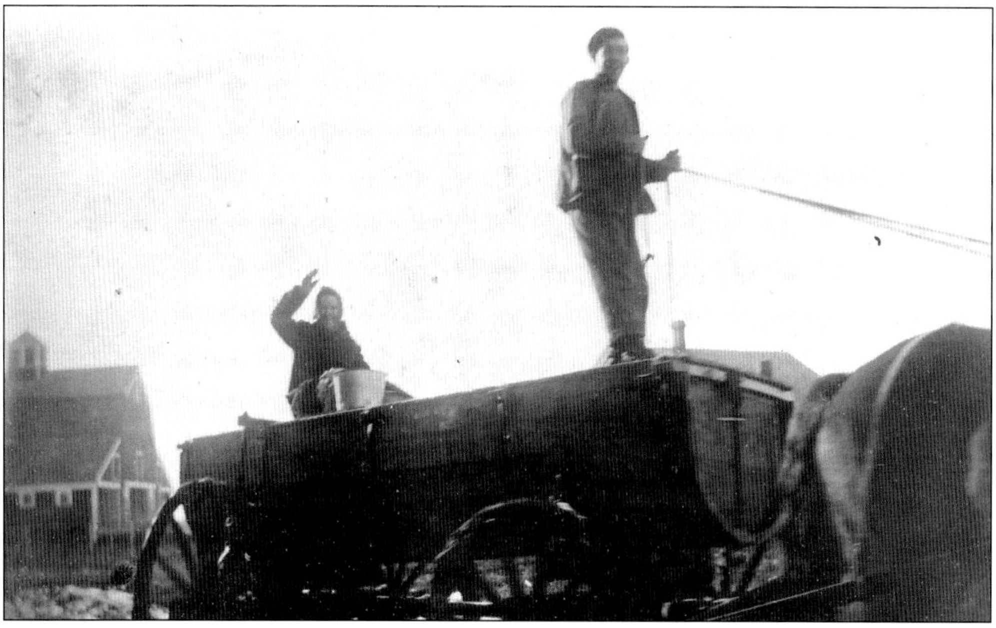

This postcard reads, "Pete and Anna hauling water from coulee in winter 1912." Swan Creek ran through Casselton south of the Northern Pacific Railroad line. West of town was a dam and reservoir where farmers would fill wagons, like the one pictured, to power steam engines and supply animals with water. The reservoir was also used by people of Casselton as a place of recreation.

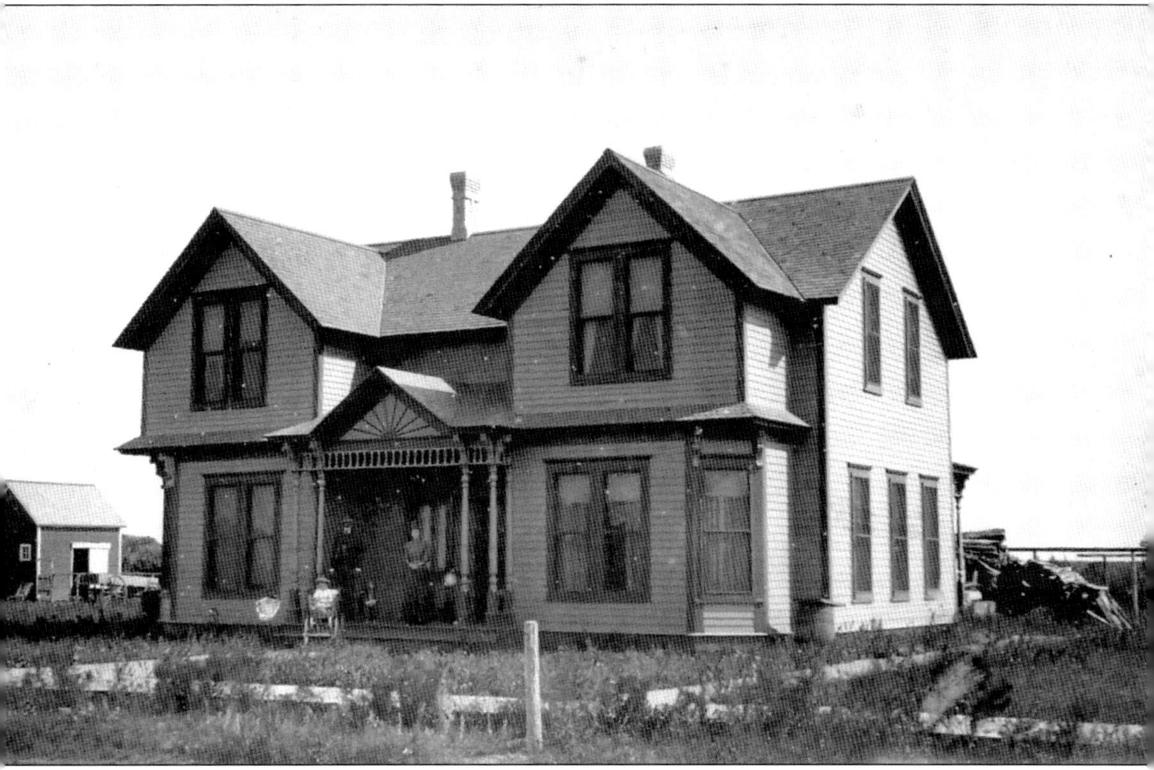

This photograph shows a large home gracing the prairie near Casselton during the 1880s. Most people who came to Cass County could not afford many comforts. For many, the work was hard and the pay was little. Dreams of becoming wealthy from land speculation and bonanza farming was just a dream for most. Some people, however, brought money and investments with them to Dakota Territory, building "mansions on the prairie" that towered over most of the humble dwellings in the area. Many of the people with money followed the railroad from the East, settling wherever the land seemed most profitable. These investors built bonanza farms or opened stores and businesses that became part of the Dakota Boom of the late 19th century. Their entrepreneurial efforts helped build many of the towns and businesses that created a lasting impression on Cass County and the entire region.

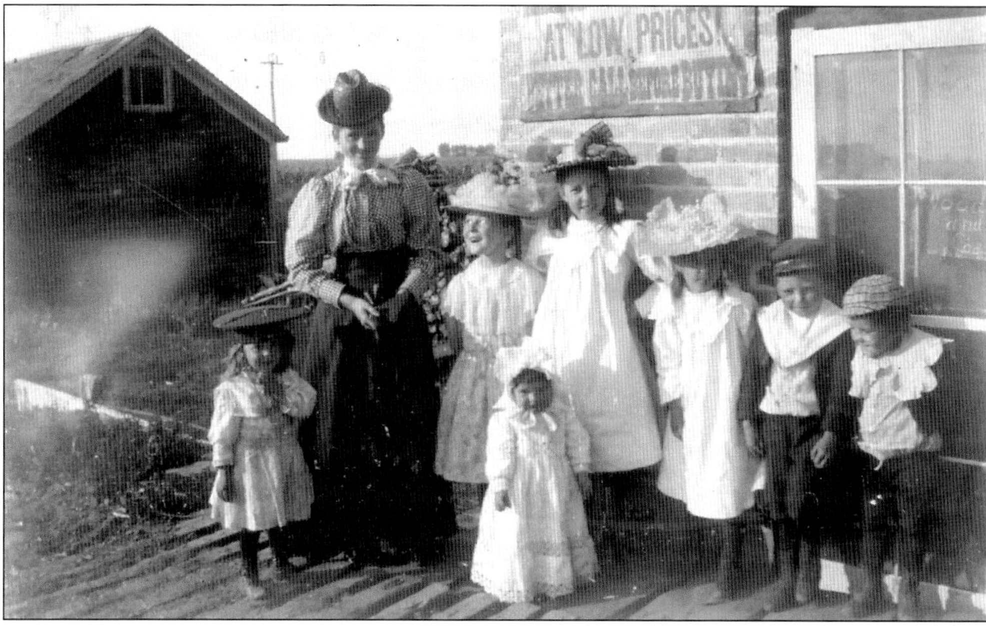


This c. 1900 photograph shows the school class of Olive Bogue Bettschen. Bettschen began teaching in Arthur in 1898 after graduating from Carleton Normal School of Minnesota in 1876. In Arthur, she was paid $35 a month and usually had around 25 students. She married Louis Bettschen in 1902 and had four children, two of which also became teachers.

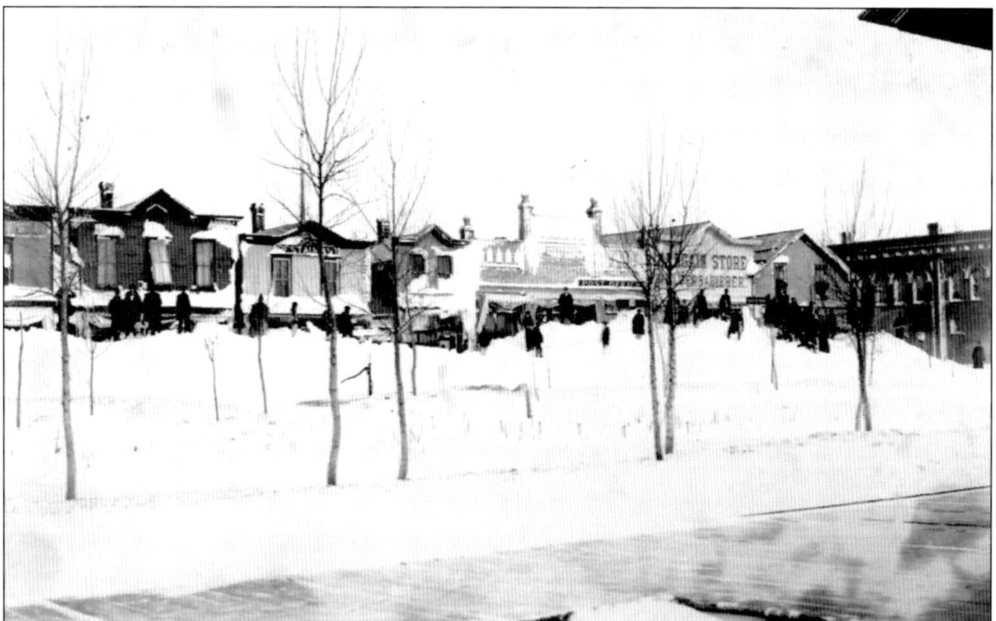

In January 1897, wind blew snow up against buildings, creating a snowdrift in the city's park across from Front Street in downtown Casselton. The flatness of the Red River Valley allows wind to blow for miles before running into any obstacles. In this case, Front Street and the city's park became a resting place for a large snowdrift that built up during the storm.

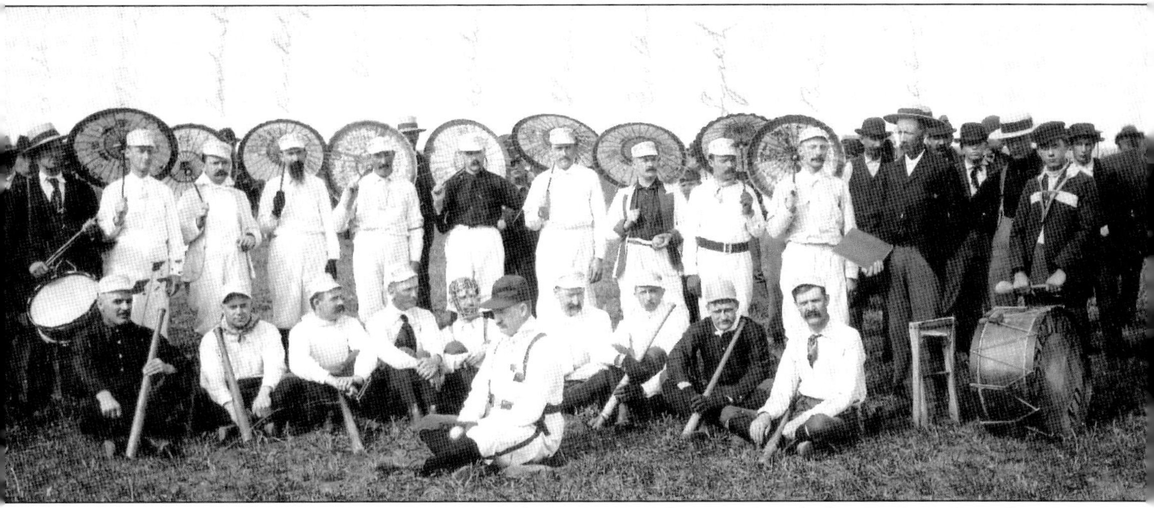

Casselton's businessmen pose for a portrait during a "gentleman's baseball game" in Casselton on July 31, 1895. Sports became increasingly popular in America at the end of the 19th century, baseball in particular. Although baseball had its roots in games of stick and ball among children playing in the street, the game quickly became common across America for adults and children. Leagues began forming in the later part of the 1800s in major metropolitan areas as well as in rural communities. Cities such as Minneapolis had teams playing baseball against opponents from the East. Baseball soon reached to the upper classes, not just as spectators but also as players. Gentlemen's games were organized with business owners and proprietors as players. Here one such game in Casselton is shown. The players in the back row of the team's lineup hold parasols for shade and to reassert their upper-class status. Teams sprouted up across Cass County. Watching, and playing, baseball became a popular form of recreation in the county.

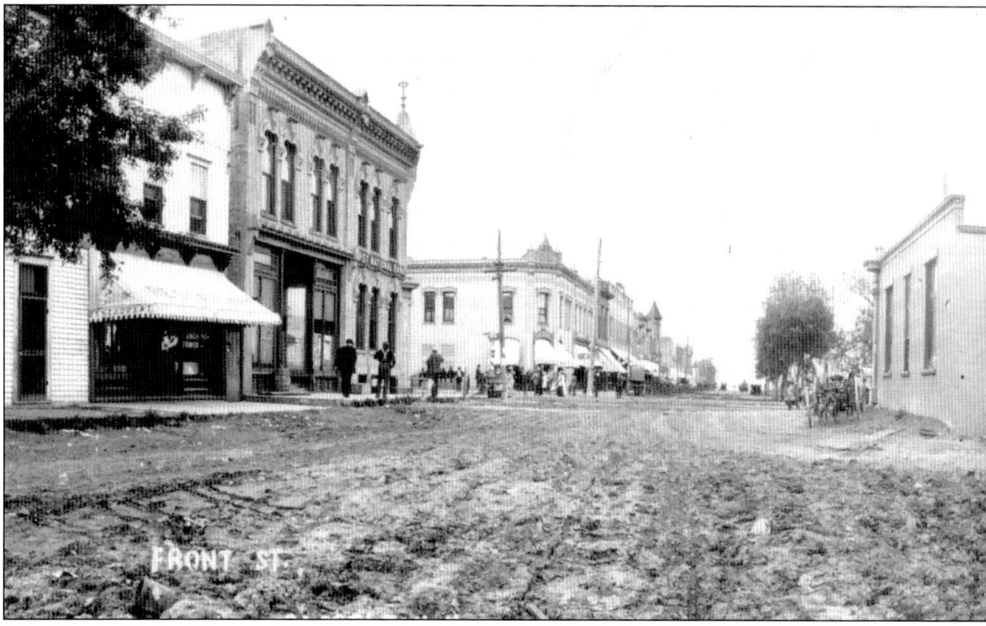


Casselton's Front Street is deeply grooved and worn in this *c.* 1910 photograph. As automobiles became more common in towns and on rural roads, street construction had to be improved. Melting snow and spring rains made many roads impassable due to muddy soil. The county's great soil for crops turned into a thick, sticky mess when wet and hampered people attempting to travel.

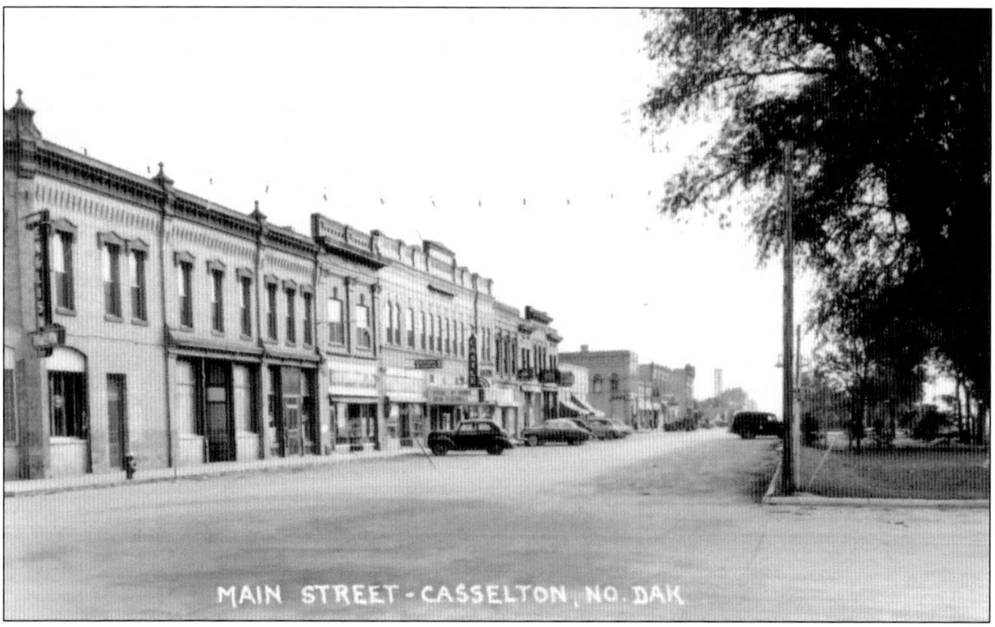


Downtown Casselton in the 1950s looked much the same as it did 50 years earlier. Many of the original brick buildings that made up the downtown were still in use. During the 1950s and 1960s, many towns throughout Cass County and the rest of the United States began tearing down old buildings for new modern construction. While some towns lost their historic buildings, Casselton remained relatively the same.

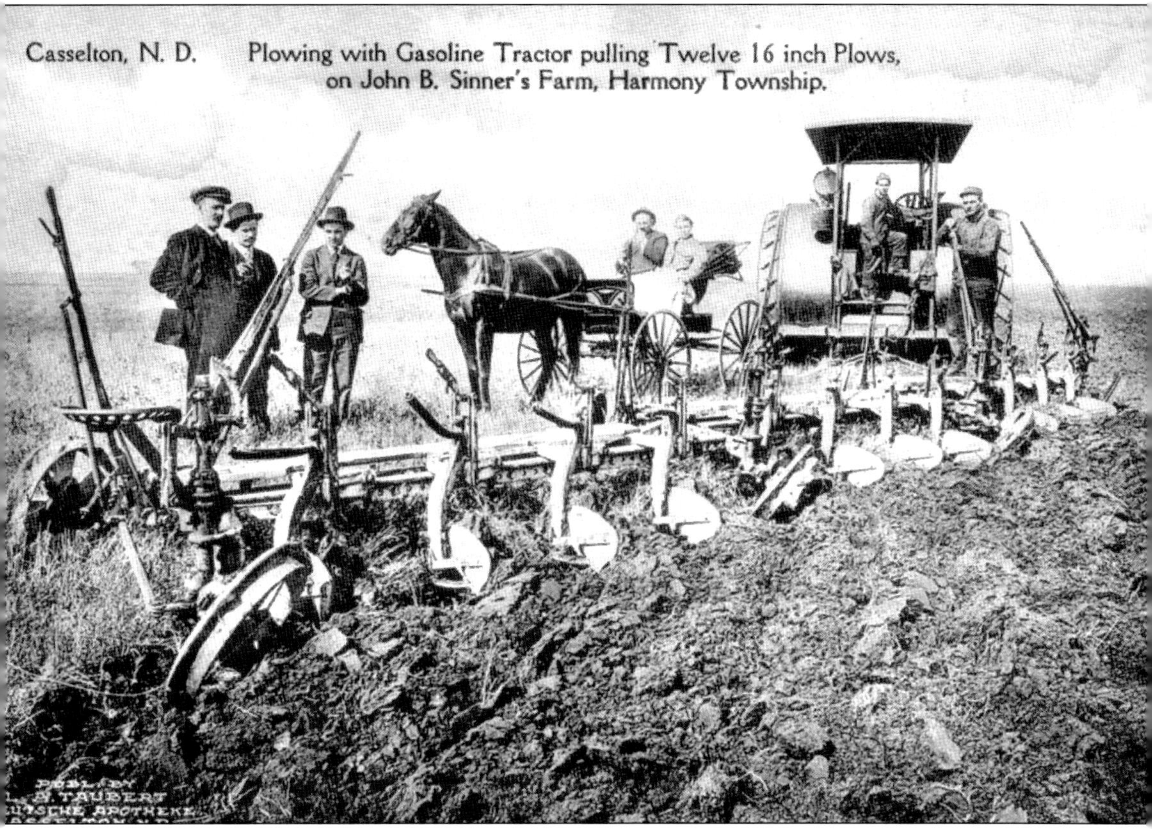


A gasoline tractor pulls twelve 16-inch plows on John B. Sinner's farm in Harmony Township near Casselton. Born in 1860 in Luxembourg as one of 15 children, John Sinner came to the Casselton area of Cass County in 1881. After seeing the farmland in the county he stated, "There are no hills or rocks and the soil is black . . . this is where I will stay." He began working on the Cheney-Dalrymple bonanza wheat farm east of Casselton and the J. J. Bond farm. Over the following decades the Sinner family purchased thousands of acres of farmland near Casselton, including the two farms that John had worked for after coming to the area. In 1919, the land owned by the family was incorporated into the John B. Sinner Farms Company Inc. Sinner died the following year after becoming ill. He and his wife, Josephine, had 12 children; all attended Sacred Heart Academy in Fargo.

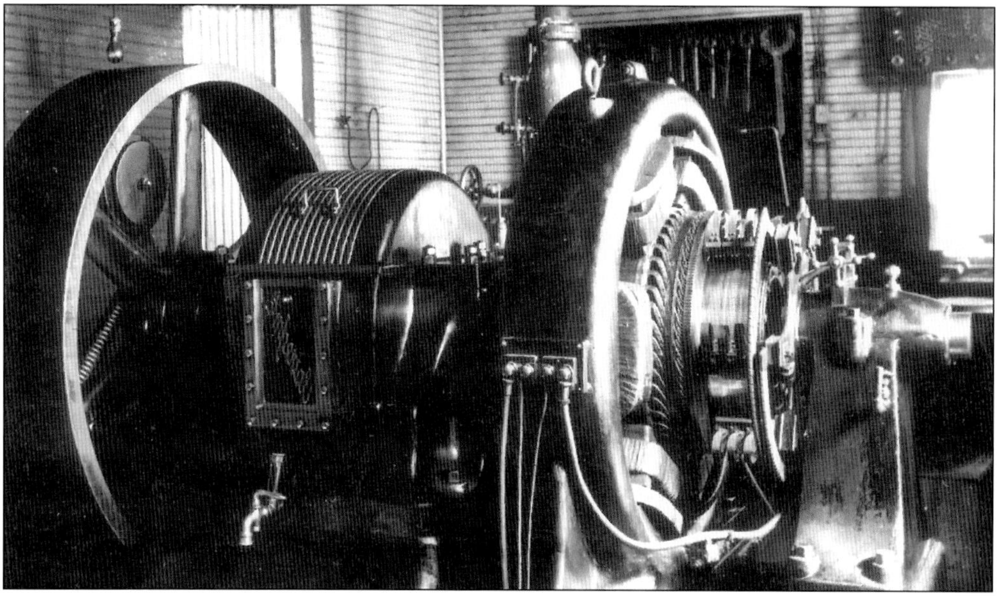

This photograph shows an Imperial generator operating at Casselton's first lighting plant in the early 1900s. At the beginning of the 20th century, some towns in Cass County were operating small generators that ran only a few hours each day, which provided limited electricity for streetlights and basic needs. Before the Otter Tail Power Company established service in Casselton in 1928, two small generators operated in town.

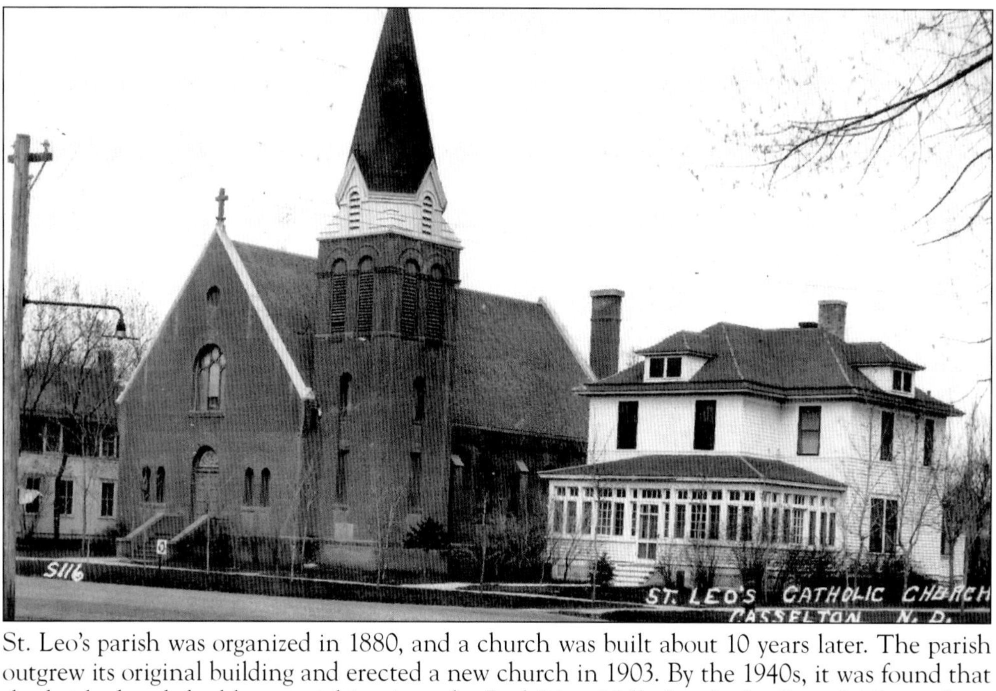


St. Leo's parish was organized in 1880, and a church was built about 10 years later. The parish outgrew its original building and erected a new church in 1903. By the 1940s, it was found that the brick church had begun sinking into the Red River Valley's soft, fertile soil. The sinking church was rebuilt in 1954. The second St. Leo's Catholic Church building is pictured here around 1932.

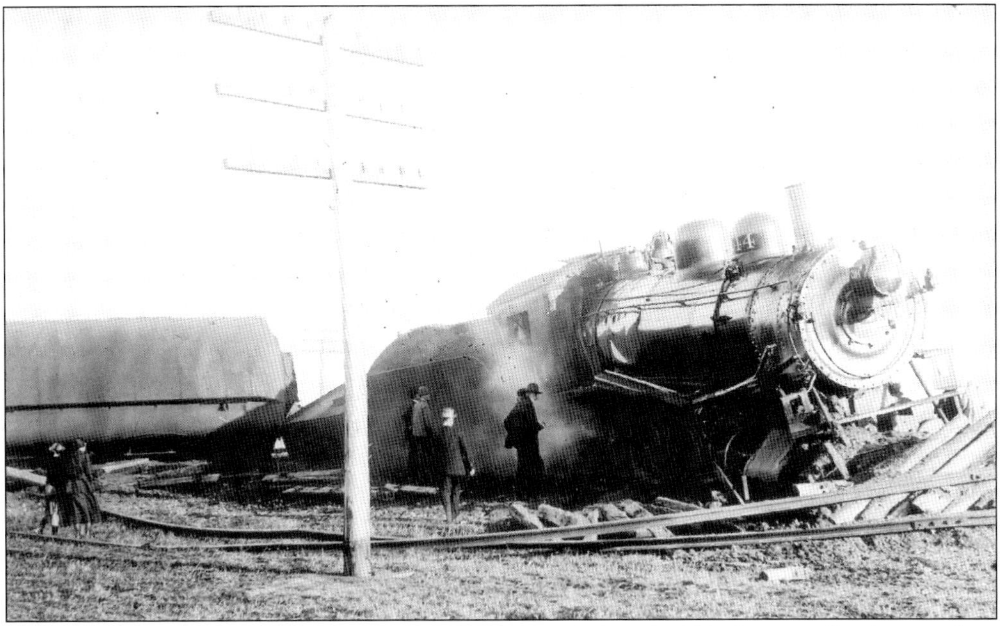

A steam engine derailed near Casselton between 1918 and 1921. Supposedly the accident was caused by two boys who had opened the switch on the tracks so "they could see a good wreck." Another train accident had occurred in Casselton about 20 years earlier when two locomotives struck each other head-on sending one on top of the other.

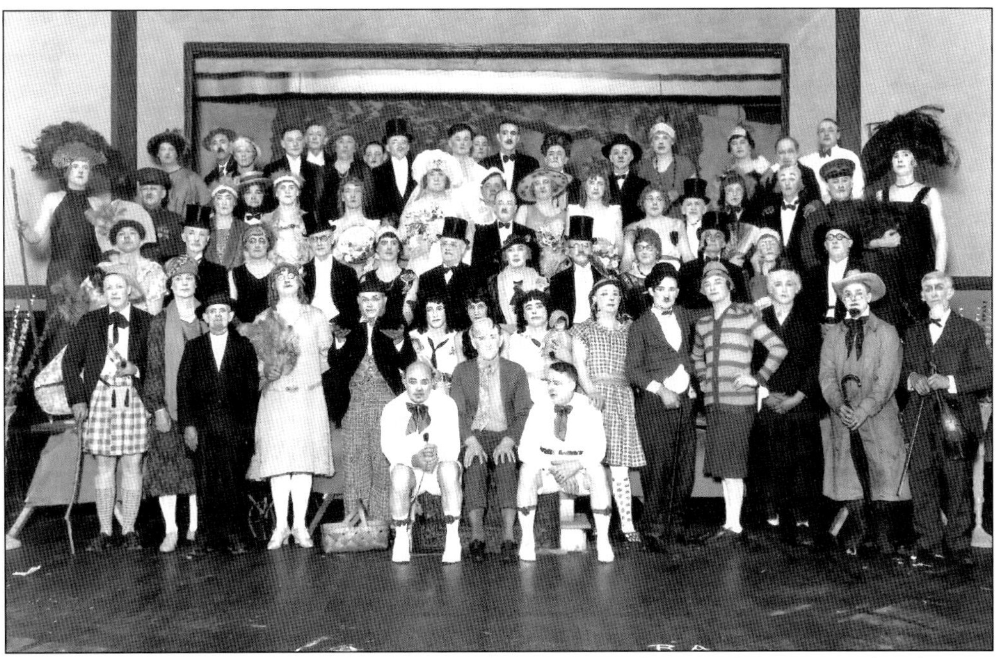

The cast of the "Womenless Wedding" poses for a group photograph in 1928. The play was performed by an all-male cast of local businessmen and well-respected citizens, including doctors and a local pastor. Casselton's high school auditorium was used as the site for the play, which was performed on February 16 and 17, 1928.

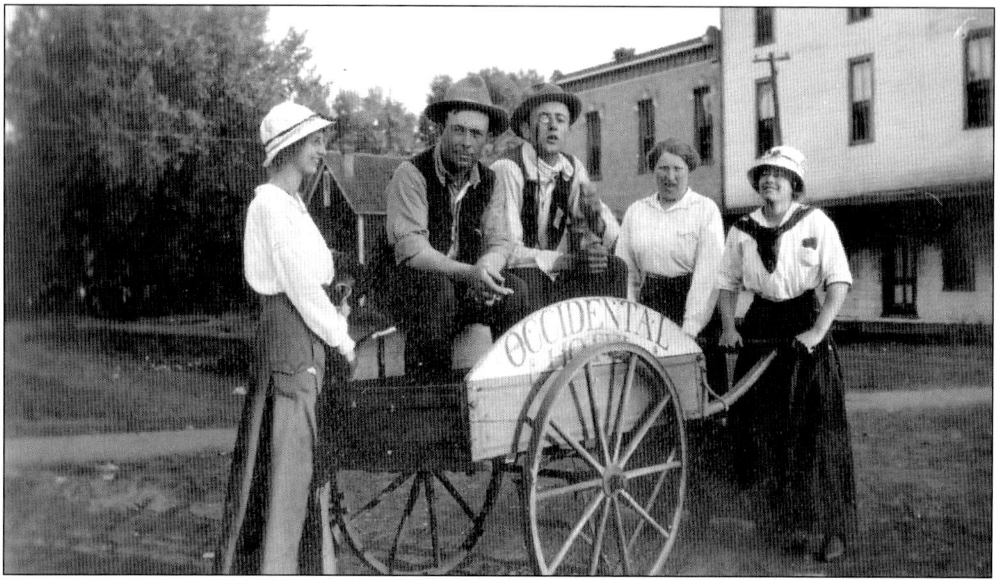


Men and women stand next to a cart from the Occidental Hotel in Casselton. The photograph is part of a scrapbook that documented the Casselton Round-Up "Rough Rider Bunch" of July 1914. The scrapbook's author came from Fargo for the event. She took various photographs and kept track of each day's entertainment.

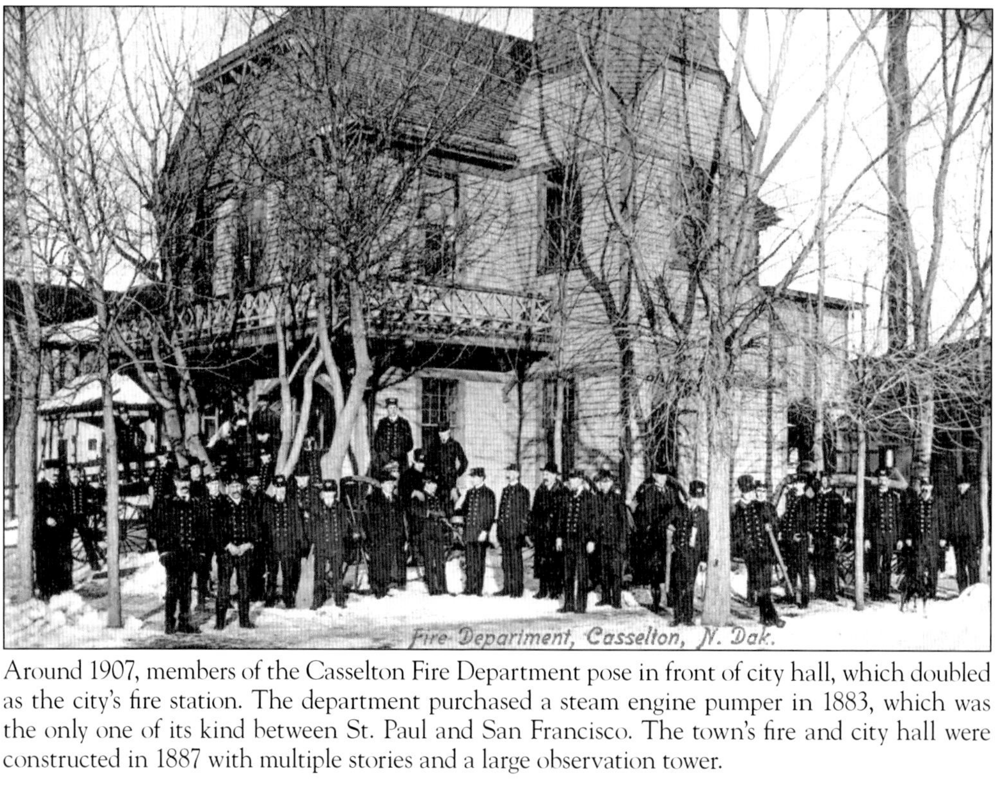


Around 1907, members of the Casselton Fire Department pose in front of city hall, which doubled as the city's fire station. The department purchased a steam engine pumper in 1883, which was the only one of its kind between St. Paul and San Francisco. The town's fire and city hall were constructed in 1887 with multiple stories and a large observation tower.

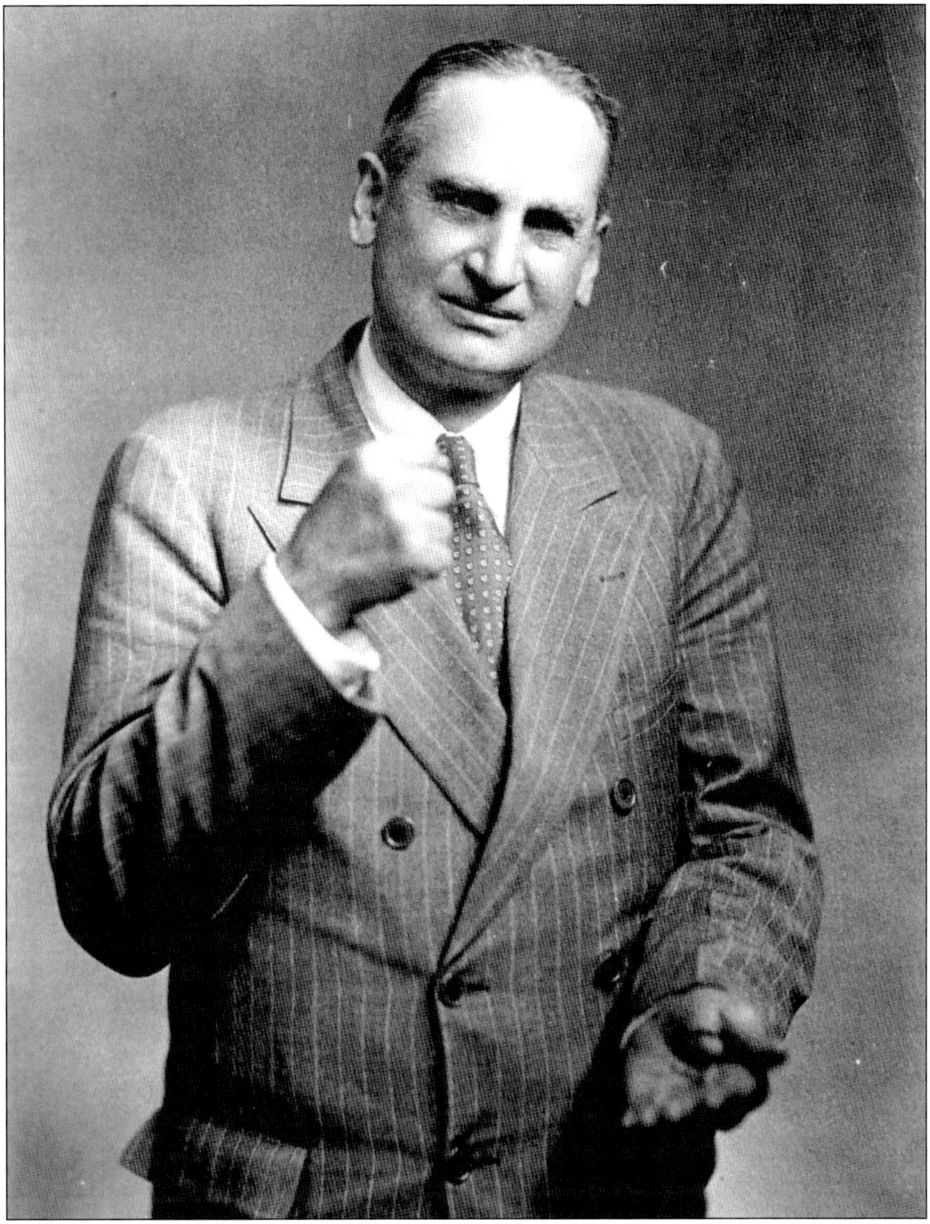

William Langer was born in 1886 and grew up in Casselton. He attended the University of North Dakota in Grand Forks before transferring to Columbia University in New York where he was valedictorian. Langer returned to North Dakota and practiced law in Mandan before being elected as state's attorney three years later. He was elected attorney general under the Non-Partisan League where he gained the nickname "Wild Bill" due to his unorthodox methods. Langer was asked to resign among suspicious activity in his office but instead ran for governor. He lost but eventually won 12 years later. Langer ran into trouble again and was indicted before a grand jury where he was found guilty of felony conspiracy but still went on to win the primary 10 days later. The state supreme court ruled he could not run for office. He was eventually acquitted and won reelection before being elected to the United States Senate where he was an outspoken isolationist and one of the state's most colorful politicians.

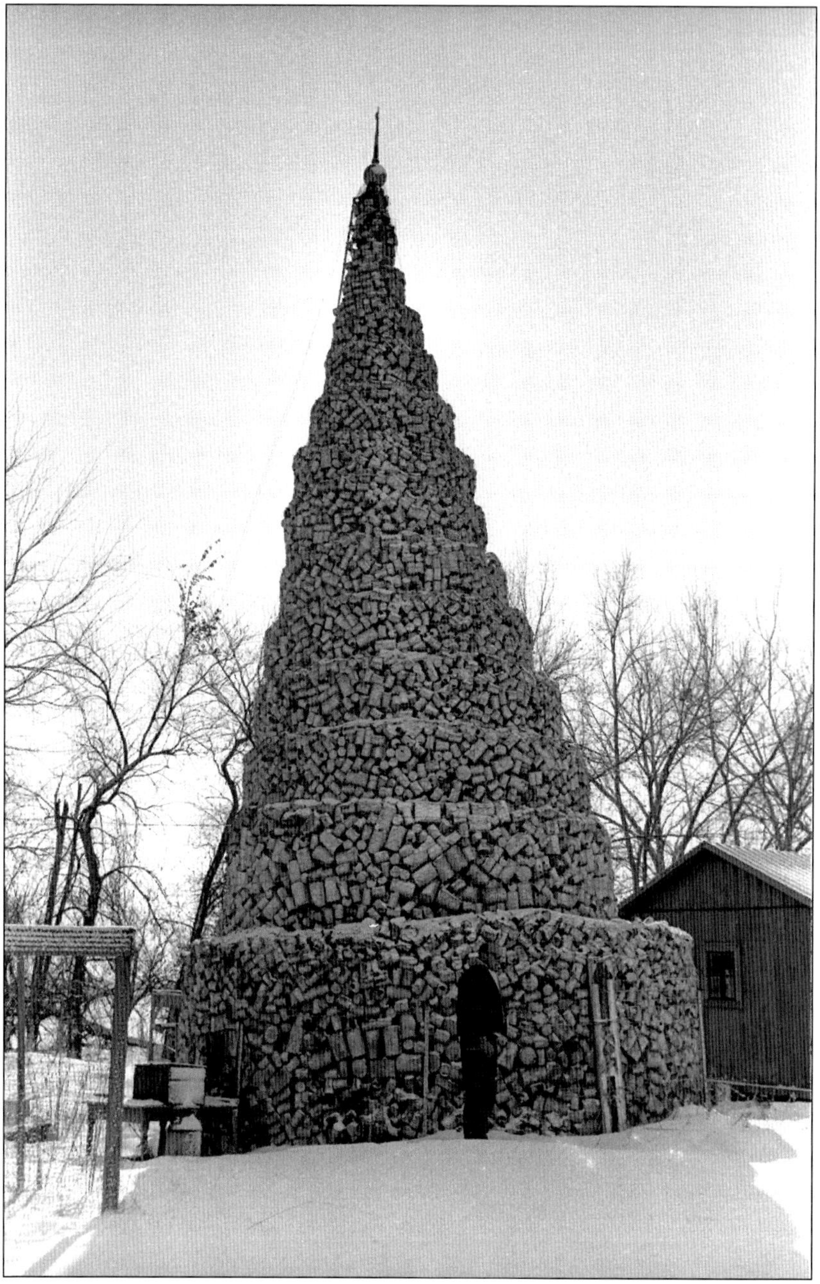

"The Can Pile," as it is known in Casselton, was built by Max G. Taubert at the intersection of Highway 10 (now Interstate 94) and Highway 18 just south of Casselton. Taubert opened a service station and lunch counter that was open 24 hours a day, seven days a week. The truck stop became popular with truck drivers hauling cattle to the West Fargo Stockyards. The restaurant, which was named after the world's largest stack of empty oil cans, was known for having the best hamburgers between Chicago and Seattle because the meat was fresh and all the cuts of the cow were used. During the dust bowl of the 1930s, the Can Pile offered free water, and sometimes coffee, which kept business going. Taubert continued operating the Can Pile, usually working the night shift, until his death in 1973.

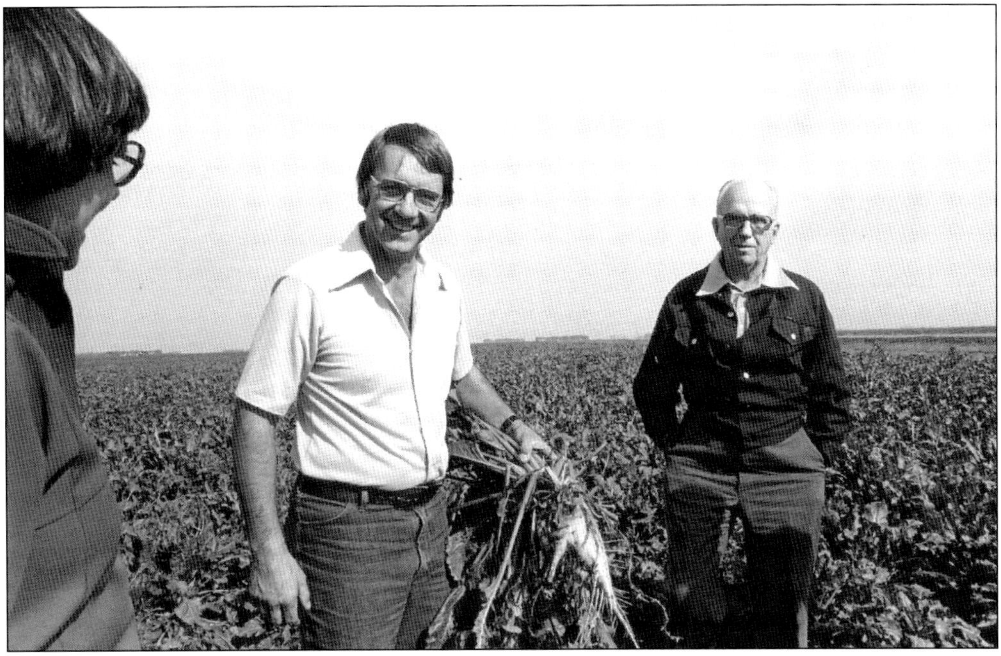

George A. Sinner was born in Fargo and raised in Casselton, which became known as "Governor City" due to a number of governors who have come out of the area. Sinner would live up to the town's title, becoming governor in 1985. He was a farmer by trade and served on many farm-related associations.

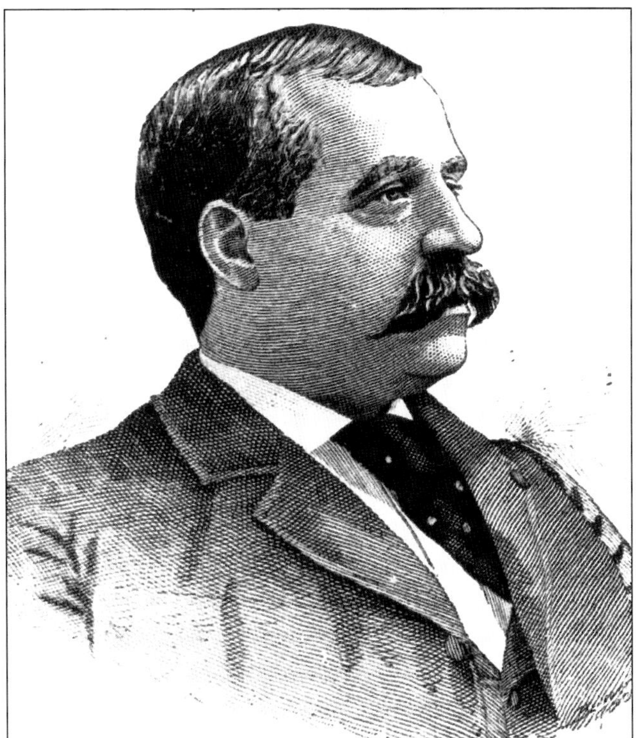

Andrew H. Burke and his wife arrived in Casselton in 1880 with no more than $65 in their pockets. He became a cashier at the First Nation Bank of Casselton. It was not long before Burke became county treasurer and eventually the state's second governor. Farmers were disappointed by him when he vetoed a law requiring railroads to lease land for buildings.

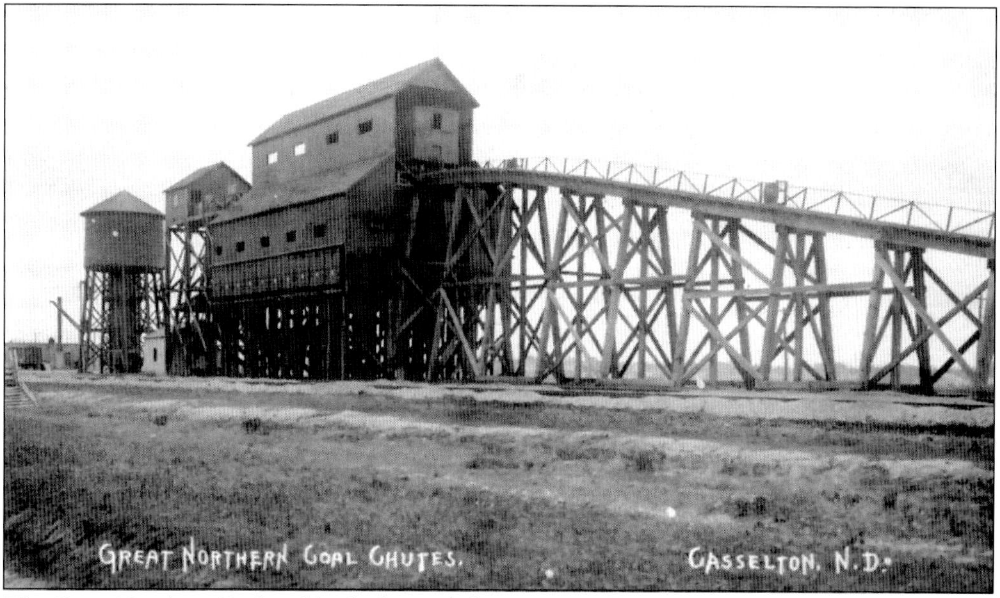


The Great Northern Railroad built the coal chute pictured here around 1905. This building was located about a half-mile from the Casselton roundhouse. Railcars were pulled up the ramp and drawn in the building. They would dump their load of coal, filling the locomotive with a new supply of fuel. This structure burned down in 1934.

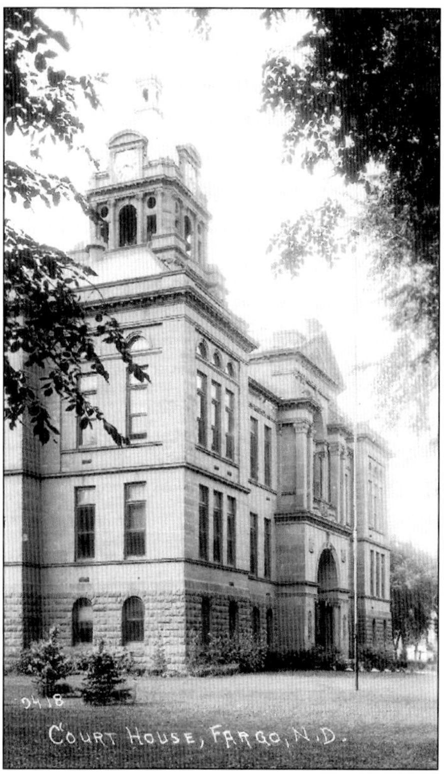


Fargo became the county seat early on due in part to its larger population and its proximity to transportation routes. Most of the county's offices were built in the city. The Cass County courthouse, pictured here during the 1920s or 1930s, was the second courthouse built by the county in the city of Fargo.

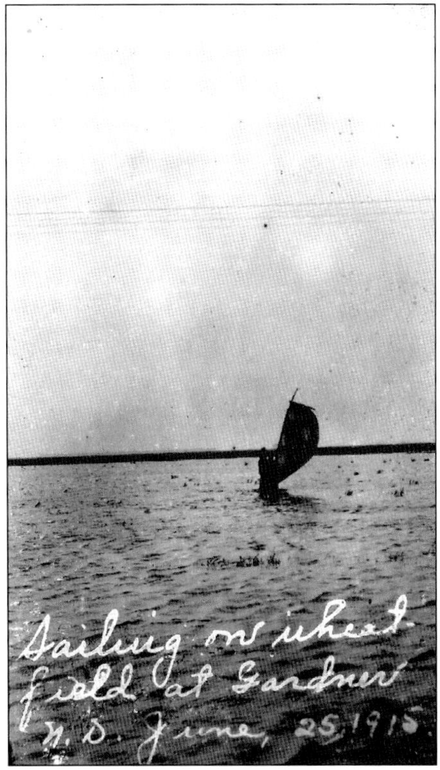


A flooded wheat field provided the perfect opportunity for these children to try out their homemade sailboat (right) on June 25, 1915. Water covered most of the land in the region, coming up to the Great Northern Railroad station in Gardner. Much of Cass County is prone to flooding from rivers as well as overland flooding. Quickly melting snow or heavy spring rains often result in water flowing over the ground toward local rivers and streams. Ice dams on the Red River are also a common factor in spring flooding. The flooded fields pictured here are probably a result of torrential rain because the flood occurred during the summer.

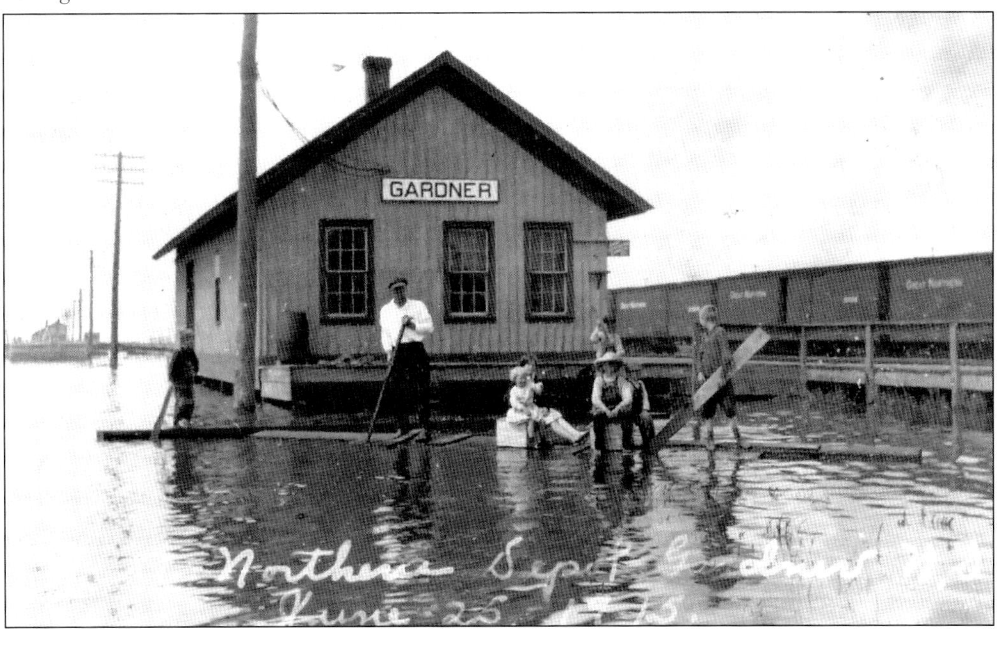

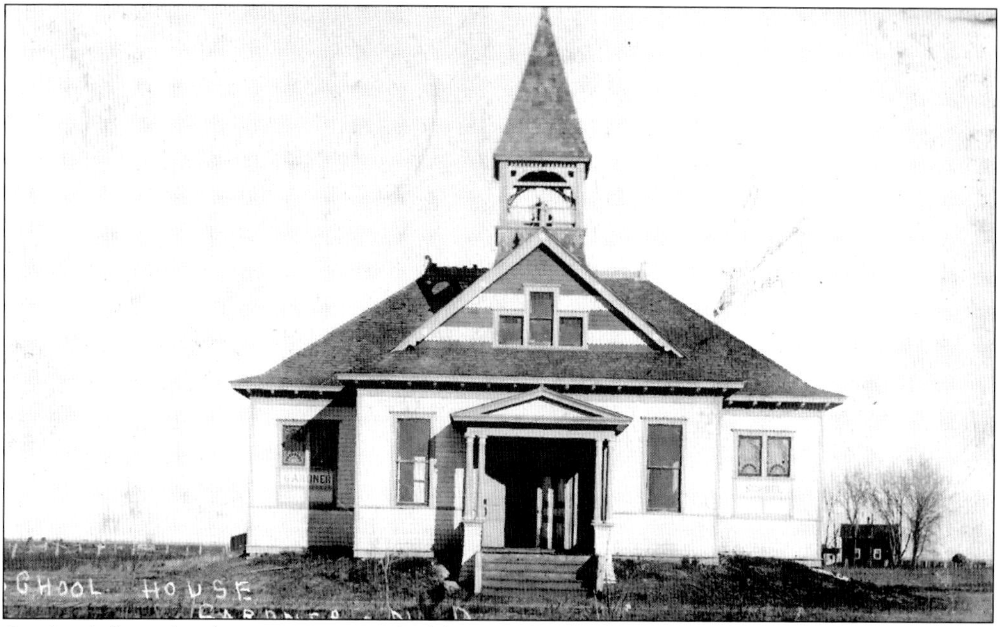

Gardner's first school was a two-room building constructed in 1895. The school's design appears to be partly taken from Scandinavian architecture. Also, notice the stained-glass windows on either side of the building. The school was used until a larger school was constructed in 1913. This photograph was taken around 1912.

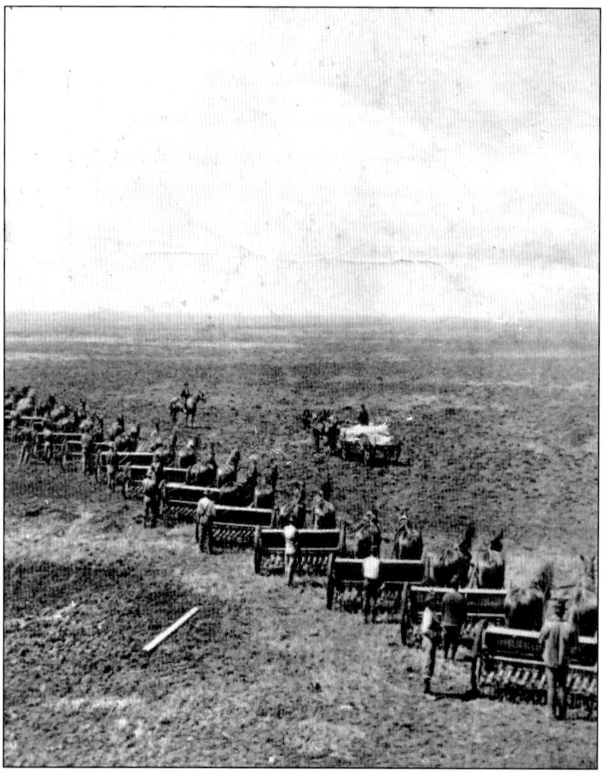

This photograph shows workers on the Rand Brown farm tilling the soil near Grandin in 1891. Large teams of men, animals, and machines were needed to work the huge bonanza farms. Land in the Red River Valley yielded itself to farms of this type in the late 1800s. The photograph illustrates the flat, fertile soil of Cass County and the Red River Valley.

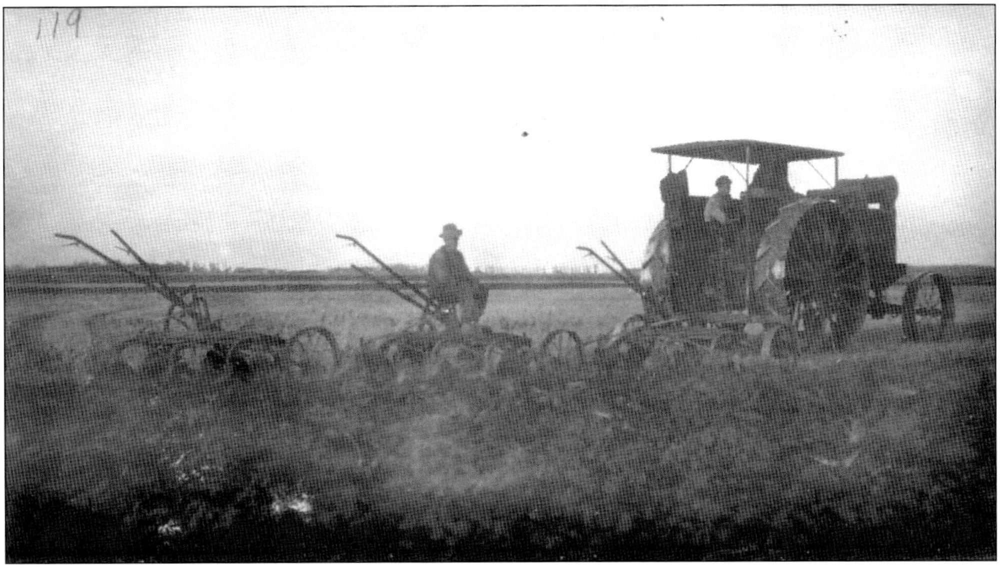

Workers on the John Herman farm, four miles north of Grandin, use a 1909 Flower City Gas Engine to plow the fields around 1910. The engineer is James J. Margach. Farmers began buying gasoline-powered tractors to replace steam tractors that had been used since the late 1800s. By the 1920s, gasoline-powered tractors had become the norm.

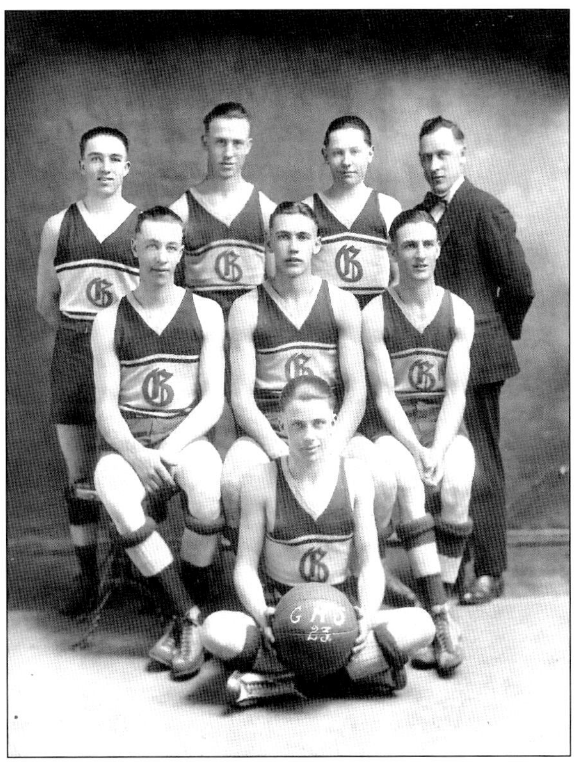

Here is Grandin's first high school basketball team, which was photographed in 1923. The first school in Grandin was built in the mid-1880s. It was eventually replaced by a two-story building that housed four classrooms. The building burned down in 1920 and was replaced by a brick structure that same year. Basketball was an extremely popular sport in the area during the 1920s. High school basketball teams were organized throughout the county.

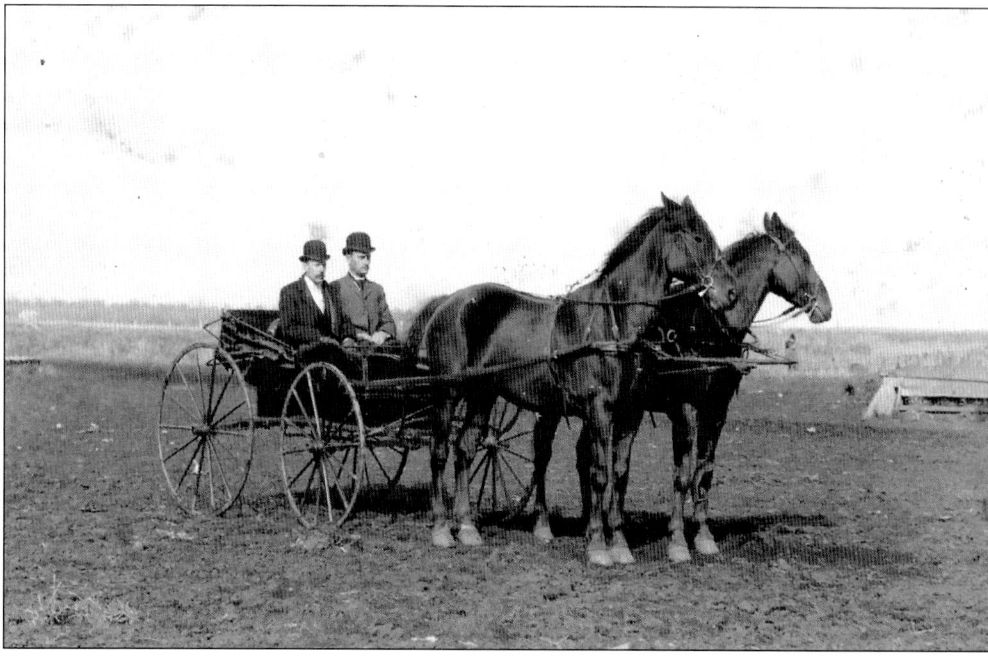

Oliver Dalrymple, sitting on the right, is pictured with his prized horses and buggy in the 1880s. The horses were reportedly the fastest team of horses in the area. They were so fast, that it was said that they beat a steam locomotive in a race. This could have been possible if the both started from a standstill.

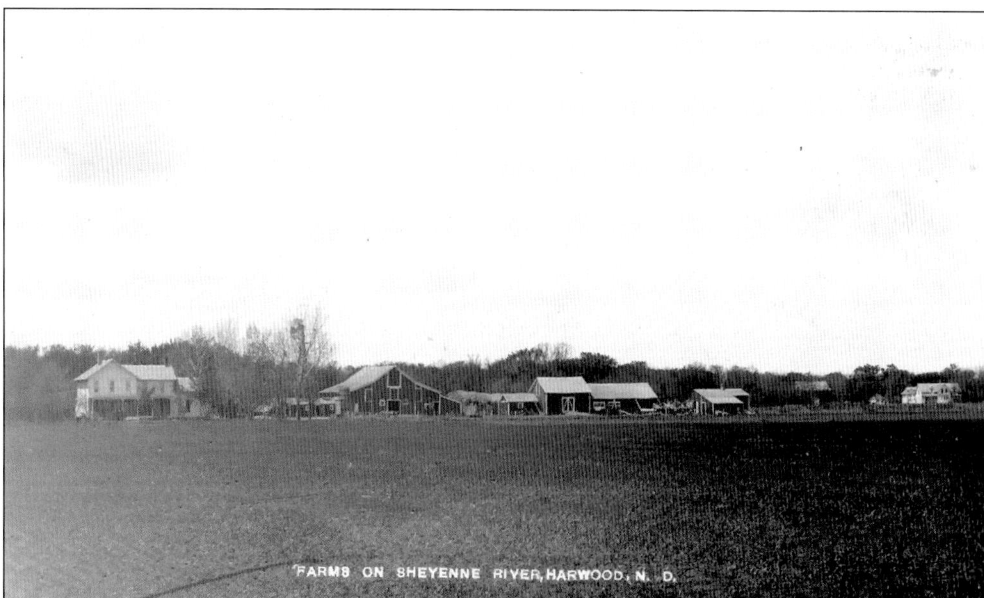


This photograph shows a farm sitting by the Sheyenne River near Harwood. The town of Harwood is situated on a thin stretch of land between the Red River and the Sheyenne River. Although the land is ideal for farming, it is also prone to flooding in the spring when it is not uncommon for both rivers to overflow their banks due to melting snow and seasonal rains.

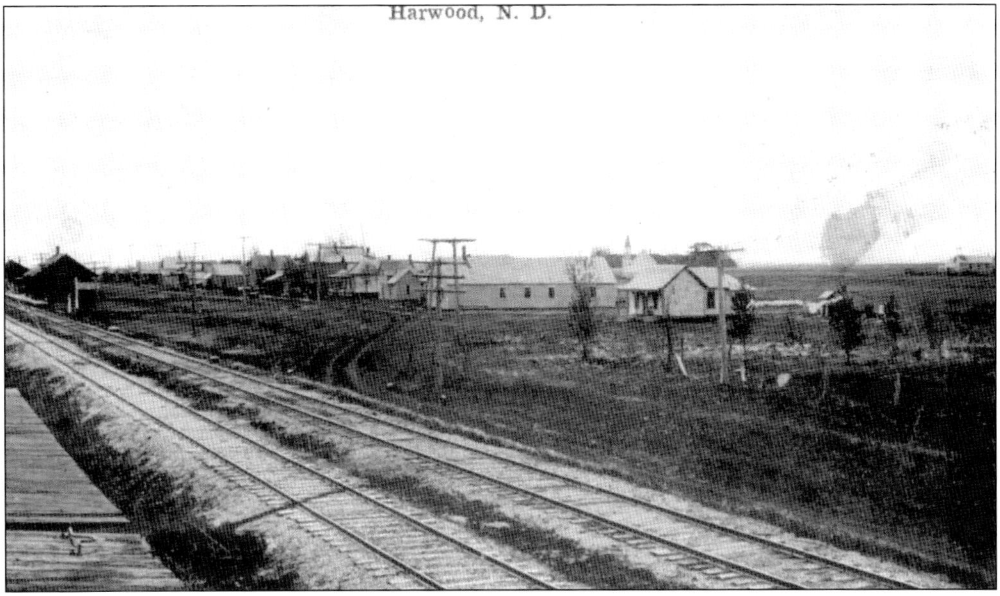


This view of the Great Northern Railroad line running through Harwood shows the depot on the left and the town in the foreground around 1912. The land where the city of Harwood now sits was originally owned by the railroad and was later sold to various investors. In 1881, Solomon Comstock, Almond White, and A. J. Harwood bought the land. A town was platted and named after Harwood.

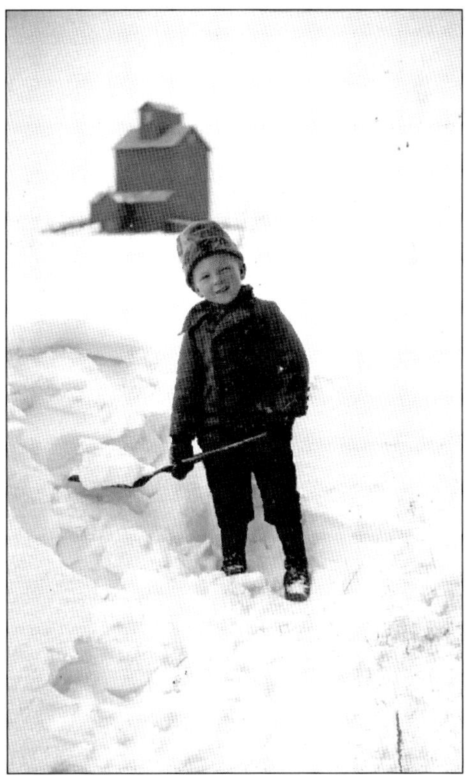

David Houston Jr. is pictured playing outside in the snow during a winter's day in Hunter. Davy, as he was called, was David and Annie Houston's only child. The family's grain elevator can be seen in the background. The Houstons owned a farm near the town of Hunter. The Great Northern Railroad's main line traveled nearby to the family's home.

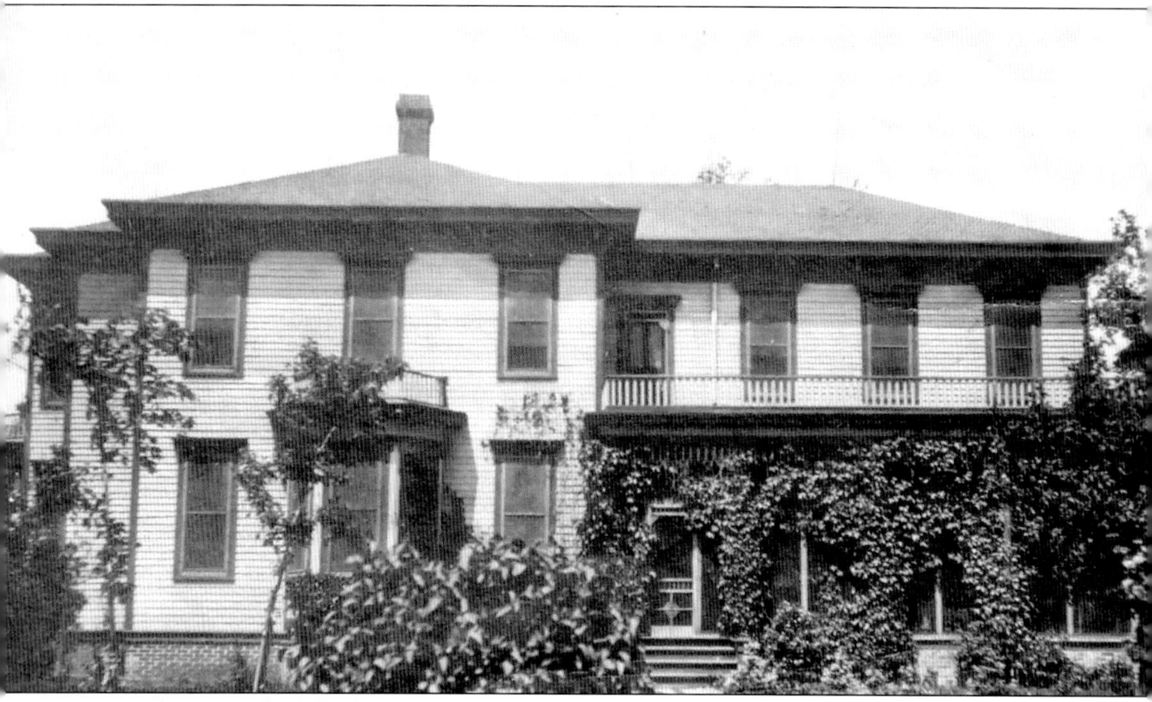

David Houston built his house near Hunter, North Dakota, in 1881. The first house he built blew down during a wind storm shortly after being completed. Houston constructed his new home using the largest nails and strongest lumber available; it also included a storm cellar that doubled as a workshop. The servants' quarters were originally located on the back side of the home. Houston divided the house in half, and the servants' house was moved down the road, separate from the living quarters of the Houston family. The servants' house eventually was destroyed. The remaining half of the Houston House was moved to its present location on the grounds of the Cass County Historical Society in West Fargo and is available for tours. Visitors will notice that there is no kitchen in the home. This is because the kitchen was located in the servants' quarters down the road.

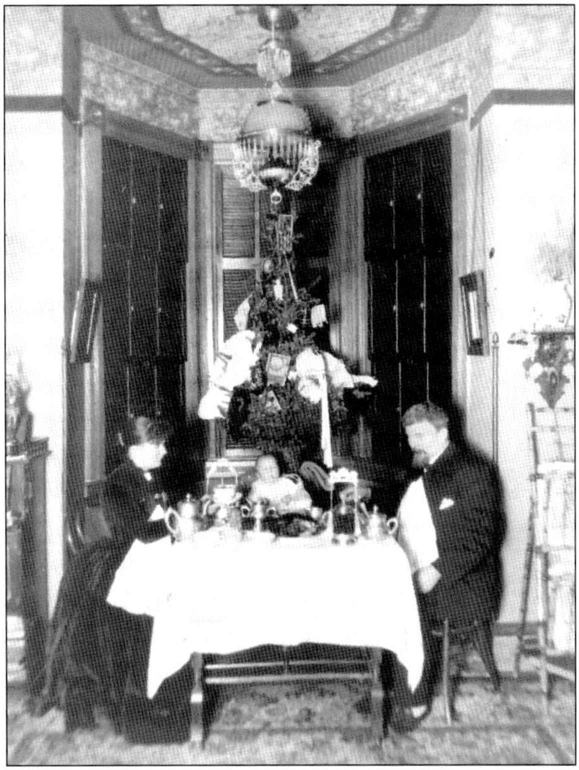

This photograph shows David Houston with his wife, Annie, and baby son, David Jr., at their home near Hunter during Christmas, around 1889. Houston was a prolific inventor and patented the roll film camera that was sold to the Eastman Dry Plate and Film Company, otherwise known as Eastman Kodak. His invention made it possible to take multiple photographs without changing the film.

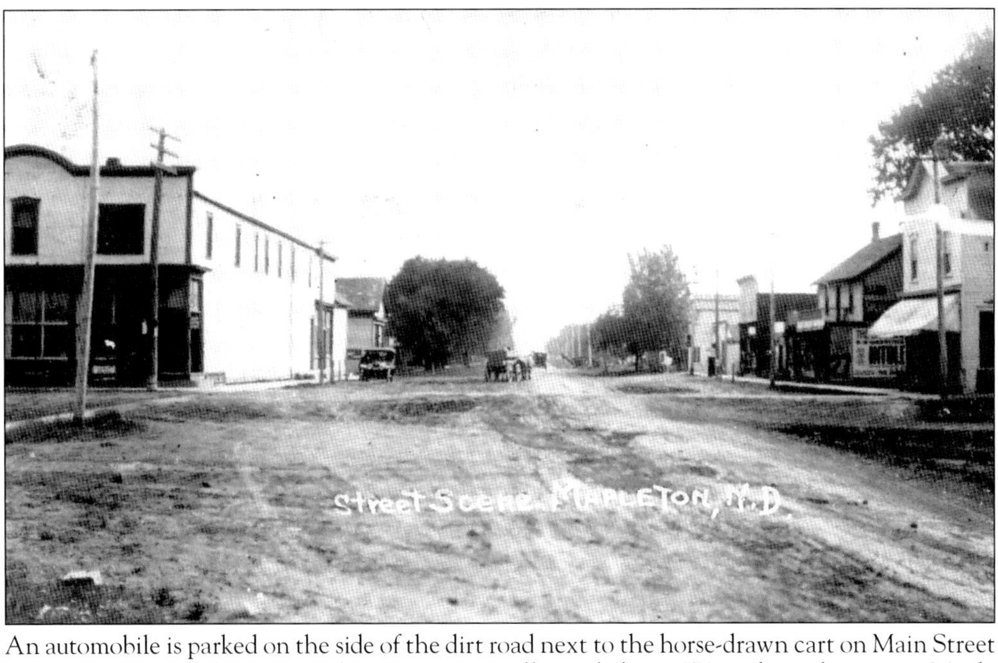


An automobile is parked on the side of the dirt road next to the horse-drawn cart on Main Street in Mapleton around 1918. Mapleton was originally settled in 1870 and was known as Maple River. The name was changed a year later when the Northern Pacific Railroad surveyed the area. In 1880, the cities of Mapleton and Fargo were approximately the same size in population and area.

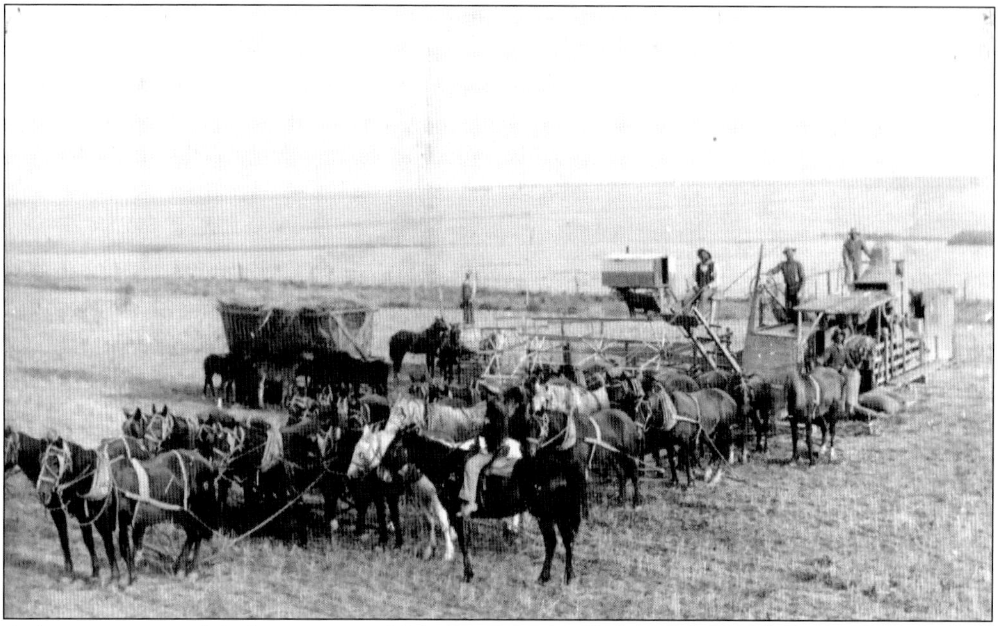

A farm crew near Mapleton uses a Holt Harvester pulled by a large team of horses around 1900. The Holt Company introduced the self-leveling combine in the 1890s, allowing farmers to harvest crops more efficiently on uneven terrain. Holt also built tractors with crawler tracks and eventually merged with one of its competitors, creating the Caterpillar Company in the 1920s.

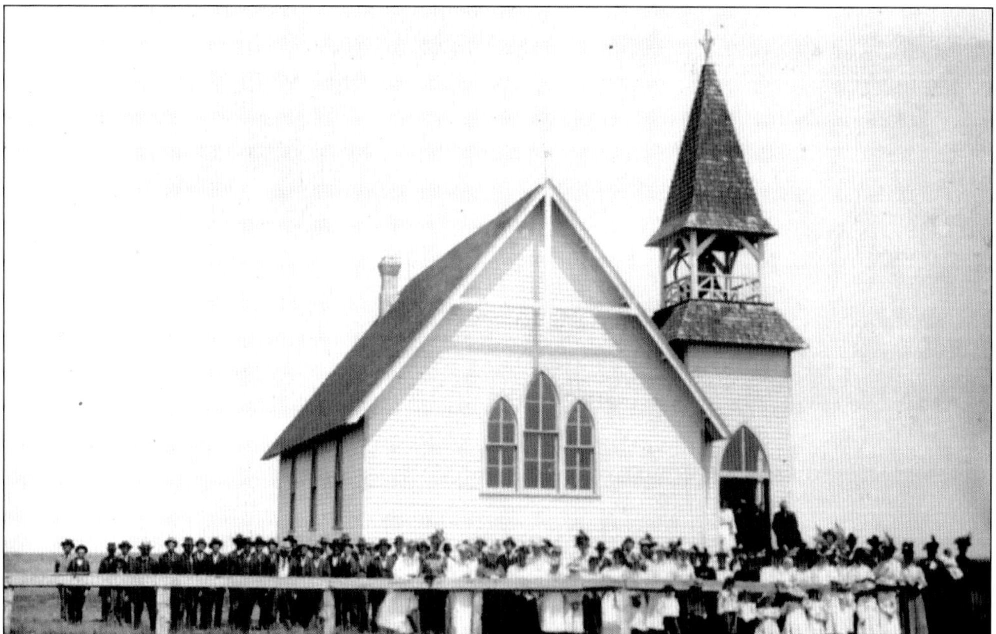

Around 85 residents of Prosper and the surrounding area gather outside the Maple Sheyenne Lutheran Church around the 1890s. The church was founded in 1878 by immigrants from Sweden who settled in the township during the 1870s. The church was constructed around 1885. A matching parsonage was also built a few years later.

# Three

# SOUTHEASTERN CASS COUNTY

Chapter 3 focuses on the towns in southeastern Cass County: Addison, Bonanzaville, Davenport, Durbin, Hickson, Horace, Kindred, West Fargo, and Wild Rice.

The land that became Addison was originally named Williams because it was owned by H. M. Williams, an area bonanza farmer. In 1882, it was renamed Addison for Addison Leech Sr., who purchased the land from Williams. Leech is said to have owned nearly 47,000 acres of land in Cass and Barnes Counties. He was also a member of the state Constitutional Convention in 1889. Addison was a Great Northern Railroad station established in 1880. Currently there is nothing left of Addison but photographs. Addison was about 12 miles southeast of Casselton.

The "town" of Bonanzaville is not really a town at all but a historical museum. Bonanzaville is the outdoor village museum of the Cass County Historical Society located at the western edge of West Fargo on Main Avenue. The Cass County Historical Society was incorporated in 1954 and spent its first years in Morrill Hall at North Dakota State University in Fargo. Bonanzaville was established in 1967 at the western edge of West Fargo. Currently there are nearly 50 buildings on the 12-acre grounds, many of which were moved to the location from rural Cass County. Some of the buildings that were moved include: Arthur Town Hall, the Buffalo Bandstand, the Checkered Years House, U-R Next Barbershop of Buffalo, the Dobrinz School, the Embden Depot, the Furnberg Store from near Osgood, the Gilby Drug Store, the Habberstad Cabin, the Hagen House, the harness shop from Addison, the David Houston House from near Hunter, the Brass Rail Saloon and Hotel from Page, the Hunter Times building, St. John's Church from near Horace, the Lokken Hardware Store from Tower City that houses the Telephone Pioneers Museum, a blacksmith shop from Tower City, the Thue-Brink General Store from Horace, and the Wheatland Township hall and jail. The museum contains several hundred thousand artifacts including a large Native American collection, antique cars, railroad engines, horse-drawn vehicles, historic farm implements, and tractors. The museum is named for the bonanza farms that made up the early history of Cass County but contains a variety of historical exhibits and displays. For more information visit the Web site at www.bonanzaville.org.

A station at the junction of the Northern Pacific and Great Northern Railroads became the town of Davenport. G. E. Channing and Henry Cooke platted the town site in 1882. Channing named Davenport for a friend of his in Massachusetts, Alice Davenport. A post office was established in 1882 with Elmer Smith as postmaster. The town incorporated in 1895. Davenport was a busy railroad town in its heyday with at least 10 trains stopping in the town every day. The town is about 25 miles southwest of Fargo and an equal distance southeast of Casselton. Unlike other small towns that are not bedroom communities, Davenport is growing and has added more than 100 residents since the 1970s, bringing its current population to 261.

The town site of Durbin was platted in 1881 when the post office was also established. It was a Great Northern Railroad station named for an employee of the railroad. The town never had more than an elevator, a post office, and a general store; it still has all three. Durbin is about 10 miles southeast of Casselton.

Hickson was built as a station on the Fargo and Southern Railway in 1883. The Fargo and Southern Railway was acquired by the Chicago, Milwaukee, and St. Paul Railroad, which became known as the Milwaukee Road. In 1883, Andrew Hicks sold the land that was to be used for the town and it was decided that the name of the town would be Hickson for Andrew Hicks. It is located about 18 miles straight south of Fargo.

Settlers first came to the Horace area in 1871–1872, and the village became a Northern Pacific Railroad loading station in 1882. A post office was established in 1875, and the village grew modestly. The town was named for newspaper editor Horace Greeley. The town site was never officially platted, but the town was incorporated in 1942. A bedroom community only a few miles south and west of Fargo, Horace has grown from 178 in 1906 to its current population of 915. The well-known Thue-Brink Store was moved from Horace to its current location at Bonanzaville in 1972.

In 1880, J. S. Huntington and William Kindred purchased the land that became the town of Kindred. They sold a strip of land, and the railroad and a station were soon built. Kindred and Huntington surveyed and platted the land and had it recorded by the end of 1880. In 1871, a group of 100 Norwegians, 19 families in all, emigrated from Houston, Minnesota, and homesteaded along the Sheyenne River near the town of Kindred. As a result of settlement, a post office was established in 1881. The town is about 20 miles southwest of Fargo and is becoming a bedroom community. The population is currently 614 and growing.

Anecdotal evidence shows that the first station on the railroad in what is now West Fargo was called Sheyenne Crossing for the nearby Sheyenne River. A post office was established in 1874 but discontinued in 1885, and mail was routed to Fargo. According to a land office map, Haggartville was the next name of the town, after John Haggert who was postmaster, the first sheriff of Cass County, a businessman, and a U.S. marshal. Future town construction was moved to the east bank of the Sheyenne River, and the town was renamed Haggert in 1884 by the railroad when they built a second line west from Fargo. In 1917, the Equity Cooperative Packing Company began construction of its plant, and in 1925, Armour and Company bought out the plant and requested housing for its employees. Residents living there were asked to move from their homes to make room for company employees, so many relocated south of the highway to form their own village. In 1937, the south area was incorporated into the village of Southwest Fargo. In 1931, the village of West Fargo incorporated, and in 1937, the village of Southwest Fargo incorporated. Confusion still existed from the different names, and in 1974, West Fargo became West Fargo Industrial Park and eventually Riverside, and Southwest Fargo became West Fargo. The two towns of West Fargo and Riverside consolidated in 1989 and kept the name West Fargo. At one point in time, West Fargo was a separate town with recognizable boundaries several miles west of downtown Fargo. It is now part of the Fargo-Moorhead metro area and is the second-largest city in Cass County with a rapidly growing population that was estimated at 17,581 in 2005. Between 1990 and 2000, West Fargo grew by more than 20 percent.

According to legend, early French travelers called the area 10 miles south of downtown Fargo Wild Oats River. The subsequent French-Canadian farming village knew it as Riceville. A post office was established in 1881, and the Milwaukee Road built a station in 1883. The town site was platted in 1884, and the name was changed to Wild Rice for the wild rice that grew along the banks of the river of the same name. As a result of the growth of Fargo, Wild Rice is now only about five miles south of the Fargo city limits.

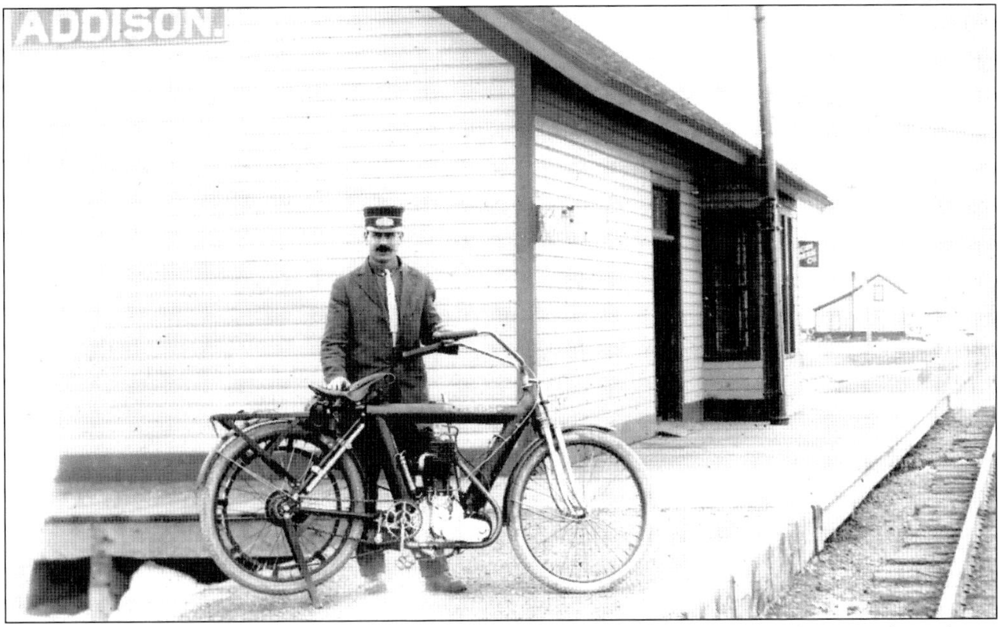


In this photograph, a depot agent poses with his motorbike at the Great Northern Railway depot in Addison. The town was originally called Williams when it was established in 1880, named for H. M. Williams who owned a bonanza farm nearby. When Addison Leech Sr. bought the farm from Williams in 1882, the town was renamed Addison. Leech owned around 47,000 acres of farmland in Cass and Barnes Counties.

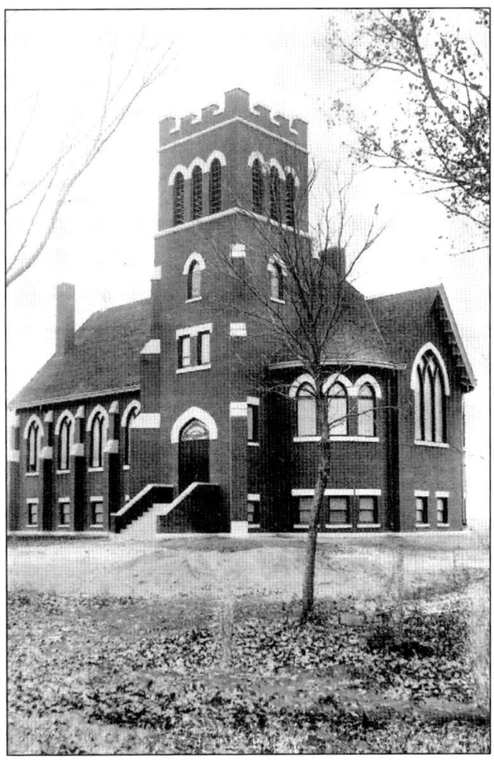

The Canaan Moravian Church is pictured shortly after its construction in 1914. German Moravian families moved to the Addison area, near the Maple River, by way of Minnesota and Wisconsin. A simple wood-framed church was built in 1886 in addition to a parsonage, school, and barn to house horses during church meetings. Services and instruction at the church were held in the German language until the 1920s.

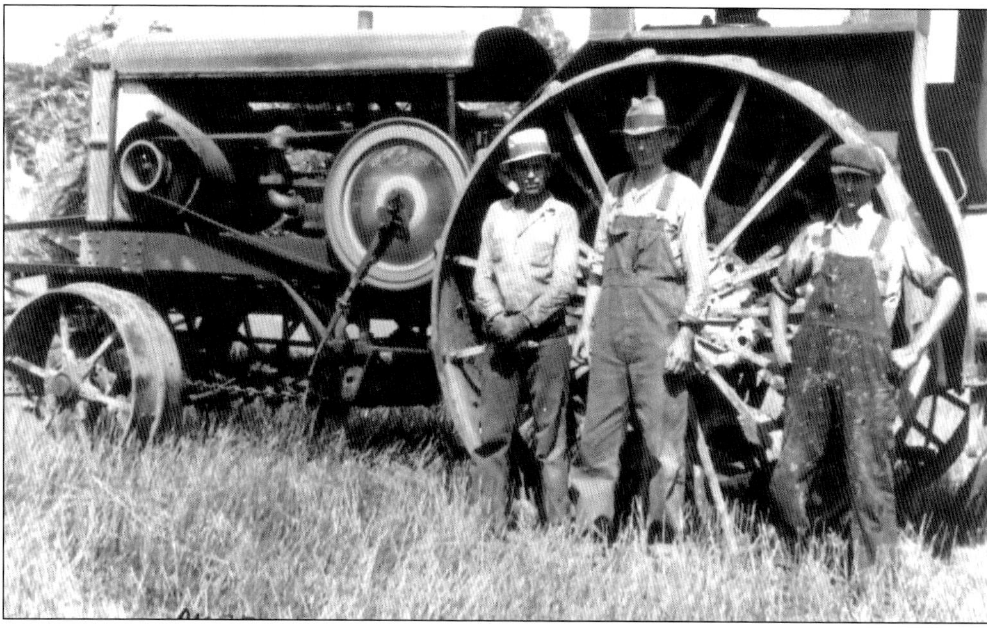

John George Plath stands between farm workers Don MacDonald and William Peterson on the Plath family farm in front of an Avery 40-80 gas tractor in the 1920s. Plath came to Dakota Territory with his family in 1879 and grew up near Davenport. *Farmer Magazine* named him a "master farmer" in 1929. Plath also served as a member of the North Dakota state legislature from 1919 to 1931.

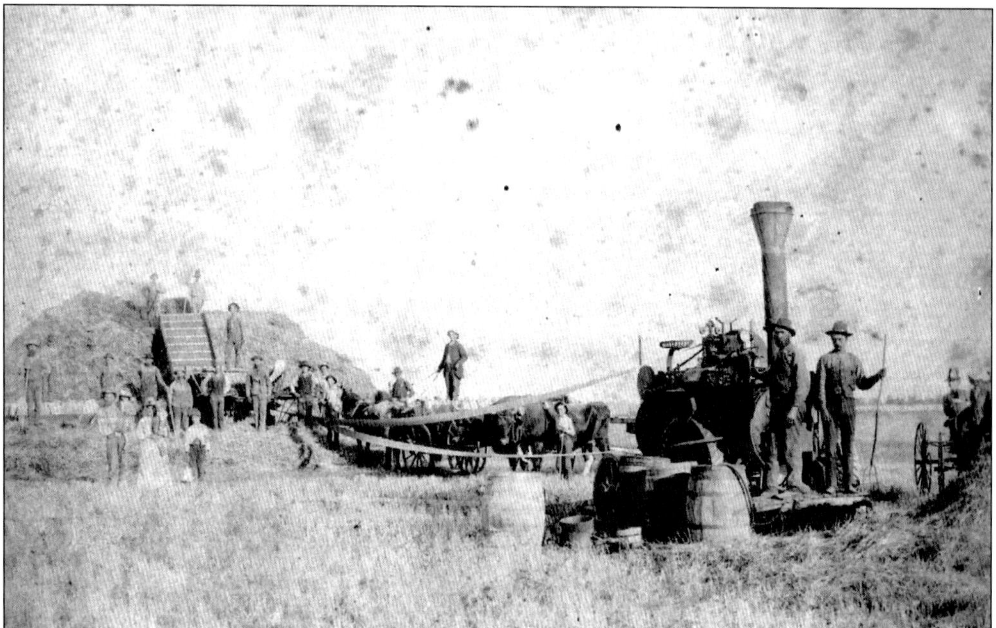

This 1890s photograph shows a steam tractor on a farm near Davenport powering a threshing machine using a long belt connected to pulleys. Giant piles of wheat would be made by threshing, which can be seen on the left. The remaining stalks of wheat would be bailed after going through the thresher.

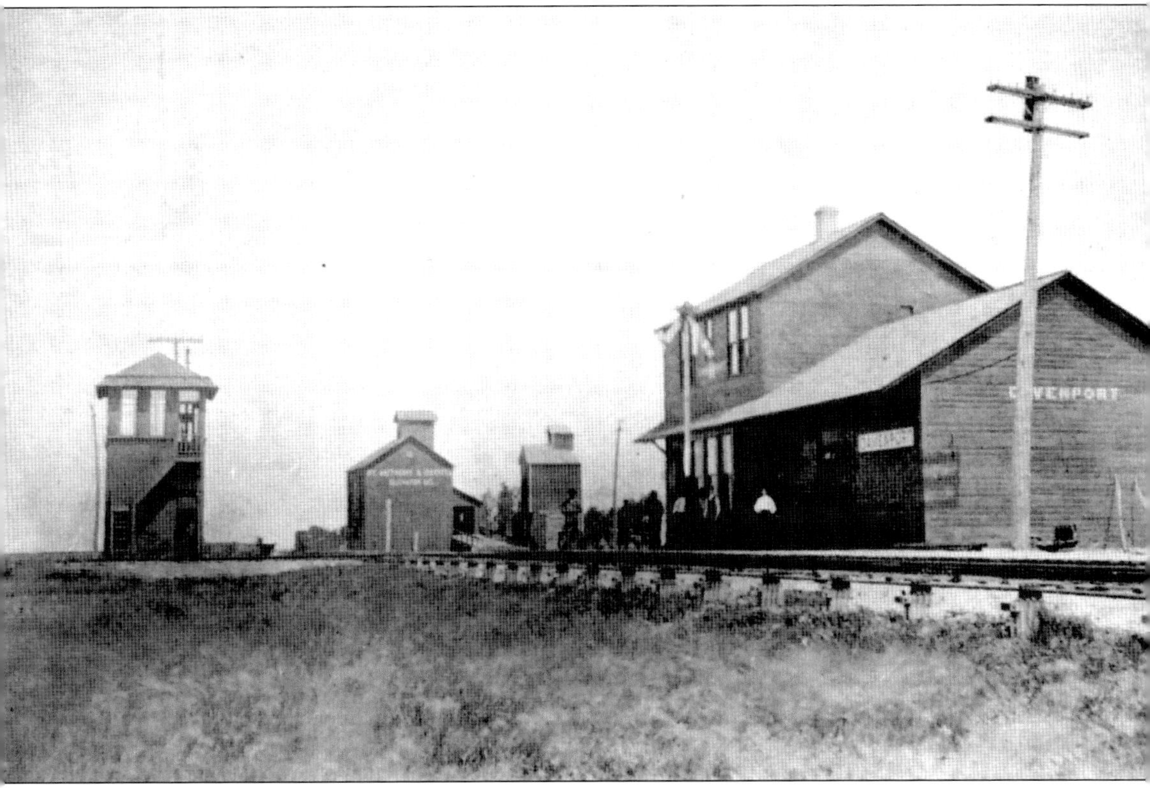

The depot and grain elevators in Davenport are pictured with a switching station around 1900. The two-story depot was located where the Great Northern Railroad and the Northern Pacific Railroad lines met. The Great Northern Railroad tracks were laid through the area in 1880, two years before the town site was platted. The same year Davenport was being formed, the Northern Pacific Railroad line reached Davenport. The two railroads led to the town adopting the slogan "All roads lead to Davenport," which was true to some extent. Six passenger trains and four freight trains stopped in Davenport each day. Salesmen from Fargo would come to Davenport by train, get a room at the hotel, and rent a horse and buggy to travel throughout the area selling their goods. The town of Davenport became a hub of activity due to the converging railroad lines and the relative location of the town between Fargo and Casselton.

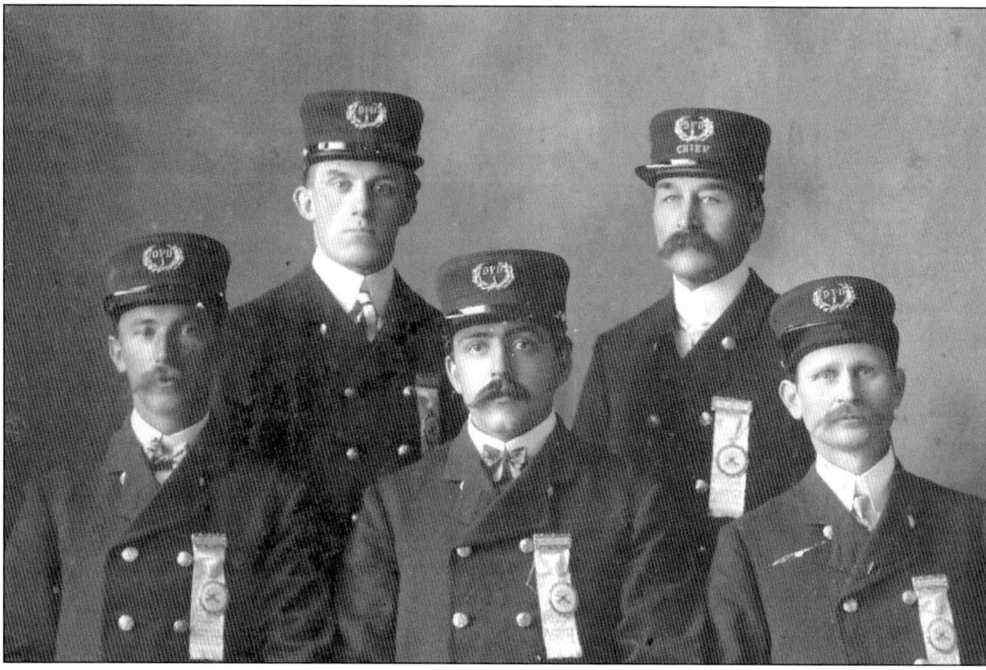

The volunteer fire department of Davenport poses for a photograph in 1903. Pictured are, from left to right, F. Friese, W. W. Borderud, J. Cole, Chief Dr. J. L. Savage, and Arne O. Tuskind. The fire department bought a hand-drawn bucket wagon in 1902 to help extinguish fires. Savage also served as the town's doctor, and Tuskind operated a general store in town.

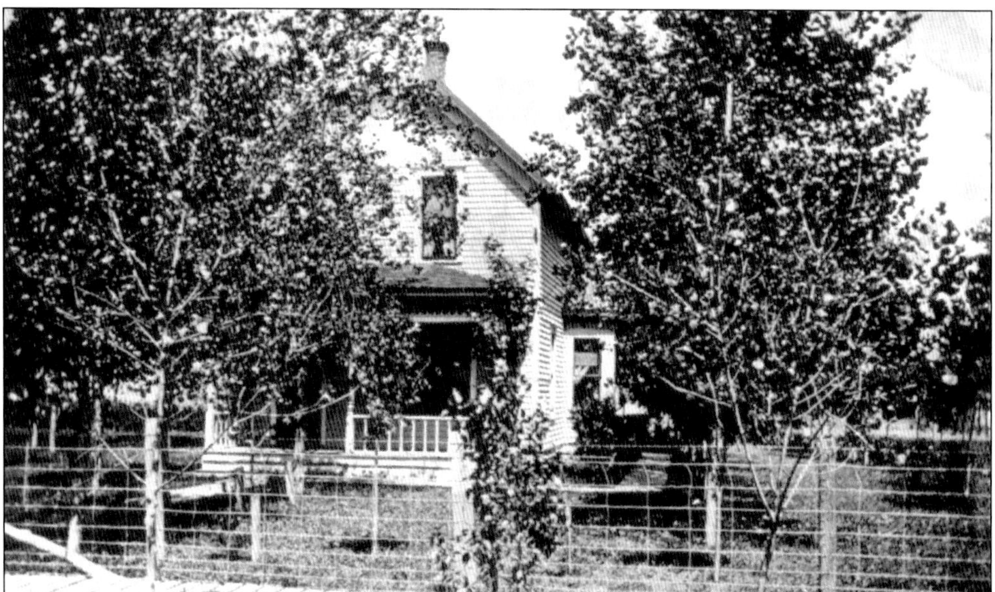

The home of Casper O. Tuskind is pictured in Davenport around 1900. Tuskind owned a general store in town with his brother Arne. The town's wooden boardwalk sidewalk can be seen in front of the house. Many towns had this type of sidewalk around 1900, to keep pedestrians out of the extremely muddy soil that was present in the spring.

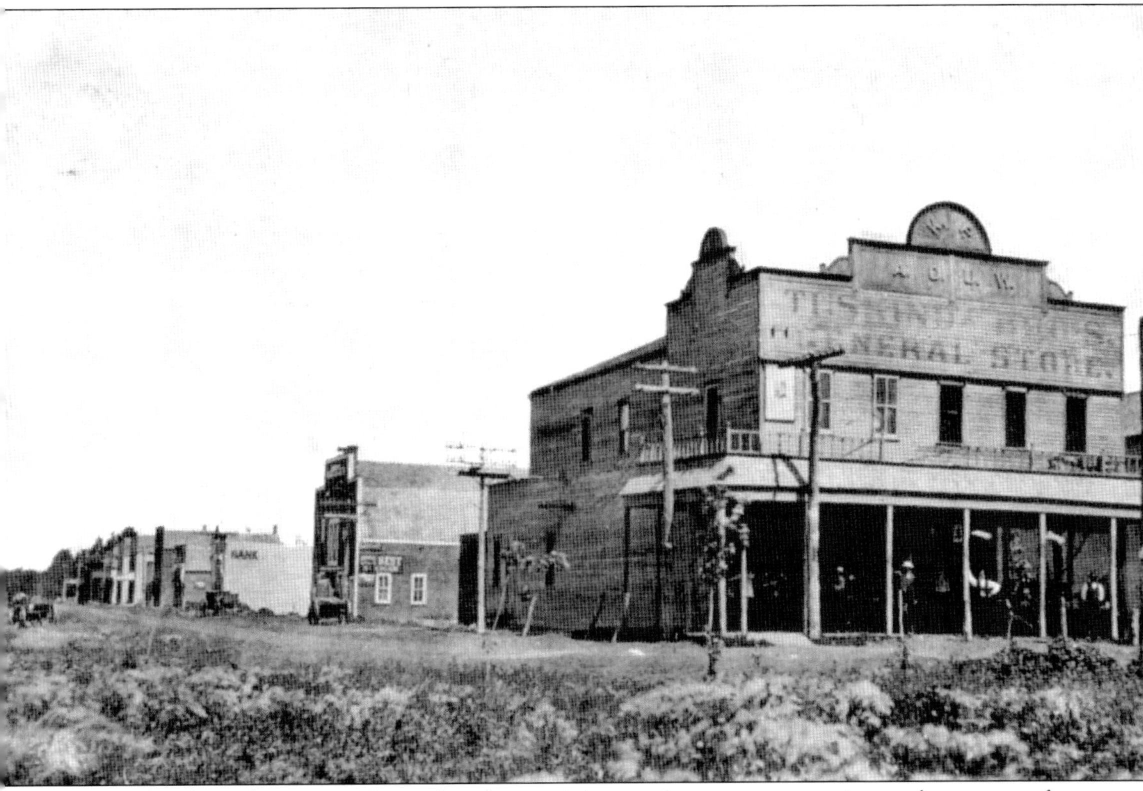


The Tuskind Brothers general merchandise and dry goods grocery store sits on the corner of Claflin Street in Davenport around 1910. The store was owned and operated by Arne O. Tuskind, who was born in Norway and moved to the United States with his parents in 1871. The family settled in Iowa before taking a claim in Dakota Territory near what later became Davenport. Arne O. Tuskind worked in the general store of Arne Borderud for a number of years before opening his own store with Axel Trangsrud as a partner. Axel eventually sold his share of the business to Casper Tuskind, Arne's younger brother, creating the firm of Tuskind Brothers. Their original store burned down but was rebuilt with a second story that was used as a doctor's office and apartment. The store was eventually taken over by Casper's sons, Orville and Gaylord, after Arne and Casper's deaths. Gaylord and Orville ran the store until the 1970s, when all the merchandise was sold at auction. The building was razed in 1977.

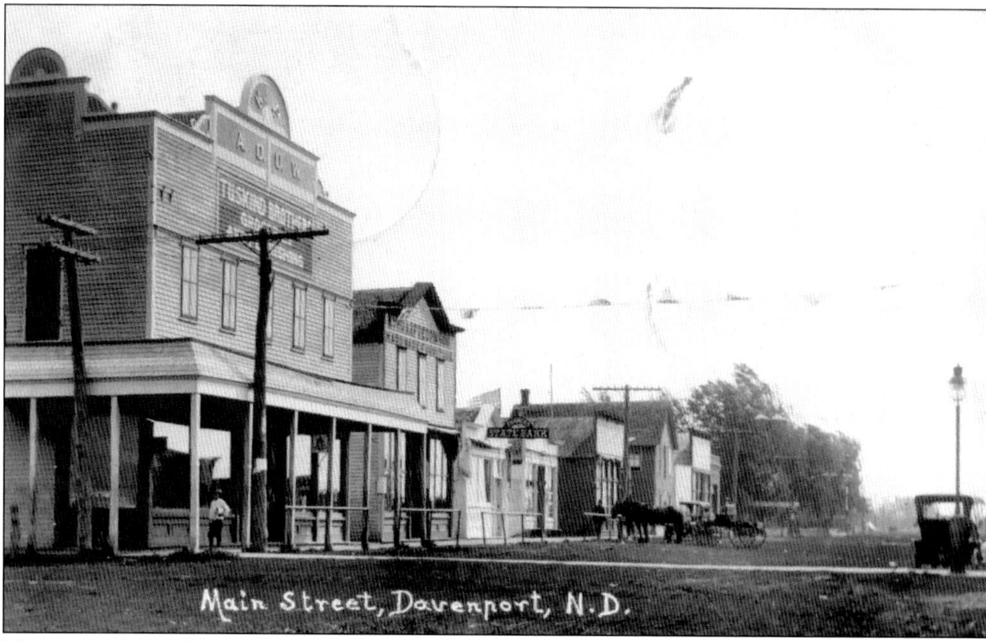


The store owned by Arne and Casper Tuskind is pictured on this c. 1915 postcard. The back of the postcard was addressed by Casper Tuskind himself and mailed to a Miss Anderson of Hudson, Wisconsin. In the letter, he writes about the health of friends and family and the drought that was present in the area at the time.

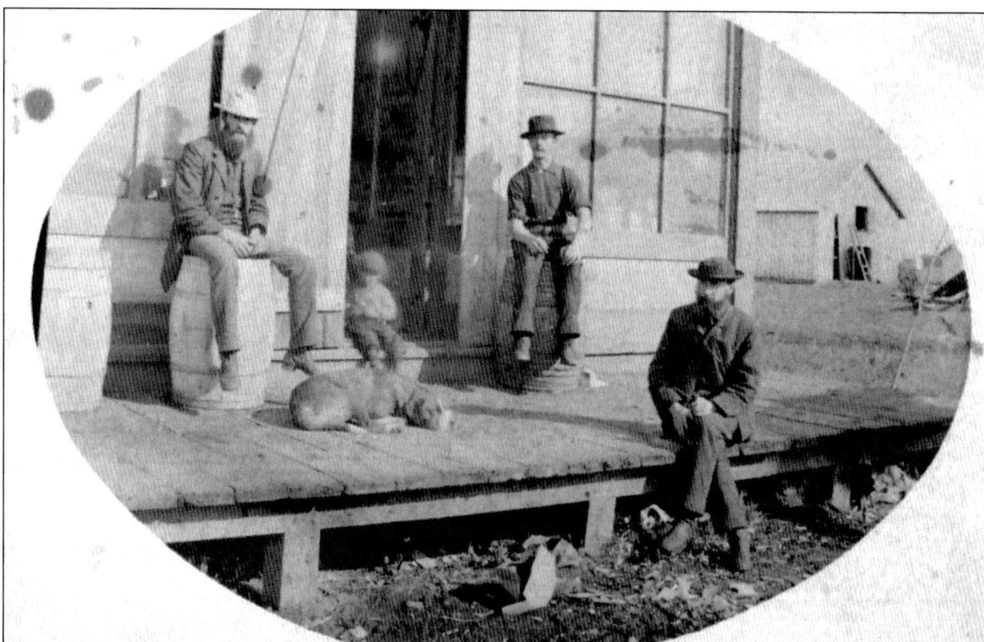

In this c. 1900 photograph, the owners of the Fout and Porterfield Drugstore sit outside their shop with friends in Davenport. Fout is on the left, sitting on the right is Porterfield, the man in the middle is Wyman W. Paige (a druggist from Steele, North Dakota), and the family dog, Barefoot, is lying down on the boardwalk in front of the store.

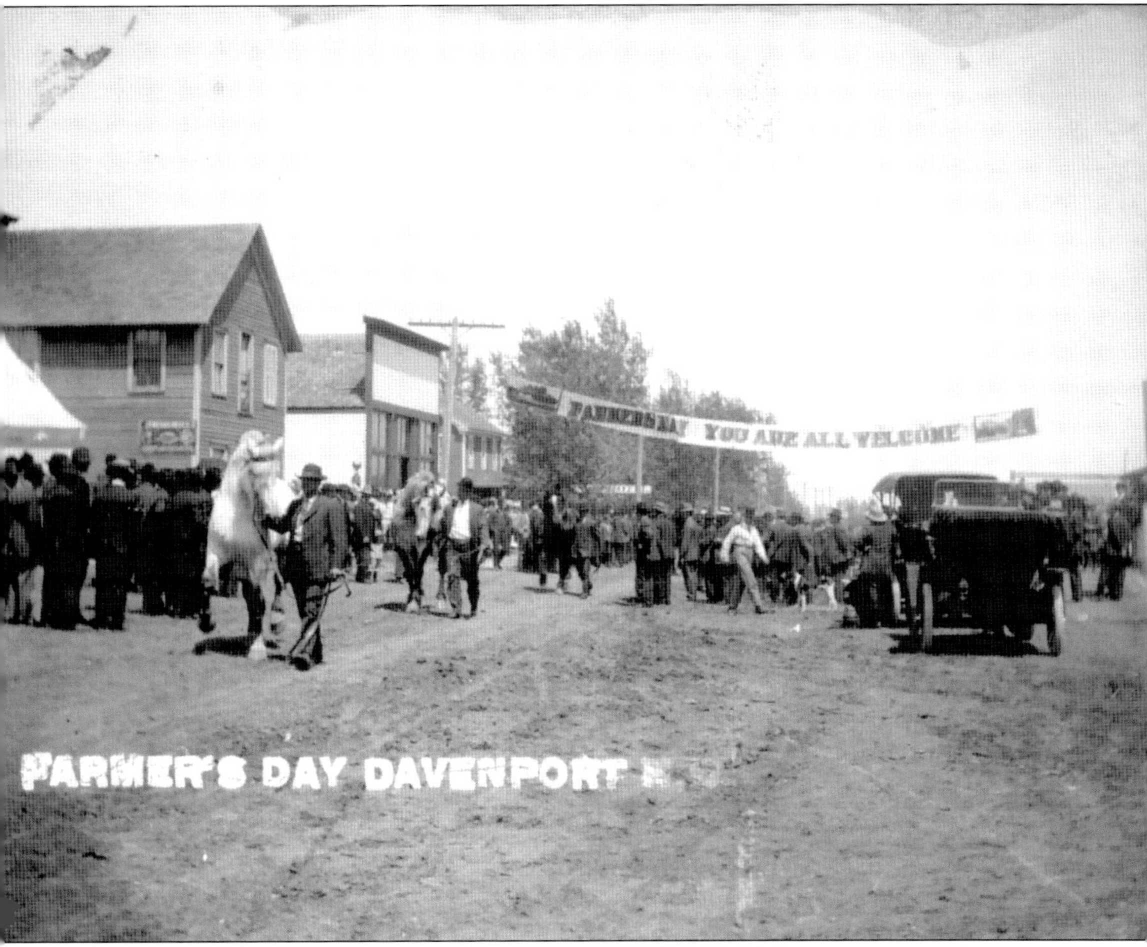


Residents of Davenport celebrate Farmer's Day in 1911. The annual community event began in 1910 when the town was visited by a train from the North Dakota Agricultural College in Fargo to honor farmers in the area. The next year, the community threw a party for itself on May 29, known as Farmer's Day. Professors from the North Dakota Agricultural College were invited to give speeches about crops and farming. Other events included band concerts, a cook-off, prizes for best livestock, free food, a tug-of-war competition, foot races, a baseball game, and an evening dance. Over 1,500 people attended the event in 1911. A tornado struck Davenport during Farmer's Day in 1943, causing damage to almost every structure in town. The cash office of the Rogers Brothers Carnival was destroyed, sending money flying throughout the town. Only around one-third of the money was found, the rest of the bills blew away with the storm.

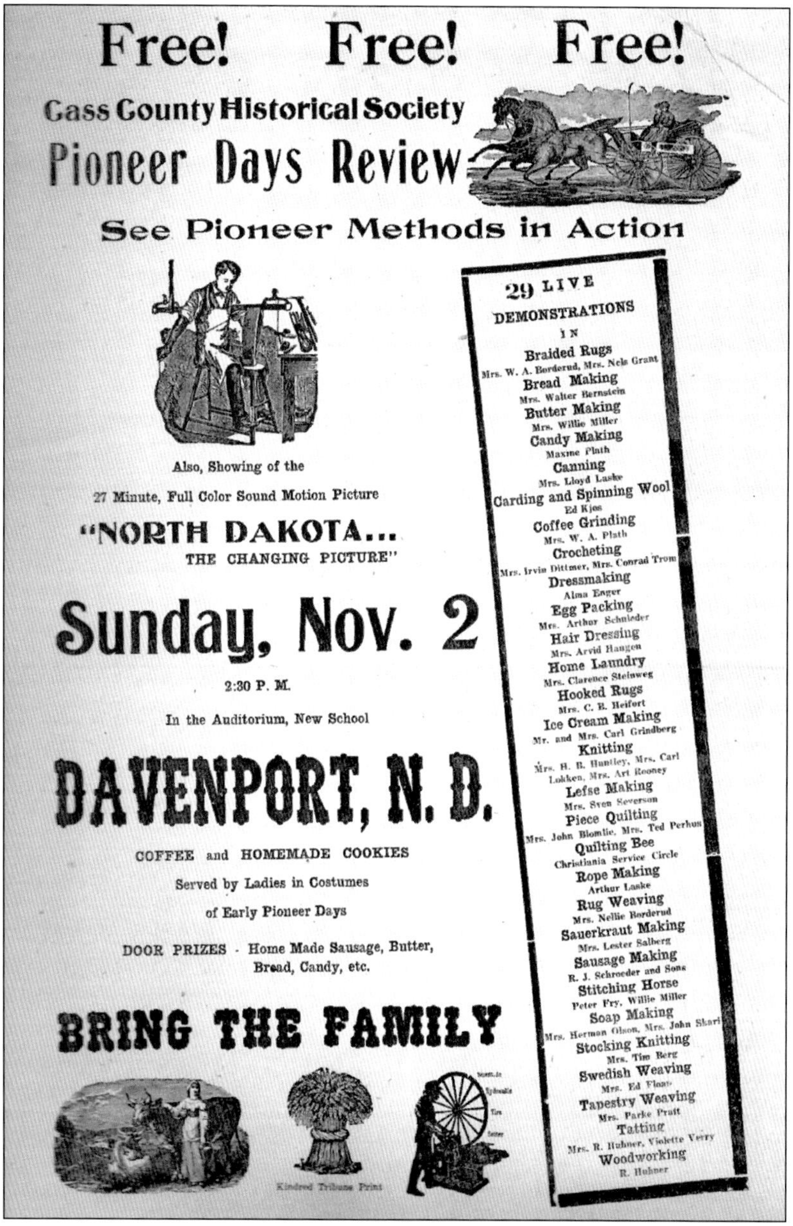


The first ever Pioneer Days Review, hosted by the Cass County Historical Society, took place in Davenport on November 2, 1958. A poster for the day lists many of the events that were scheduled to take place. More than 200 demonstrators were on hand at the town's new school auditorium to exhibit historical methods of doing daily activities such as making butter, washing clothes, quilting, and other skills. The demonstrations were accompanied by music and food. It is reported that more than 3,500 people showed up for the day's festival. The event was so successful that the historical society decided to have the event every year. Pioneer Days continued to be held in Davenport for the following three years. It was eventually moved to Bonanzaville near West Fargo where the Cass County Historical Society has a museum and historic village with buildings from throughout the county. Attendance during Pioneer Days in 1981, which by then was a two-day event, was counted at over 20,000 people.

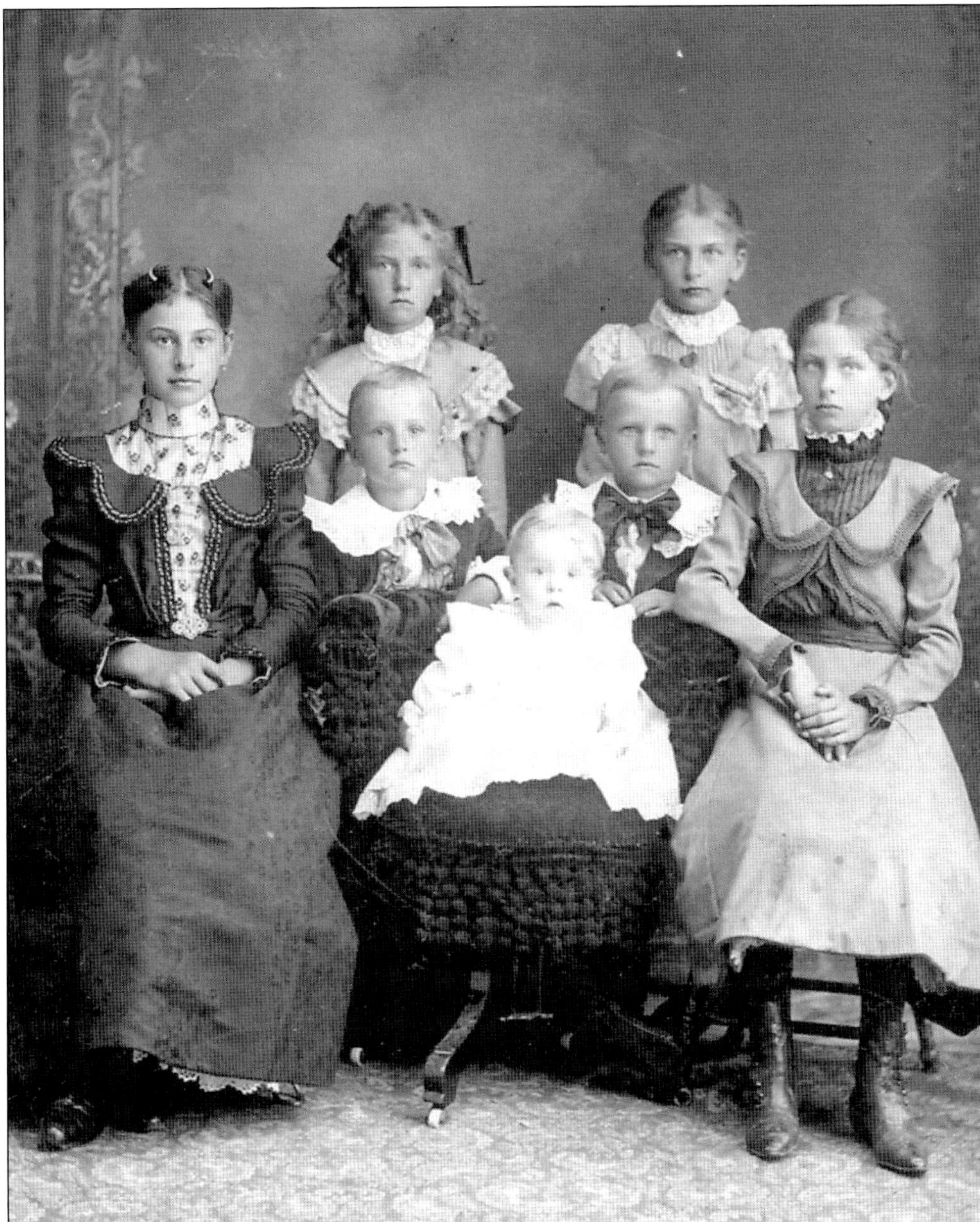

The four daughters and three sons of Ernest and Anna Baumgarten are seated for a portrait in the late 1890s. The Baumgartens left Germany together with a blessing from their parents to marry, and settled in Everest Township in 1885. The couple was married at the Goshen Moravian Church and bought land just north of the town of Durbin where they farmed until the 1920s. The area in and around Durbin was originally settled by German immigrants from Minnesota, Iowa, and Wisconsin who belonged to the Moravian Church. Many other areas in Cass County were also settled by immigrants who belonged to the Moravian Church. The town was named after a Great Northern Railroad employee who worked on locomotives where Durbin now stands. The city's hotel was widely renowned for its restaurant's steaks. Another popular site to visit near Durbin was the Weaver's buffalo farm.

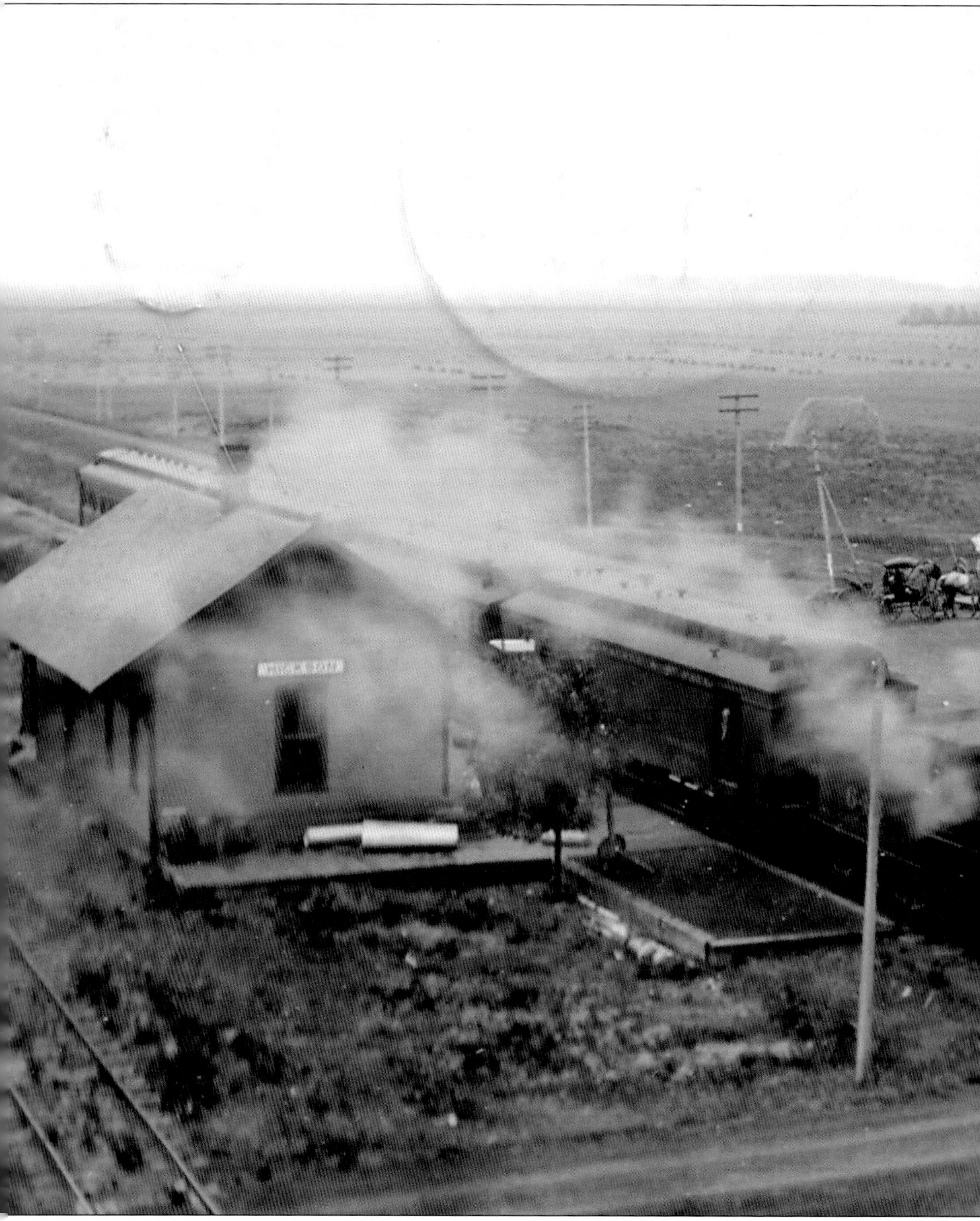

This photograph shows a steam locomotive taking off from the Hickson depot between 1907 and 1910. The Fargo and Southern Railway laid tracks through the area from 1883 to 1884. The railroad was bought by the Chicago, Milwaukee, and St. Paul Railroad in 1885. T. T. Kinneberg Fruit and Confectionary, seen on the right of the photograph, opened in 1895 and sold sweets

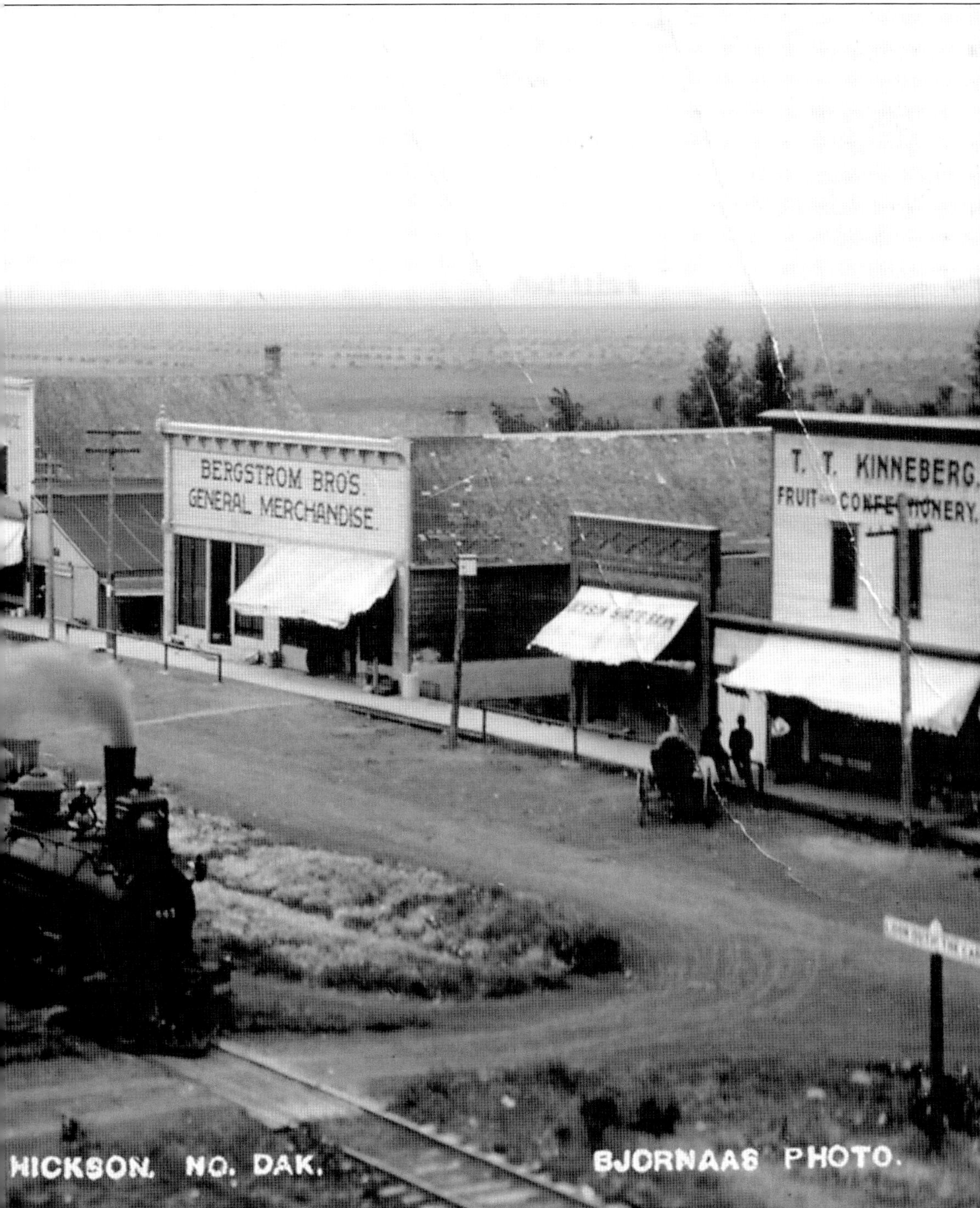


and candy. The upstairs of the building had a stage and dance floor where traveling shows, community events, and dances were held. To the left of Kinneberg's store is the Hickson State Bank. Two general merchandise stores complete the block on the left. Bergstrom Brother's is in the middle, and J. A. Blegen is on the left.

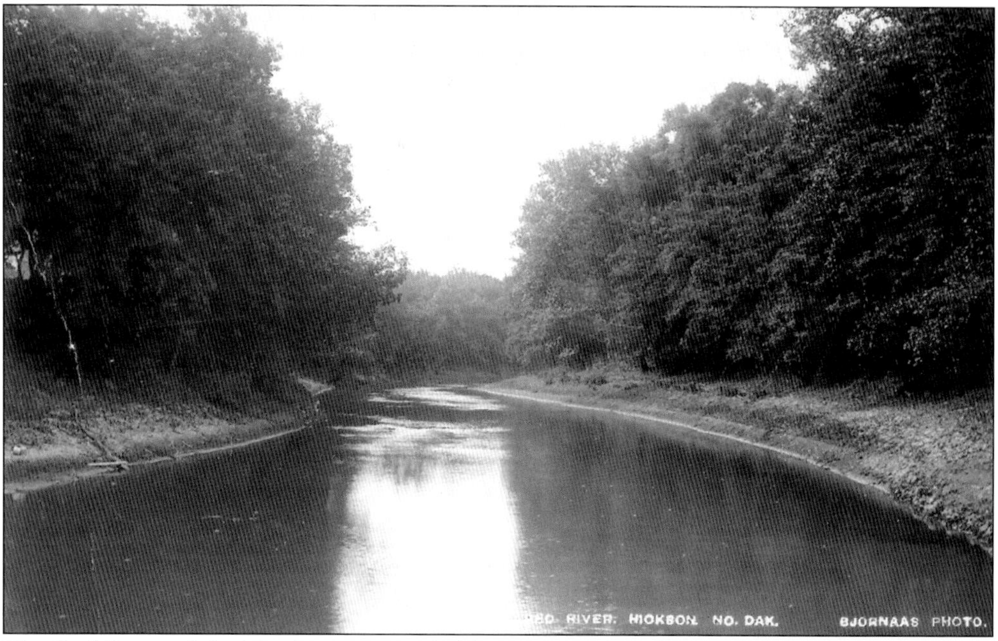


The Red River of the North is surrounded by trees in this photograph taken near Hickson. The river begins near Wahpeton, North Dakota, where the Bois de Sioux and Ottertail Rivers converge. As the water flows north, it empties into Lake Winnipeg in Canada. Throughout history, the river has been a thoroughfare for travel, connecting Cass County with Winnipeg, Canada, and other communities along the river valley.

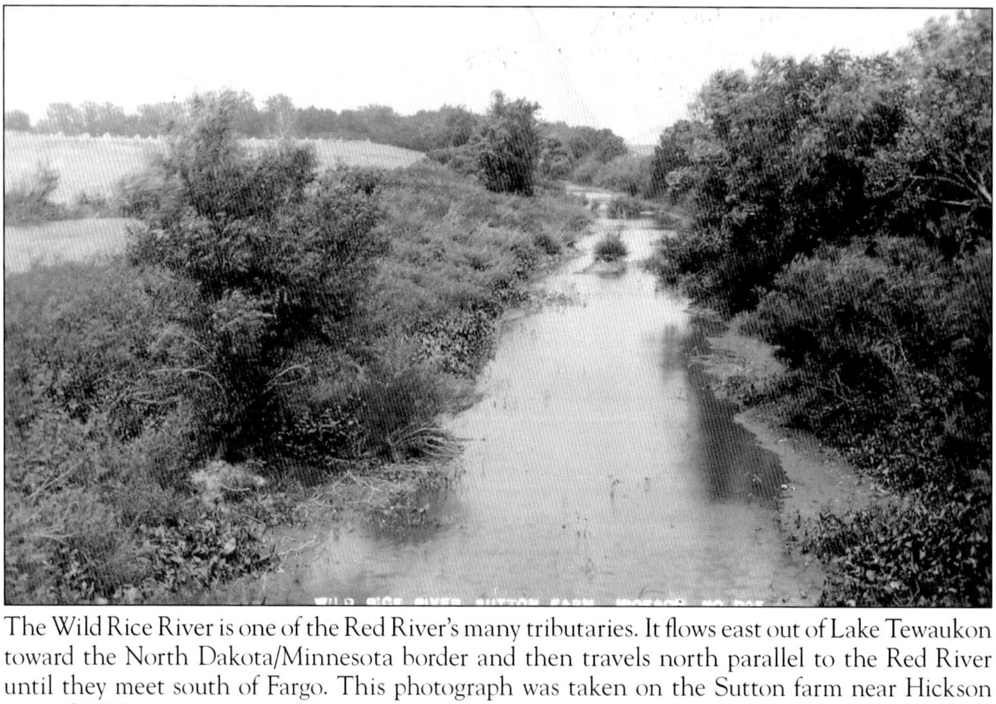

The Wild Rice River is one of the Red River's many tributaries. It flows east out of Lake Tewaukon toward the North Dakota/Minnesota border and then travels north parallel to the Red River until they meet south of Fargo. This photograph was taken on the Sutton farm near Hickson around 1910.

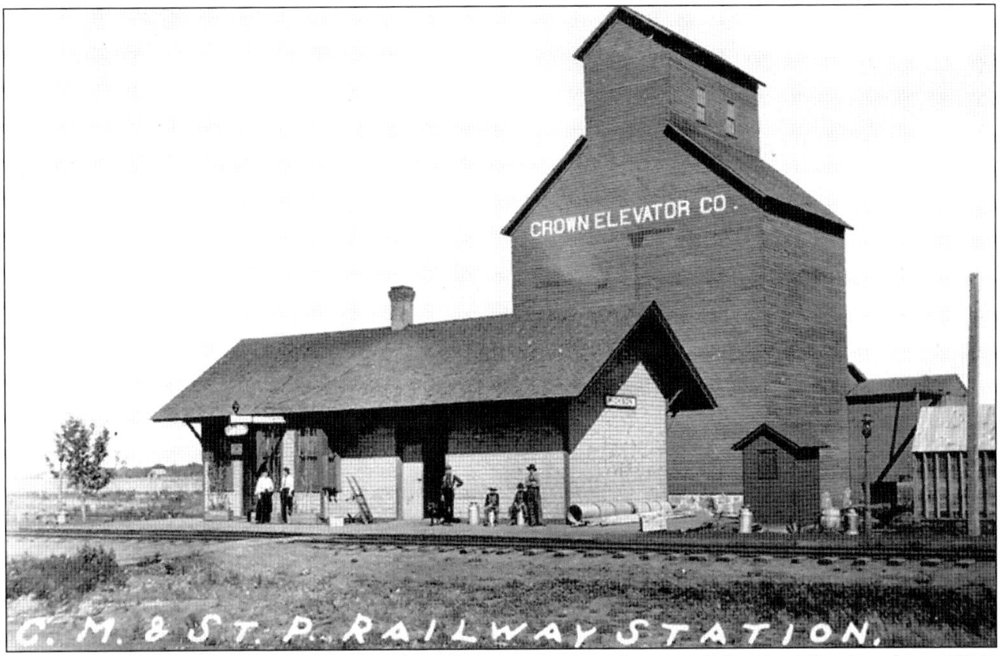


The Hickson depot was built along the Chicago, Milwaukee, and St. Paul Railroad in 1900. This photograph of the depot and crown elevator was taken some time around 1908. Both the depot and the elevator caught fire and burned in 1919. A new train depot was built the following year.

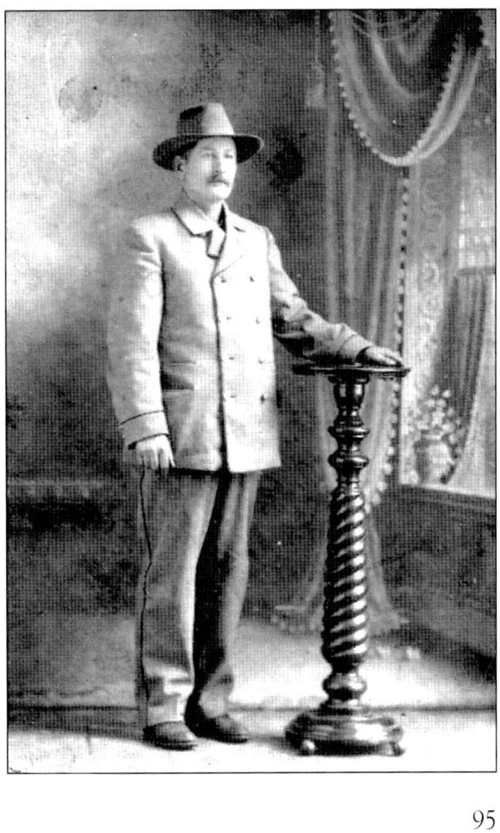

Peder Peterson stands by a pedestal in this portrait from about 1905. Peterson is dressed in his postal carrier uniform. He delivered mail on a route in the Hickson area. Mail was originally brought by the town's pastor from the post office in Normanna Township until an office was established in Hickson on June 23, 1884.

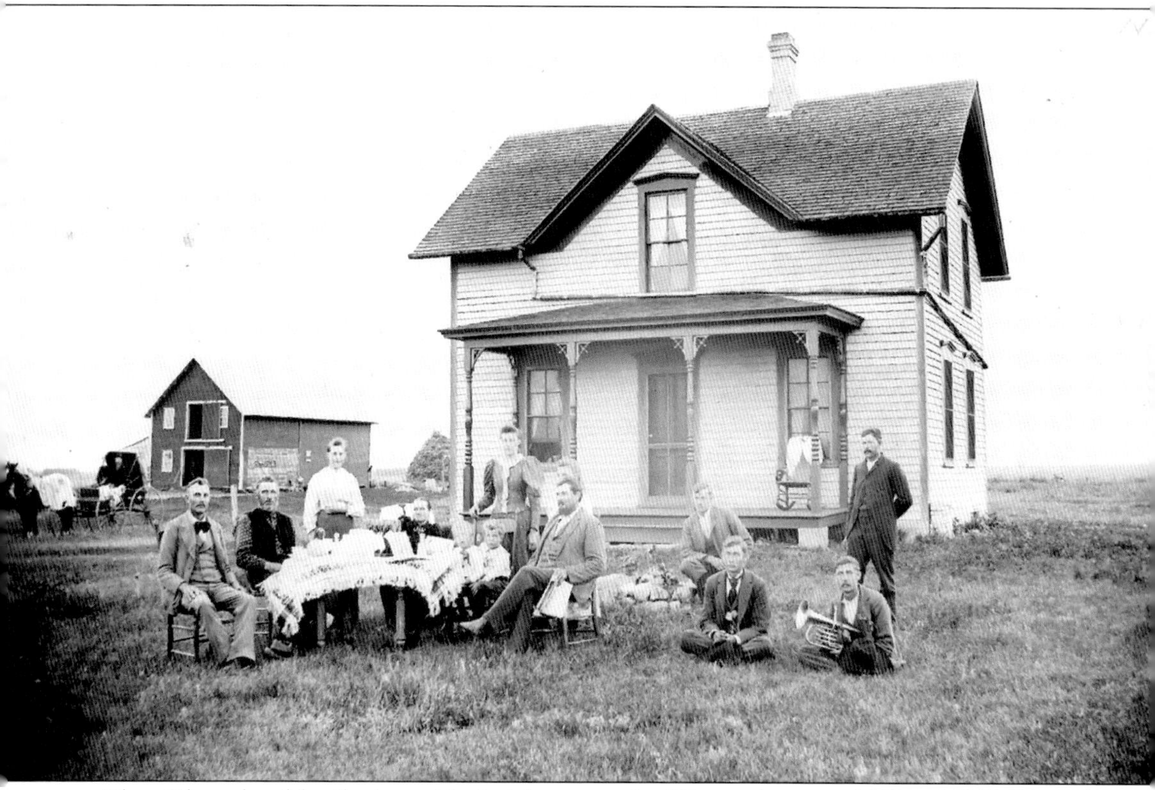

Claus Glasrud and family sit outside their home south of Horace between 1905 and 1907. Glasrud was the son of a Civil War veteran living in Spring Grove, Minnesota. With his father and brother, he made the 400-mile wagon trek to Cass County and homesteaded north of Kindred in 1878. His family returned to Minnesota, but Glasrud stayed on the homestead to farm. During an 1882 threshing accident, he nearly lost his leg and was rushed by train to La Crosse, Wisconsin, to receive treatment for his injuries. He returned to his homestead five months later and continued farming. Eventually, Glasrud sold the land near Kindred and bought a quarter section of land near Horace where this photograph was taken. In 1905, he married Hannah Thompson of Moorhead, Minnesota. She died two years later, leaving Glasrud with a daughter from Hannah's previous marriage. In 1910, he married Anna Skrove and bought a 240-acre farm in Minnesota.

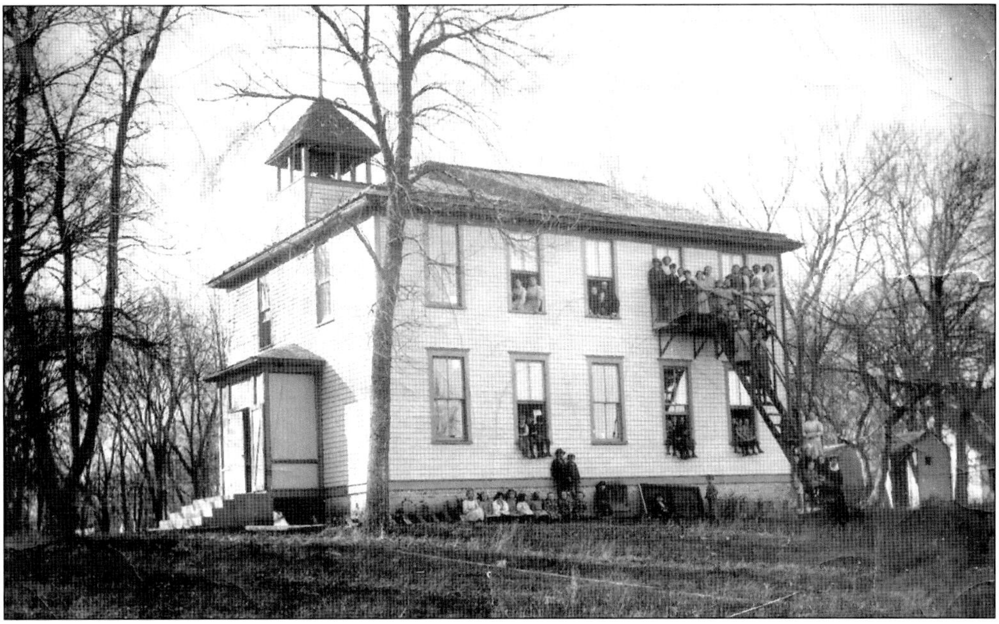

During the 1890s, three schools were being operated near Horace. In 1898, the school board voted to build a centralized school, closing the other three schools, and this two-story building was constructed. Two horse-drawn buses were used to transport children to school who did not live within easy walking distance. The children posed for this photograph around 1910.

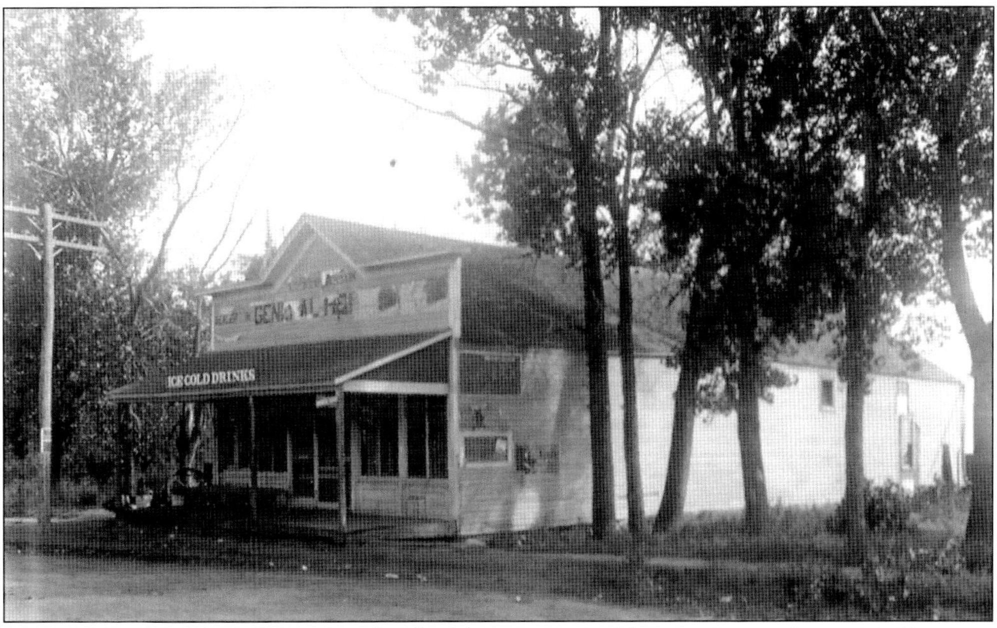


C. Fredrickson's General Merchandise building is pictured here in September 1926. Christian Fredrickson was born in Wisconsin before coming to Dakota Territory with his family in 1871. He worked as the postmaster of Horace during the 1890s and operated a store from 1901 to 1915. Over the years, the building has been used as a pool hall, community building, and agricultural research station by North Dakota Agricultural College.

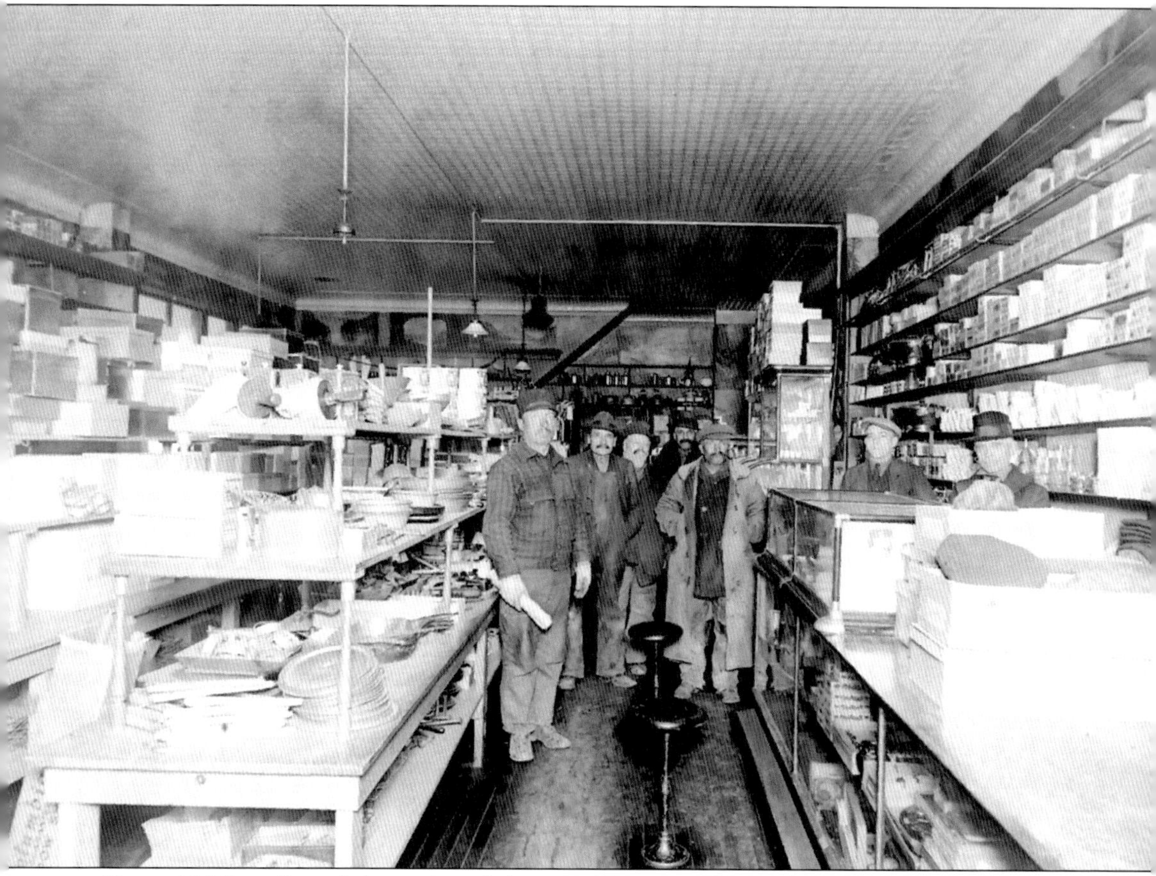

Henry H. Thue (far right) stands with his son Christian Thue to his right, behind the counter of the Thue and Brink Store in Horace, North Dakota, during the early 1900s. Henry H. Thue opened a general merchandise store in 1888. Two years later his father-in-law, C. O. Brink, became his business partner. In 1896, Thue and Brink built a larger store across the street from their old shop. The main floor housed a general store, warehouse, and post office while the upstairs was used as a dance hall. Local residents noted that the needs of customers were always met. The store operated a gas pump, meat counter, and lumberyard when no other shop offered those services in the area. In 1973, the building was moved to its present location on the grounds of the Cass County Historical Society in West Fargo.

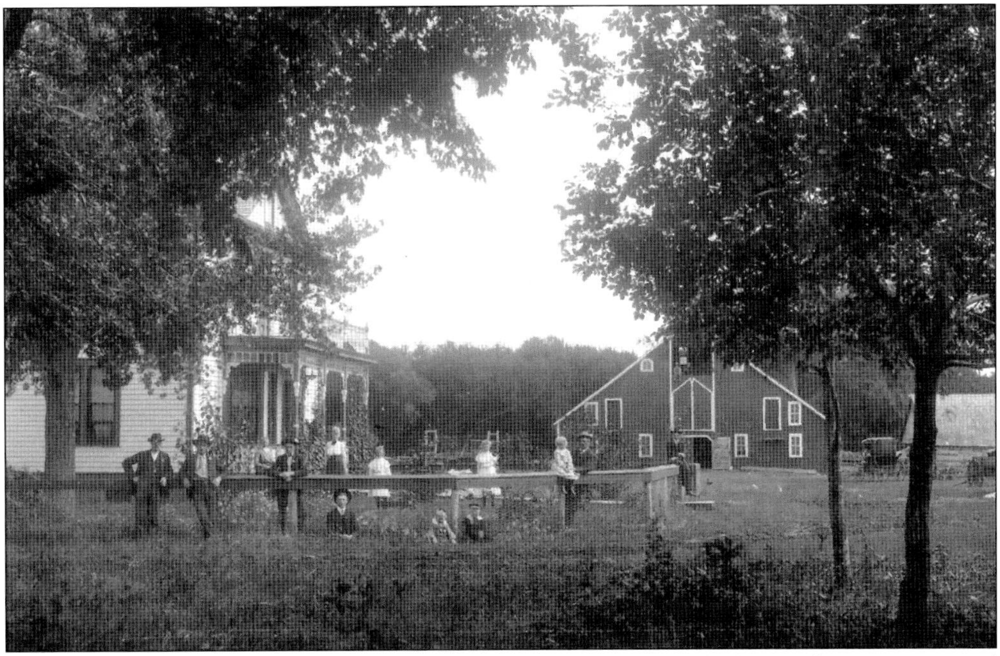

Knut J. Hertsgaard poses with his family on their farmstead near Kindred around 1900. Hertsgaard left Norway and came to the United States with his mother and siblings in 1868. The family settled along the Sheyenne River in 1871. They were some of the first residents to settle in the area.

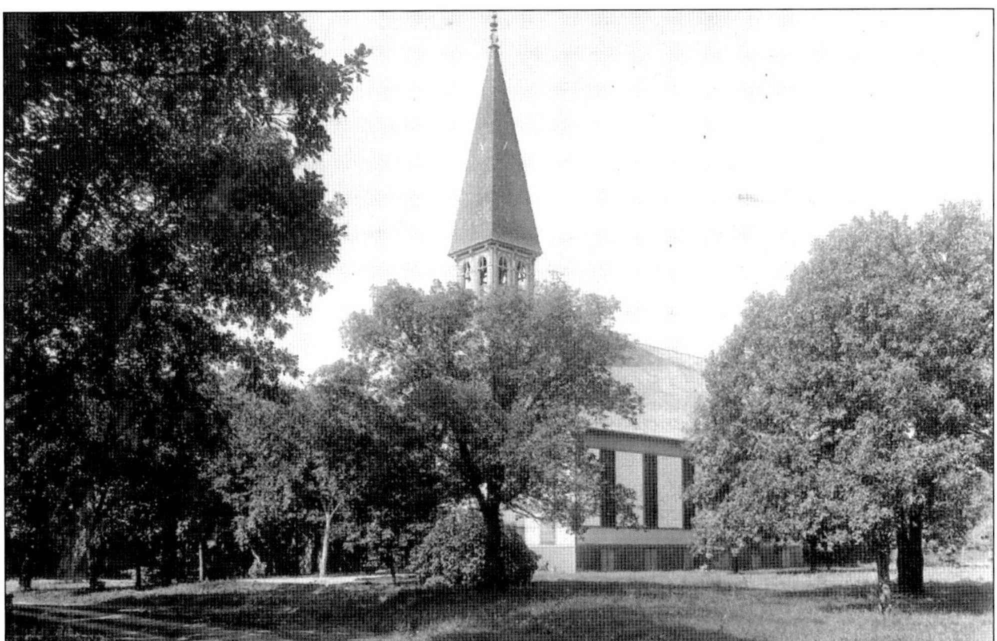

The Sheyenne Lutheran Church began holding religious services in local residents' homes in the early 1870s. A building was constructed in 1889 near Kindred but burned down a few years later. It was quickly rebuilt in the same location using the plans from the original church. The church's name changed in 1912 to the Norman Lutheran Church.

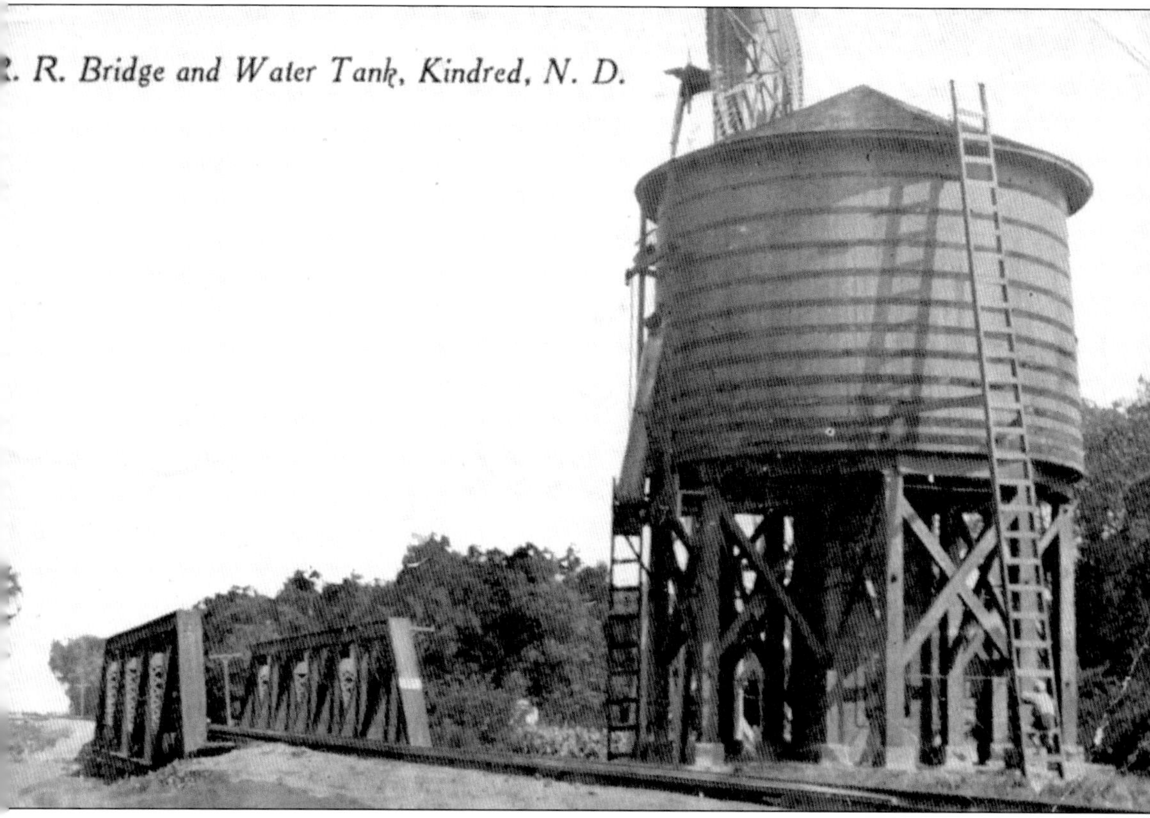


Railroad water tanks were usually constructed near rivers or lakes to provide an ample supply of water to steam locomotives before the advent of diesel engines. The tank in this 1930s postcard was located one mile south of Kindred in Ransom County where the Great Northern Railroad crossed the Sheyenne River. The water filling station was operated by Clarence Twedt who worked at the tower full time and lived in a house nearby. The railroad originally wanted to build a town at the point where the tracks crossed the river but was moved one mile north after a dispute erupted when the railroad would not pay the amount the landowner requested. The town site near the river had a few buildings, but the depot was built further down the tracks, away from the river, creating the town of Kindred.

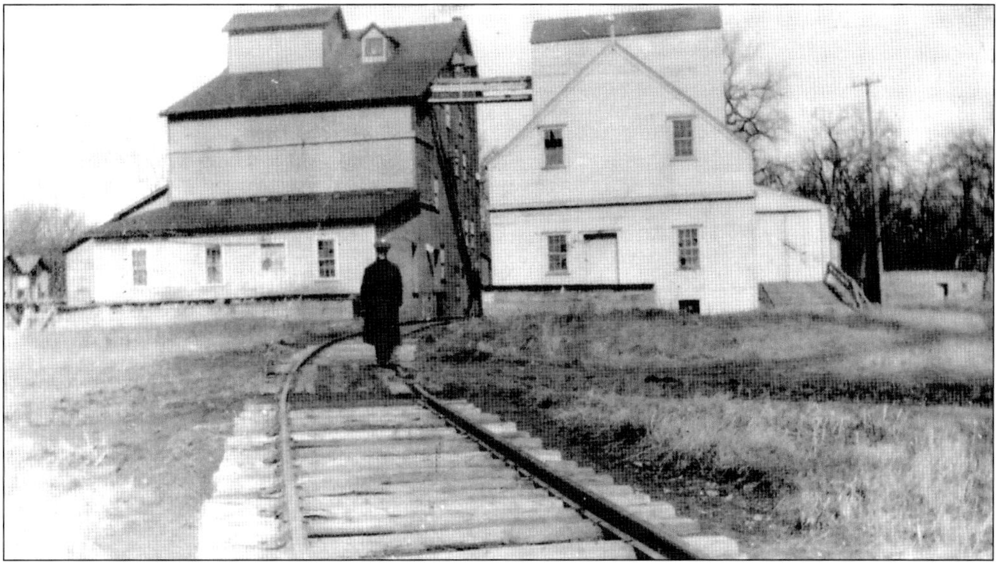

In the above photograph, a man walks down the tracks between the Queen of the Valley flour mill and elevator around 1910. The mill was originally built a few miles from where Kindred now stands in the town of Norman, but was moved after the Great Northern Railroad crossed the Sheyenne River. The mill was powered by a dam built on the river. Flour was delivered to surrounding communities by horse-drawn wagon and by train. The mill closed shortly after the town of Kindred was founded. The elevator continued to operate until 1917, when fire destroyed the elevator, mill, and dam. The photograph below shows the mill's dam on the Sheyenne River during operation.

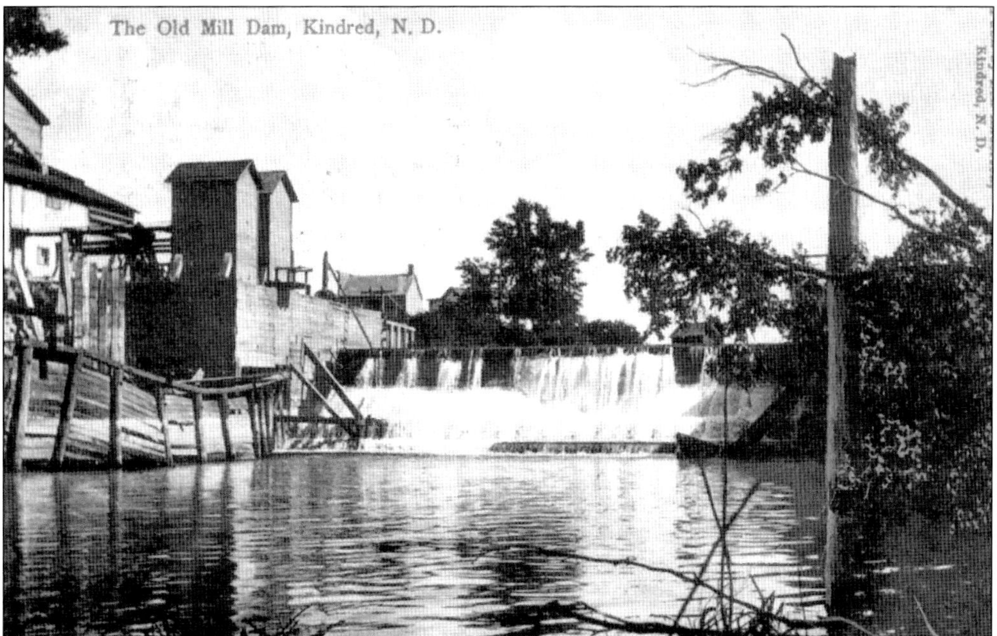

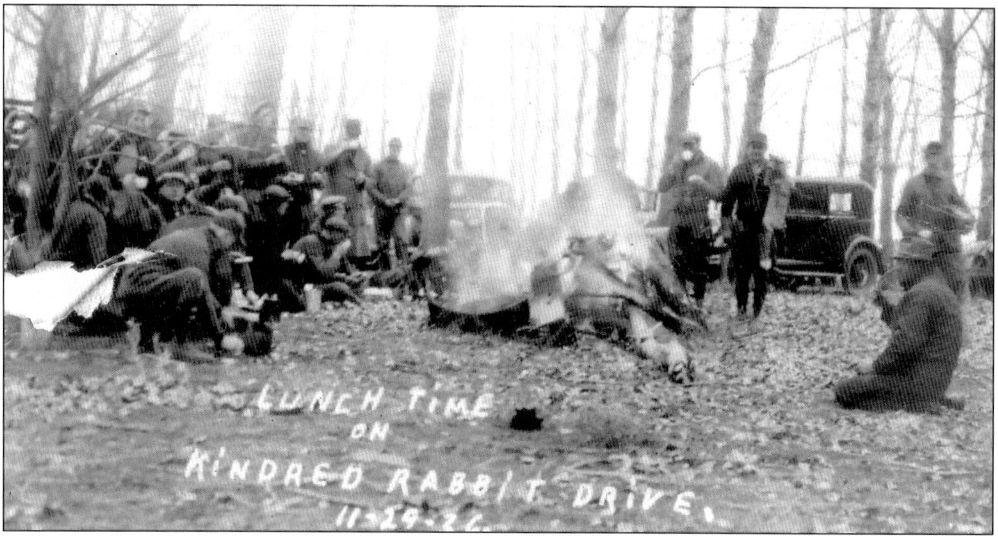


Men sit around a fire for lunch during the Kindred Rabbit Drive held on November 29, 1936. The Great Depression caused a lot of hardship for people in the Midwest. The rabbit drive was probably an inventive way for families to have enough food to survive the tough North Dakota winters. The postcard claims the group caught 937 rabbits and one fox.

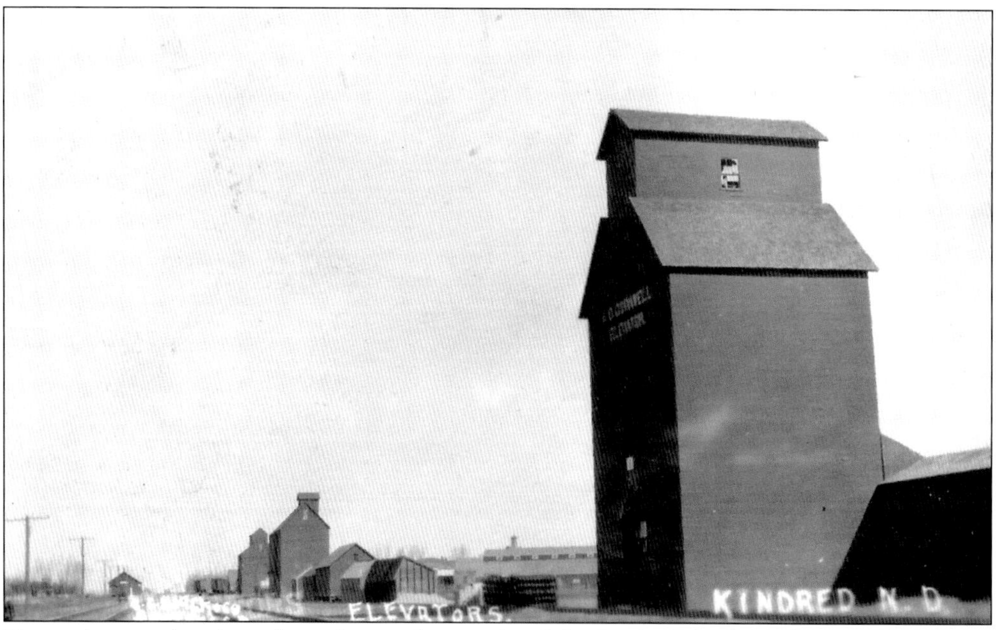


Grain elevators lined up along the northeast side of the tracks helped Kindred continue to be an important railroad stop along the Great Northern Railroad. The Kindred depot is on the left side of this photographic postcard from the early 1900s. The Cornwell Elevator is on the right side of the photograph in the foreground.

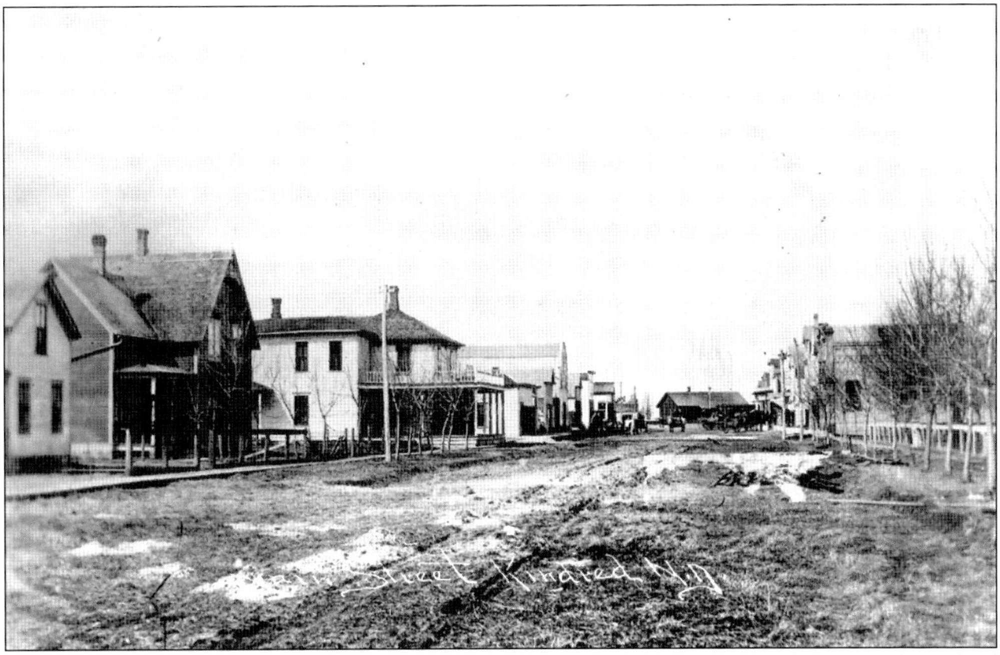


Originally owned by the Great Northern Railroad, the area that is now the town of Kindred was bought by J. S. Huntington and William A. Kindred only to be sold back to the railroad later that year. The postcard above shows a mix of businesses and homes along Kindred's Main Street sometime around the 1890s. The postcard below shows the same street about 15 or 20 years later when horse-drawn wagons gave way to early automobiles. Fire swept through Kindred in 1910, destroying 22 buildings in the downtown area. Many of the town's commercial buildings were then rebuilt using brick and masonry.

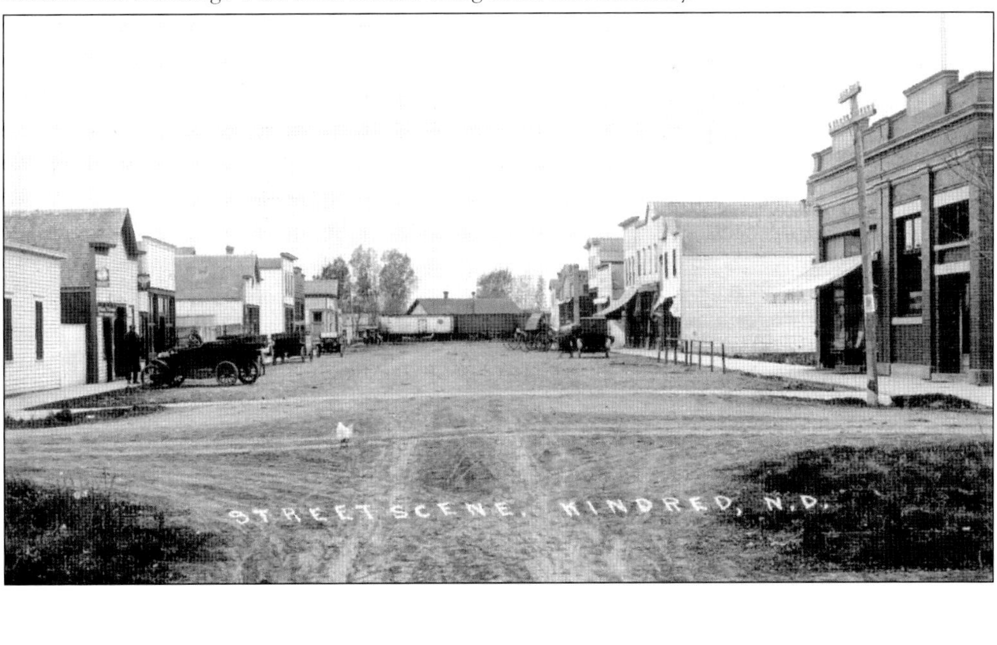

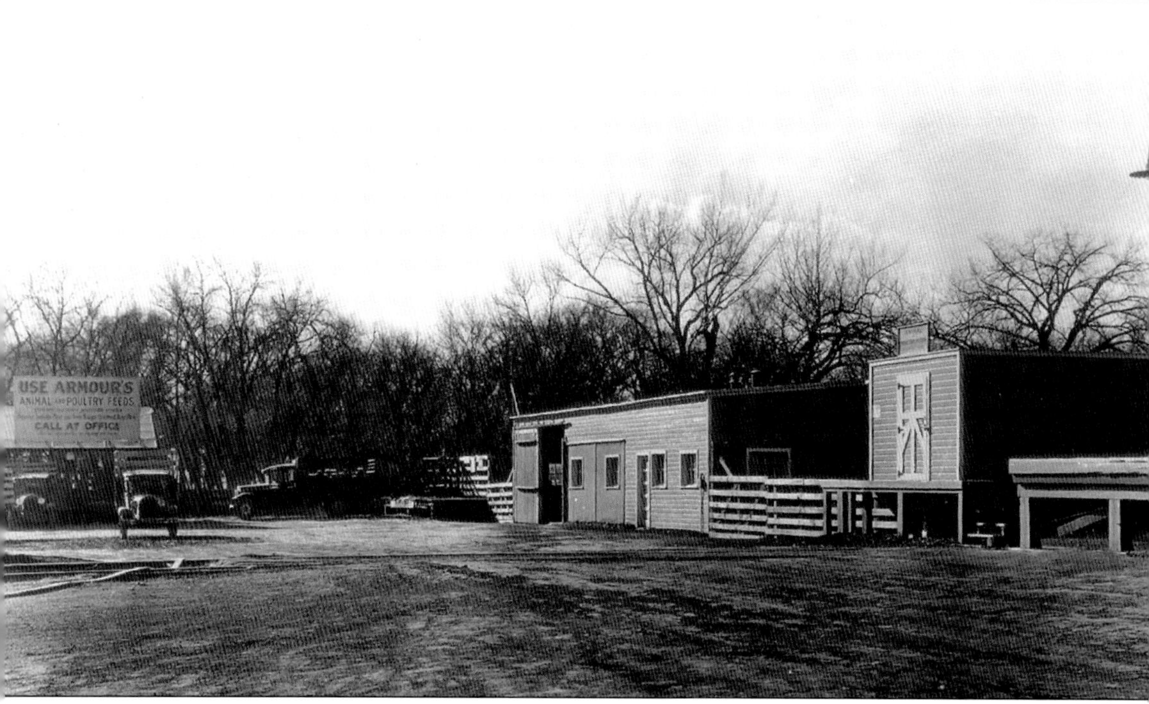


In 1871, John Haggart homesteaded on land near the Sheyenne River. The Northern Pacific Railroad built its main line through the area and eventually constructed a feeding and watering station for cattle being transported on railcars. On October 4, 1916, a small group of farmers formed the Equity Co-op Packing Company. They purchased land from John Haggart and built the Equity Packing Plant in 1917 near the old railroad cattle station. The co-op operated a packing plant, slaughterhouse, and feed yard in addition to trading cattle, hogs, sheep, grains, fruit, vegetables, and other products and selling real estate property. Their products were sold under the names Fargo Brand and Valley Brand. The Equity Packing Plant filed for bankruptcy in 1922 and was sold, along with the land around the plant, to Lewis Altenbernd, who in turn sold the plant to Armour and Company in 1925. The original Armour and Company buildings are shown here during the 1920s.

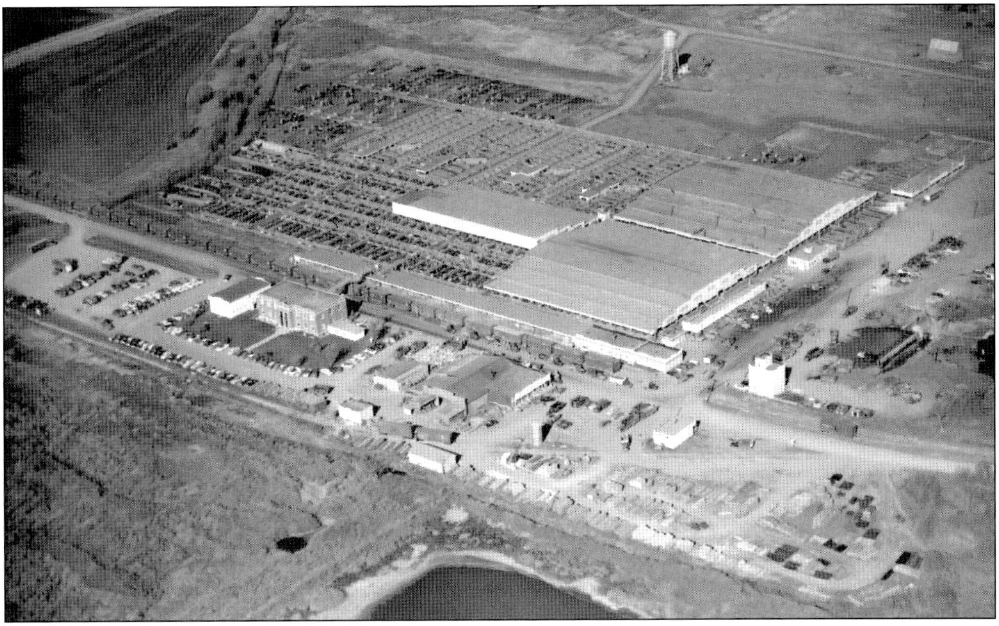

In the early 1930s, a representative of the Midwest Union Stockyard Company of St. Paul, Minnesota, was sent to establish a livestock market in North Dakota. Land was purchased west of Fargo, and construction of a facility began in 1935. The Union Stockyard began operating in October later that year and became one of West Fargo's largest industries. The stockyard became one of the largest livestock markets in the United States.

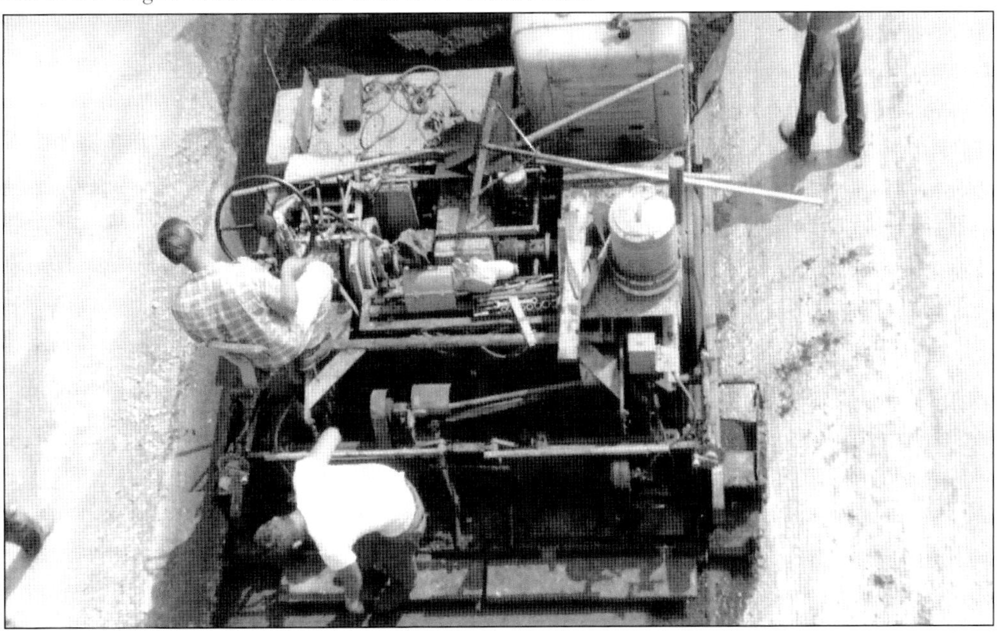

After opening the Midwest Union Stockyard Company in 1935, trains were the main method of transporting livestock. As roads improved, the use of trucks increased, although trains were still used to ship livestock further distances. With more and more trucks driving to and from the stockyard, roads had to be maintained on a regular basis. In this photograph, crews work laying asphalt for a heavy truck road leading to the Union Stockyard in 1955.

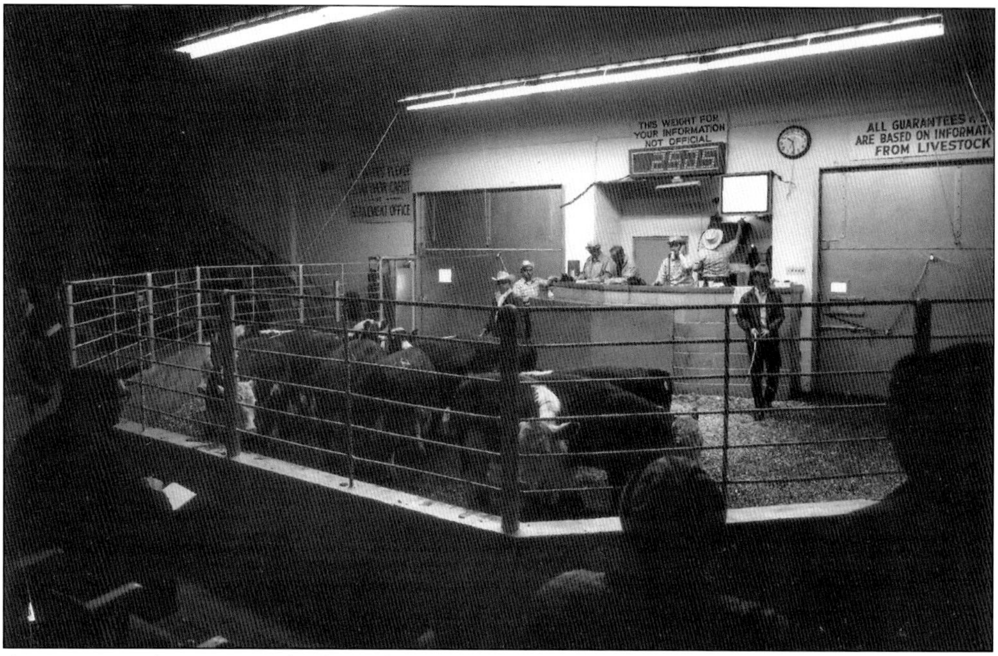


An auction sales ring was built in the 1960s to hold live auctions indoors with the animals entering and exiting through doors in the arena. The auctioneers sat in the middle of the ring with the animal pen between the auctioneers and the buyers who sat on stadium-style benches. Stockyard employees show off a group of cattle during an auction in 1969.

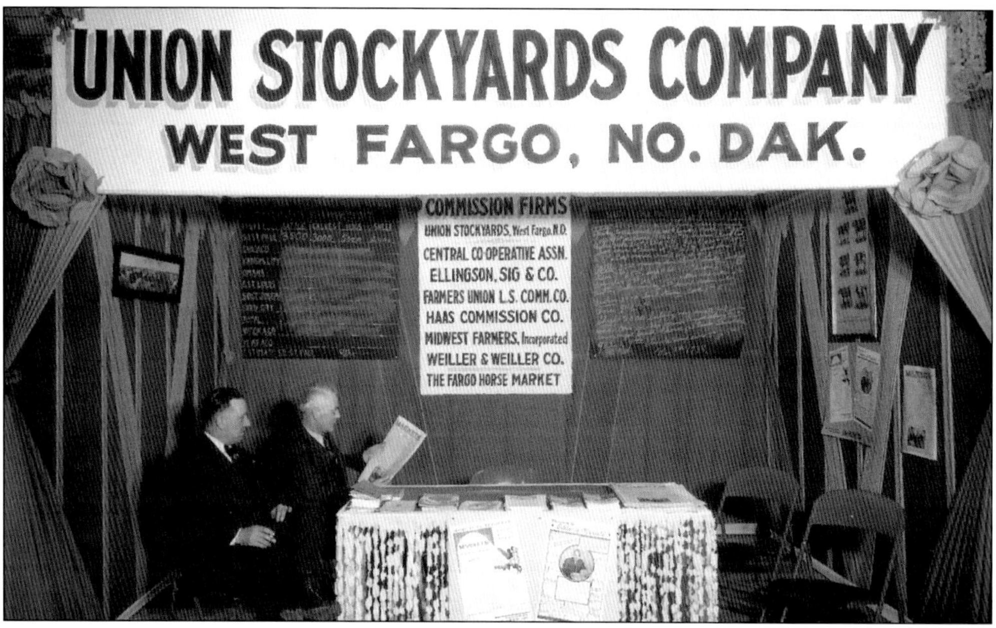


Two men wait for passersby at a West Fargo Union Stockyard booth at the state fair in 1938. The stockyard was still relatively new, and promotions like this one helped the West Fargo business to grow. Two chalkboards on either side of the booth show the market for livestock in South St. Paul, Minnesota. Businesses that worked with the stockyard are listed between the chalkboards.

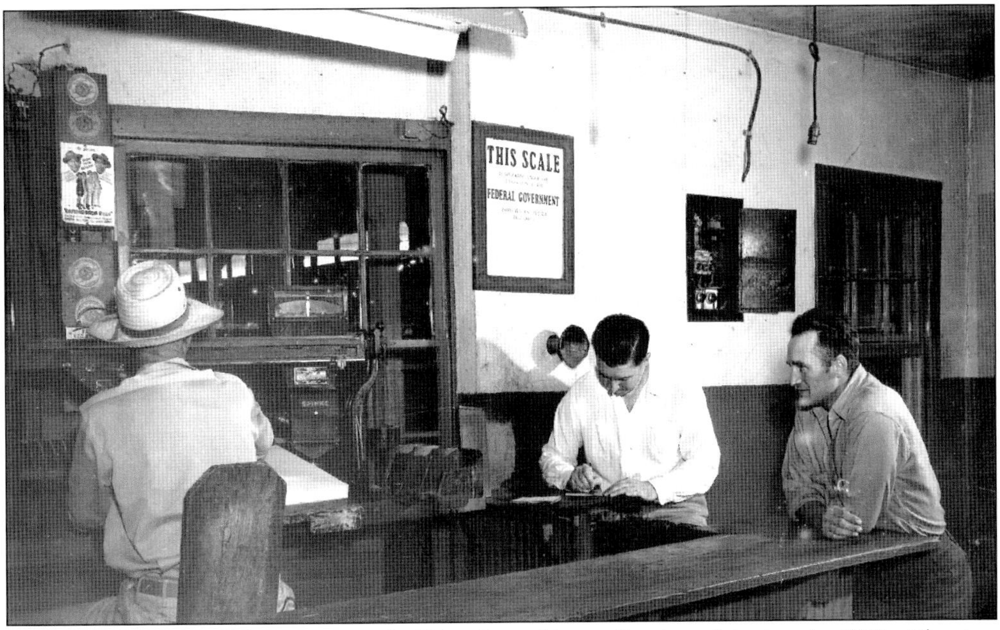


Livestock are weighed for auction at the West Fargo Union Stockyard during the 1930s. The sign hanging in the middle of the photograph reads, "This scale is operated under the supervision of the Federal Government. Inspected and tested regularly." A digital scale was installed shortly after the auction ring was built. This type of scale produced more accurate measurements.

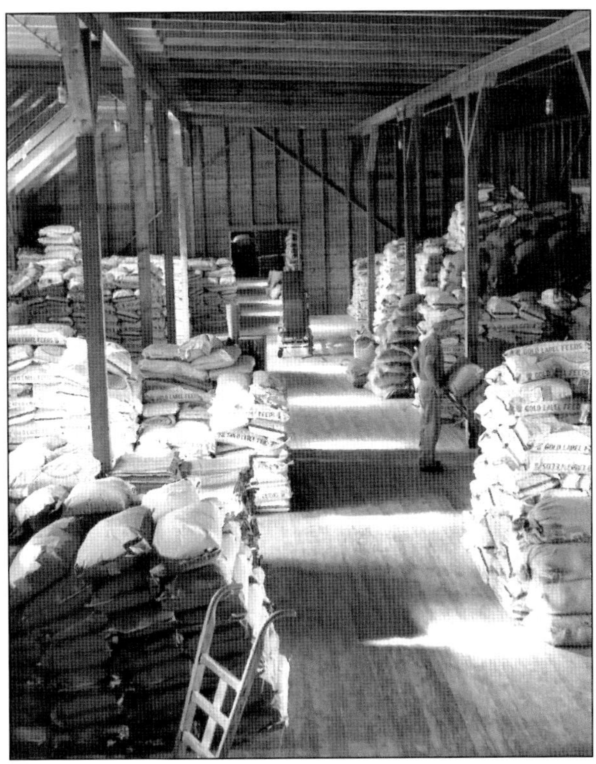

Shown here is the interior of Goldberg Feed and Grain Company/Gold Label Feeds. Workers pile sacks of grain and animal feed at the packaging warehouse of the Goldberg Feed and Grain Company in West Fargo. The business filled and shipped bags of grain under the name Gold Label Feeds. This photograph was taken in the late 1940s or 1950s.

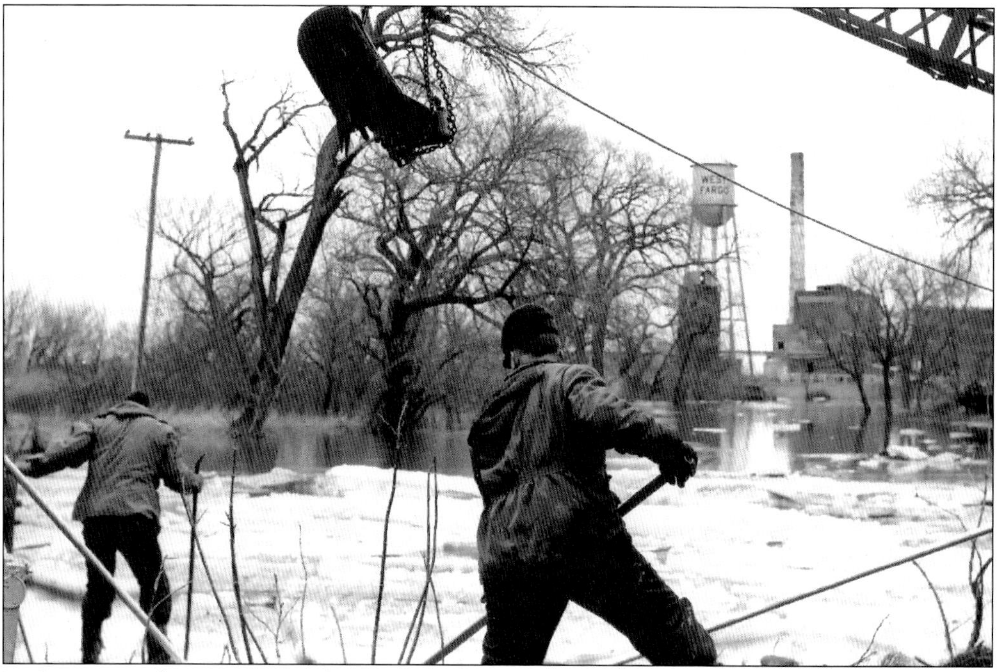


In the winter of 1964–1965, workers attempt to clear ice dams on the Sheyenne River by blasting the ice with dynamite and using heavy machinery. Warmer weather in the spring causes ice on the river to break into pieces and float down river. This causes a problem when blocks of ice get stuck and dam the river, resulting in the river overflowing its banks. The Sheyenne River drains into the Red River, both of which flow north and empty into Hudson Bay in Canada. The ice begins melting on the southern part of the rivers and flows north where the rivers are still frozen. Ice dams, combined with flat open prairie, often produce major flooding in the Red River Valley, as can be seen in this aerial photograph of West Fargo in 1954.

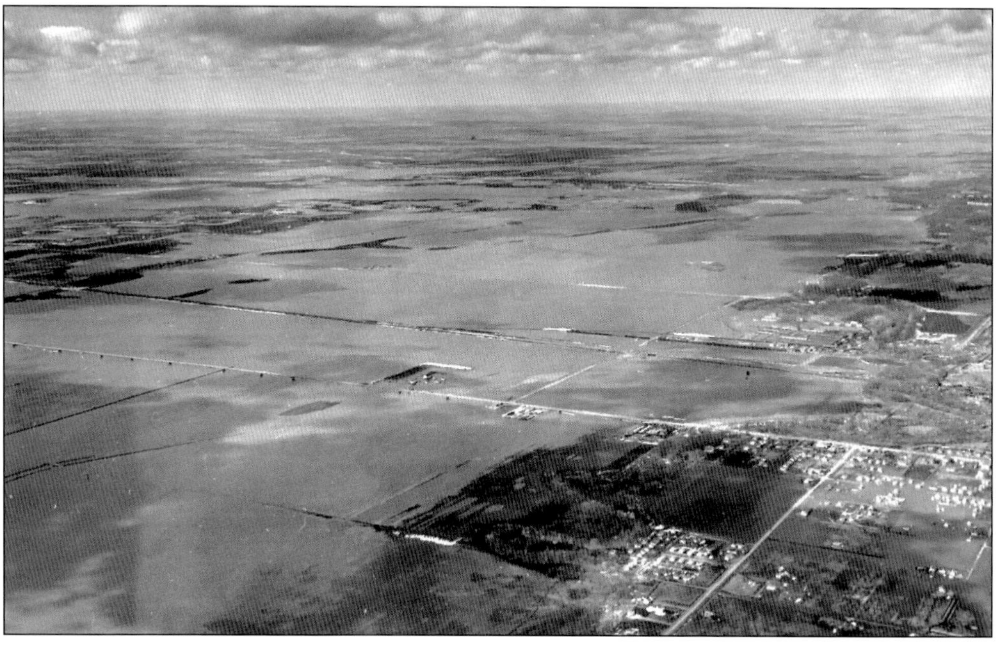

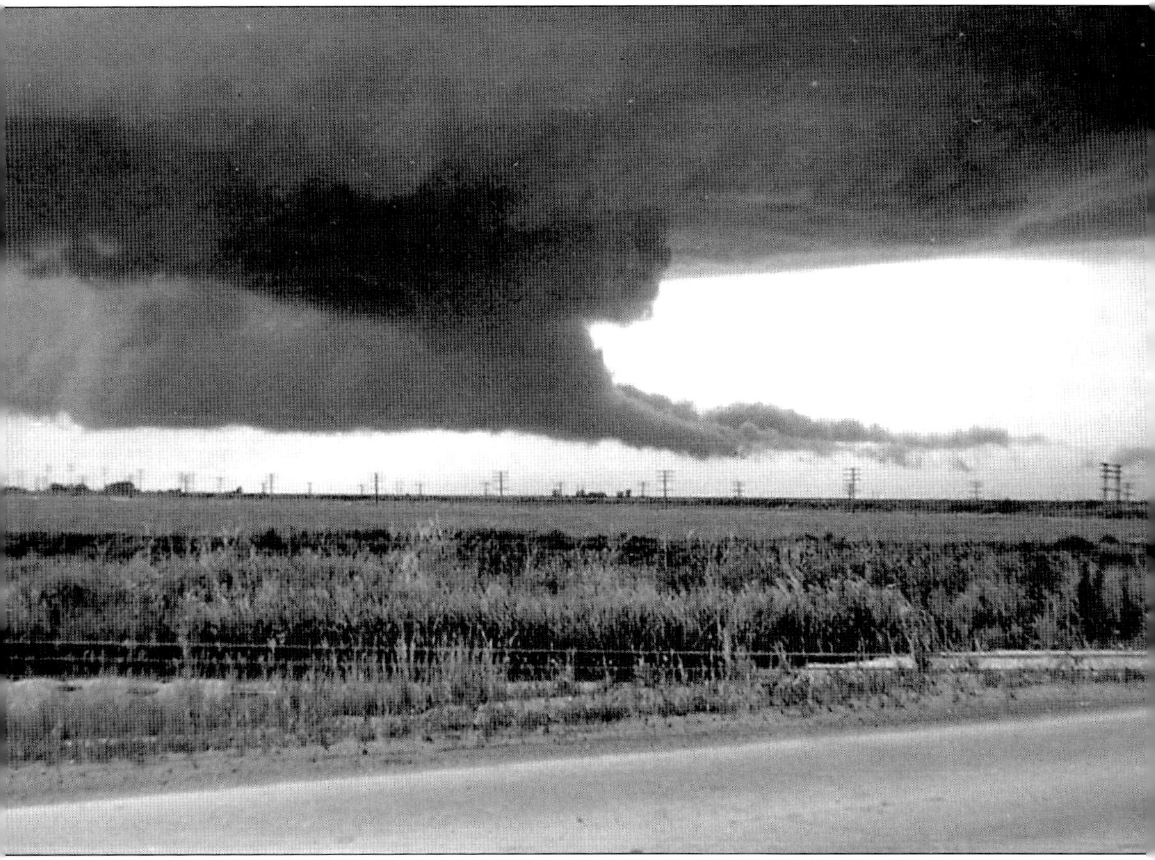

A tornado roars through the fields west of Fargo on June 20, 1957. The storm began west of Fargo, entering town in the Golden Ridge area, which was almost completely destroyed. The tornado continued through town, stopping in north Moorhead. Ten people died in the storm, six children from one family alone. More than 100 people were injured, 300 homes were destroyed, and another 1,000 were damaged. About 2,000 people were displaced due to the storm. In addition to damaging homes, four churches, three schools, and a handful of commercial buildings also suffered serious damage. The tornado was one of the most studied storms in history. Hundreds of photographs and home video were taken as the storm advanced through town. This helped Dr. Ted Fujita, a meteorologist from the University of Chicago, develop the Fujita Scale, which measures the severity of tornados. Fujita determined that the storm that hit the Fargo-Moorhead area was a category F-5 tornado with wind speeds close to 300 miles per hour.

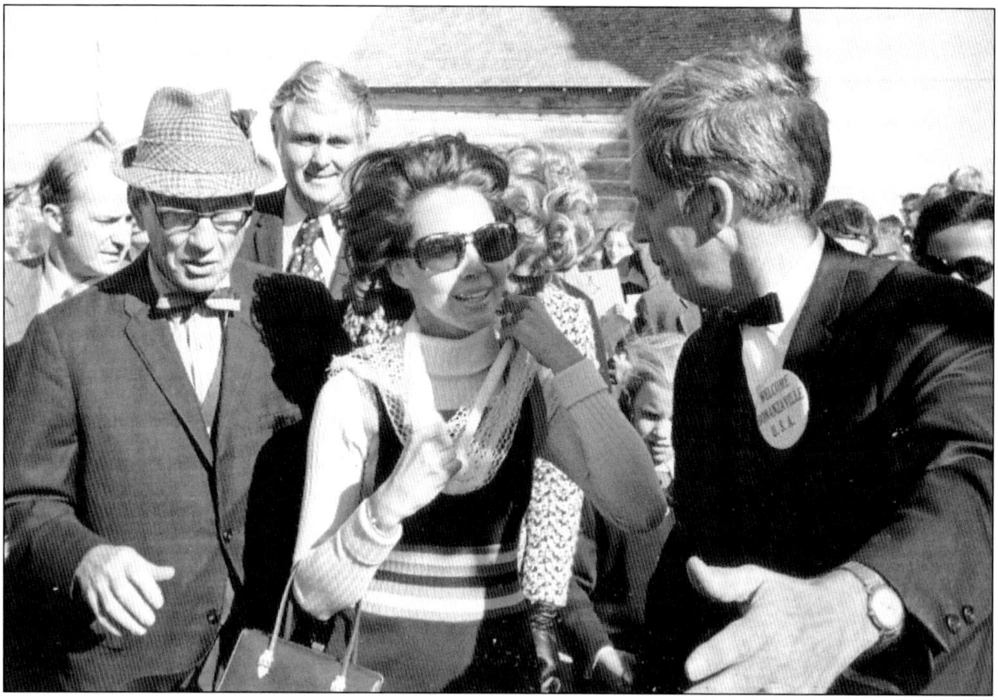


Julie Nixon Eisenhower (above) visits Bonanzaville at the Cass County Historical Society in West Fargo on September 22, 1972. A crowd of people, including reporters, swarmed the historic village to get a glimpse of the president's daughter. During her visit to the museum and village, Eisenhower taught a class of students in the historic Dobrinz School during the museum's annual Pioneer Days event, which incorporates two days of historic demonstrations, crafts, food, and music. Pioneer Days was later moved to the third weekend of August every year. The Dobrinz School is pictured (below) in its original location shortly after being built in 1895 in Mapleton Township.

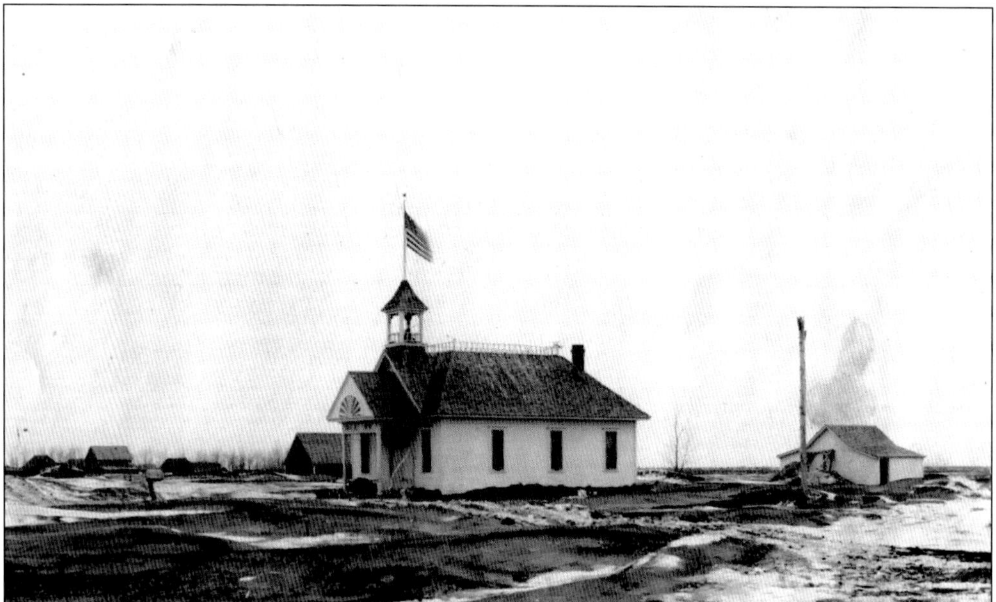

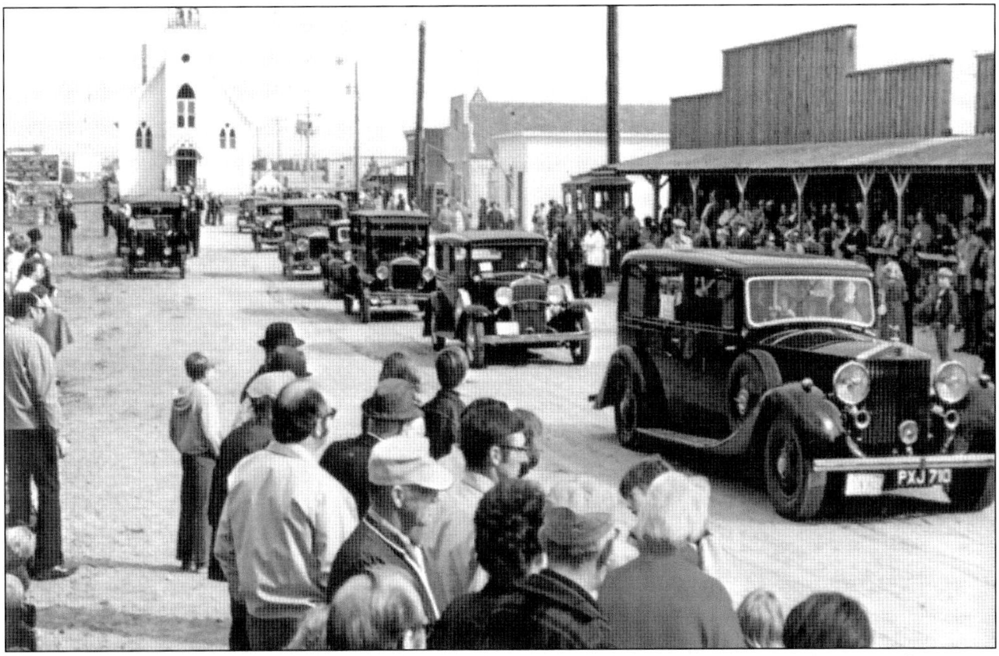


Pioneer Days has been held at Bonanzaville in West Fargo since the 1960s. The event began in Davenport but was eventually moved to Bonanzaville where the Cass County Historical Society established a museum and historic village. People line up along the parade route in Bonanzaville during Pioneer Days during the 1970s.

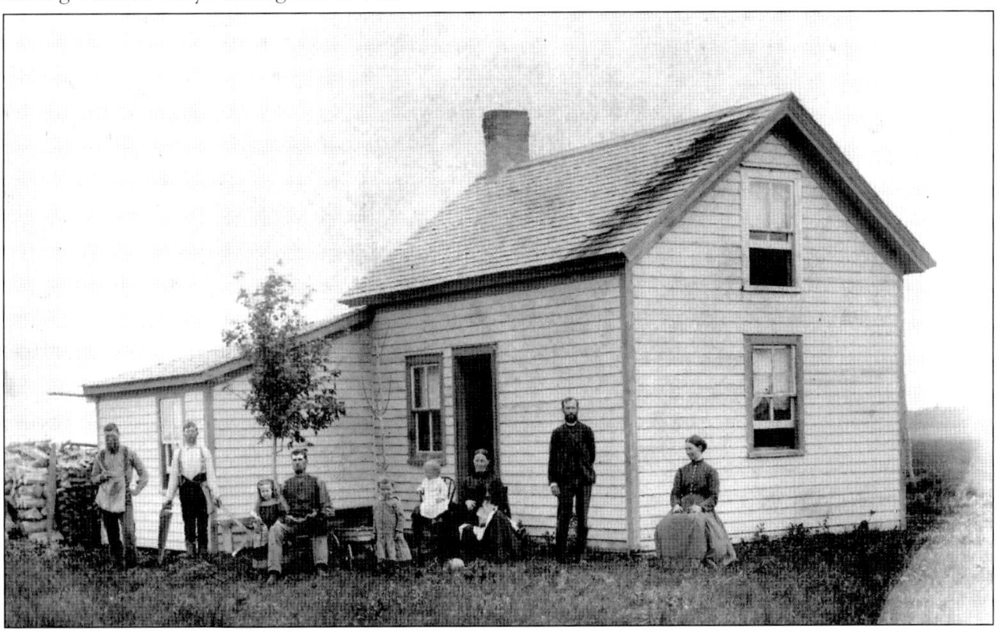

Francis McKenzie, the man sitting in the chair, is pictured with friends and family on his homestead farm in 1884. His brother Thomas boarded a steam boat traveling south on the Red River from Manitoba in 1871. When the boat stopped near Wild Rice, Thomas wandered west and found a grove of wild roses in bloom where he decided to make his home. Francis joined Thomas in 1879, and operated adjoining farms.

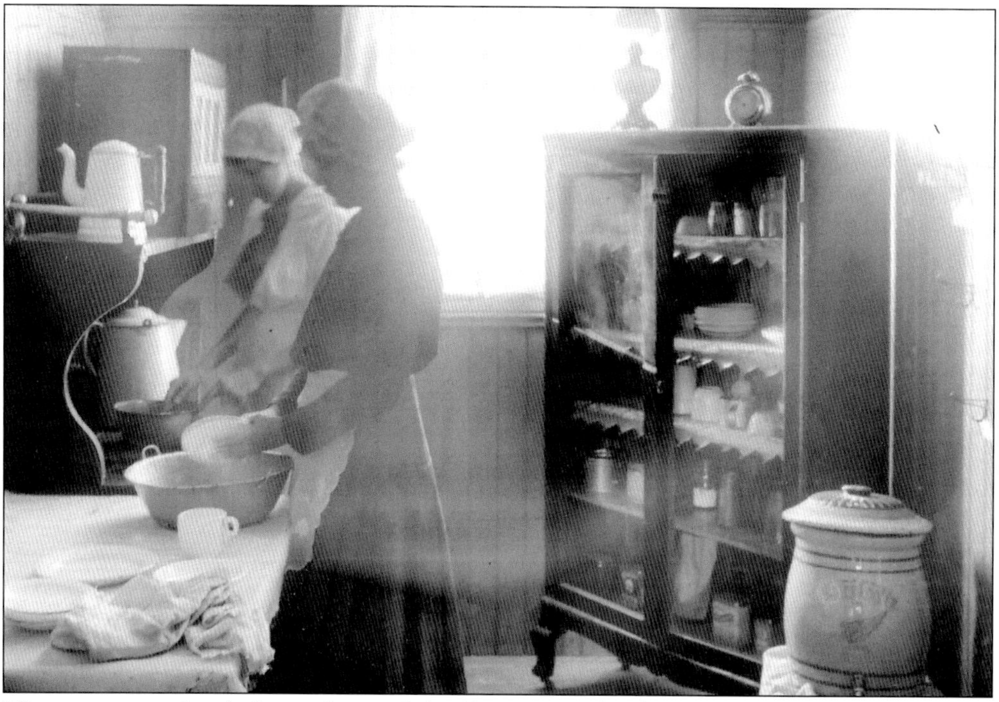

Women prepare lunch for students of the District 4 School near Wild Rice in the school's kitchen. During the town's most prosperous time, Wild Rice had a public school as well as a Catholic school at St. Benedict Church. The church began when the French missionary Fr. Jean Baptiste Genin opened the Holy Cross Mission in the late 1860s. Many French homesteaders settled in the Wild Rice area.

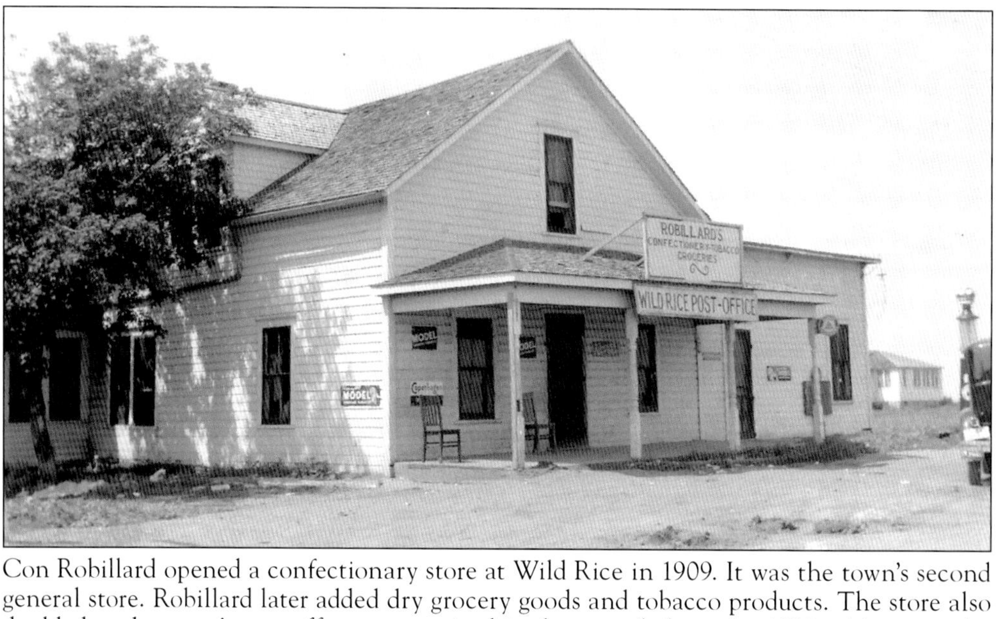


Con Robillard opened a confectionary store at Wild Rice in 1909. It was the town's second general store. Robillard later added dry grocery goods and tobacco products. The store also doubled as the town's post office, as seen in this photograph from the 1920s. Also note the automobile and gas pump on the right side of the photograph.

# *Four*

# Southwestern Cass County

Chapter 4 focuses on the towns in southwestern Cass County, the least populous quarter: Alice, Chaffee, Embden, Leonard, and Lynchburg.

Alice was a Northern Pacific station established in 1900. The town site was platted by Frank Blasl and was incorporated in 1925. The town was named Alice by R. S. Lewis, a Fargo banker and former lieutenant governor of North Dakota, for his wife and daughter who were both named Alice. The population of the town is currently 56, down from a high of 181 in 1940. It is about 25 miles west and south of Casselton.

Chaffee was a station constructed on the end of the line of the 12-mile-long Red River Valley and Western Railroad that served the Amenia and Sharon Land Company bonanza farm. Eben Chaffee, president of the land company, named the town Rita after his niece. In 1884, the Great Northern Railroad took over the railway and renamed the town Chaffee in honor of Eben Chaffee. The town site was platted in 1898. Although small and created to serve a bonanza farm, residents of Chaffee boasted of its amenities. Like other small rural towns, they had an elevator, depot, bank, post office, cream station, school, machine dealer, two mercantile stores, cement block factory, barbershop, hotel, butcher shop, hardware store, harness shop, lumberyard, stock loading pens, bulk gasoline plant, blacksmith shop, and even a doctor. Chaffee is about 15 miles southwest of Casselton.

The town of Embden is located 17 miles west and south of Casselton. Enos Gray, a homesteader who settled in the area in 1879, named the location for his home of Embden, Maine. He established the post office at his farm home in 1883, but mail was discontinued in 1891. The Northern Pacific Railroad established a station in Embden in 1900, and the town and post office were reestablished with the same name. The former Embden Depot is now a historic attraction at Bonanzaville in West Fargo.

There are three different versions of how the town of Leonard was named. The first is that the township and town site were named for Leonard Stroble, an early settler. The second is that it was named for Leonard Stiles, the first postmaster when the village was established in 1881. The third is that Mary Hewitt, owner of the land that became Leonard, named the town after a friend of hers. Whatever the source of the name, the town was a Northern Pacific Railroad station in 1882. Leonard officially incorporated in 1951 and has a stable population of 255. It is located about 18 miles south of Casselton.

When the Red River Valley and Western Railroad built 12 miles of road from Addison to Chaffee, Lynchburg became the midway point. When the Great Northern took over the railroad, it built a station there in 1893. The town was named for Frank Lynch, who was president of the Red River Valley and Western Railroad. The post office ceased operation in 1911. Lynchburg is 10 miles south and west of Casselton.

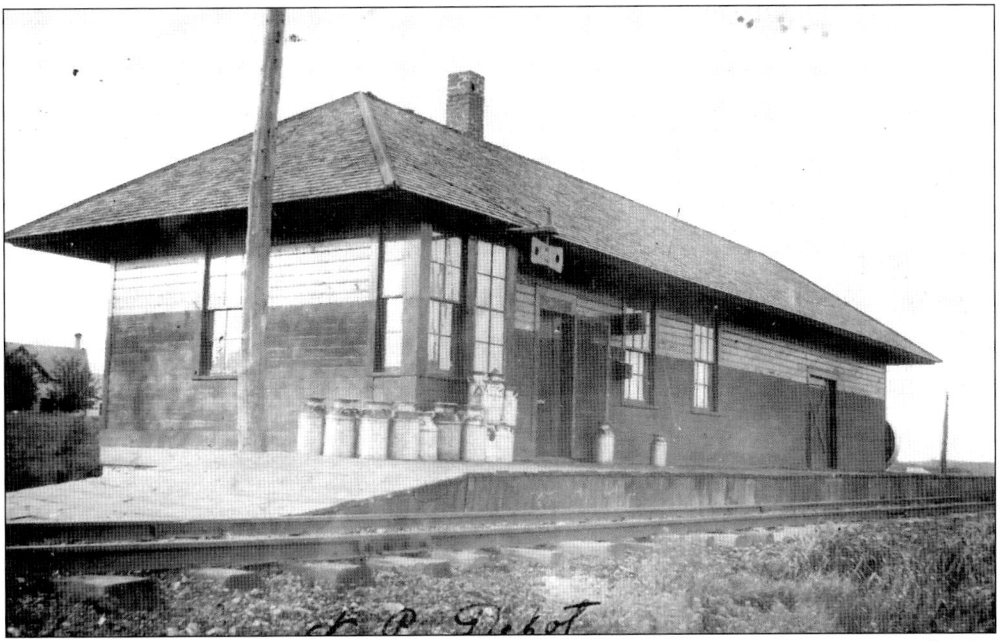

The Northern Pacific Railroad reached the land where Alice now stands in 1900. Reportedly, the first train depot in the town was nothing more than a railroad boxcar. A permanent depot was built along the tracks later that same year. The town was named by Fargo banker Robert B. Lewis, who named it Alice after his wife and daughter.

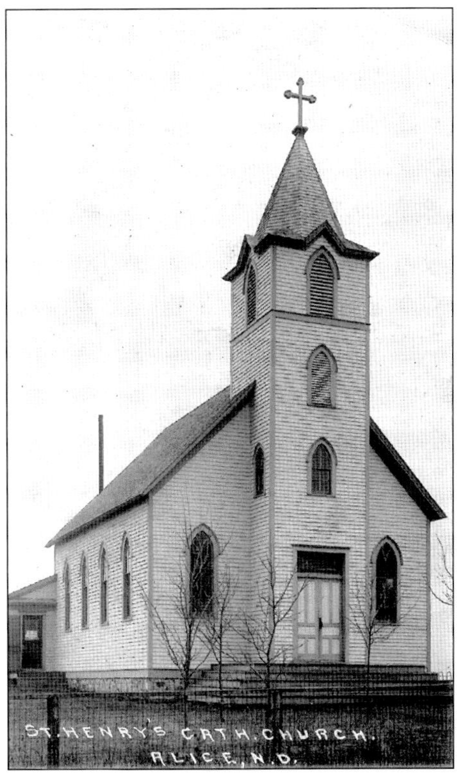


St. Henry's Catholic Church in Alice was built in 1903. This photograph was taken around 1910. Mass was held by visiting priests from Casselton and Fingal (Barnes County) until Fr. William Schimmel was appointed to the parish in 1914. A new church building was constructed of brick in the 1950s.

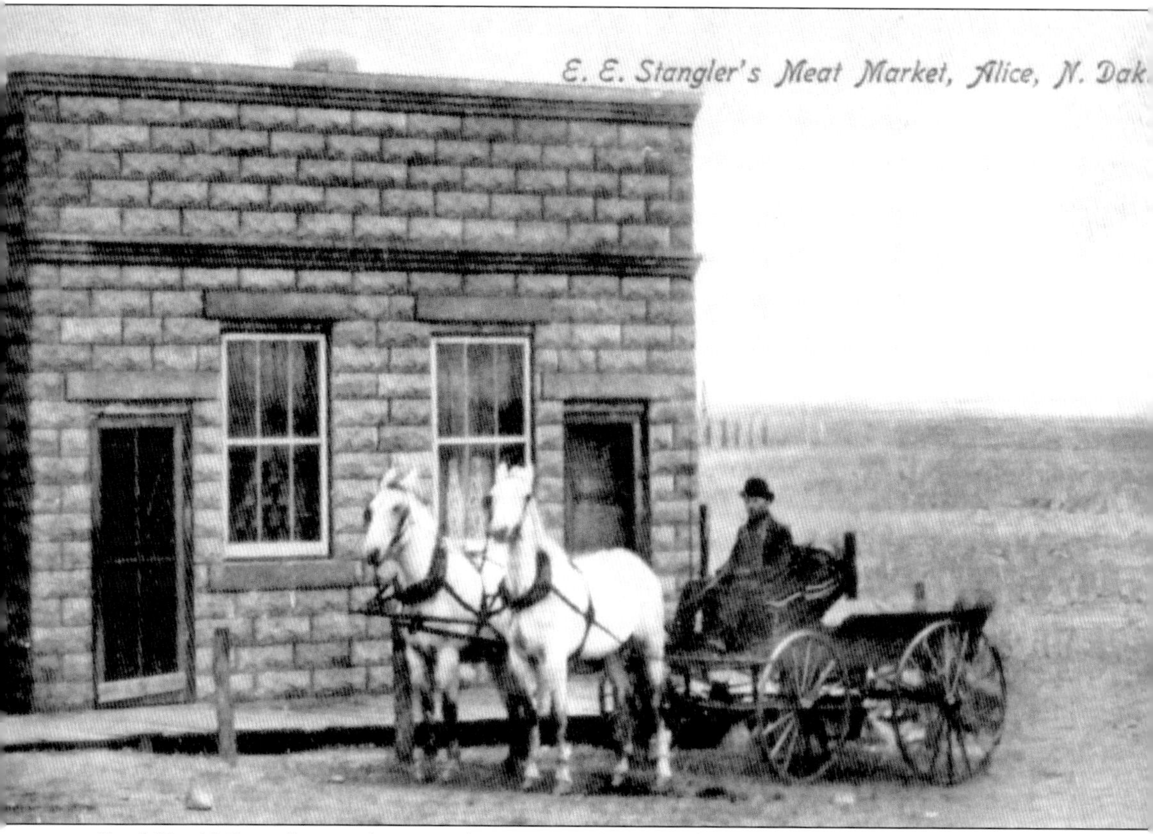


Emil Ewald Stangler was born in Austria in 1879. As a boy, he worked as an apprentice to a butcher for three years. At the age of 17, he moved to the United States and settled in Casselton. In 1905, Emil opened a meat market and the Stangler name became known throughout the country for quality meat products. Maple wood from Minnesota was used to smoke the meat, and spices were imported from Jamaica to use for seasoning. The market became so popular that Alice became a regular stop for men working for the Northern Pacific Railroad who wanted to buy meat. A large icehouse was built to store and ship the meat products. The meat market was destroyed by fire in 1910. Stangler built a sturdier building, pictured here, one year later. Emil continued operating the market until his death in 1965. His son Roman took over the business but died two years after his father.

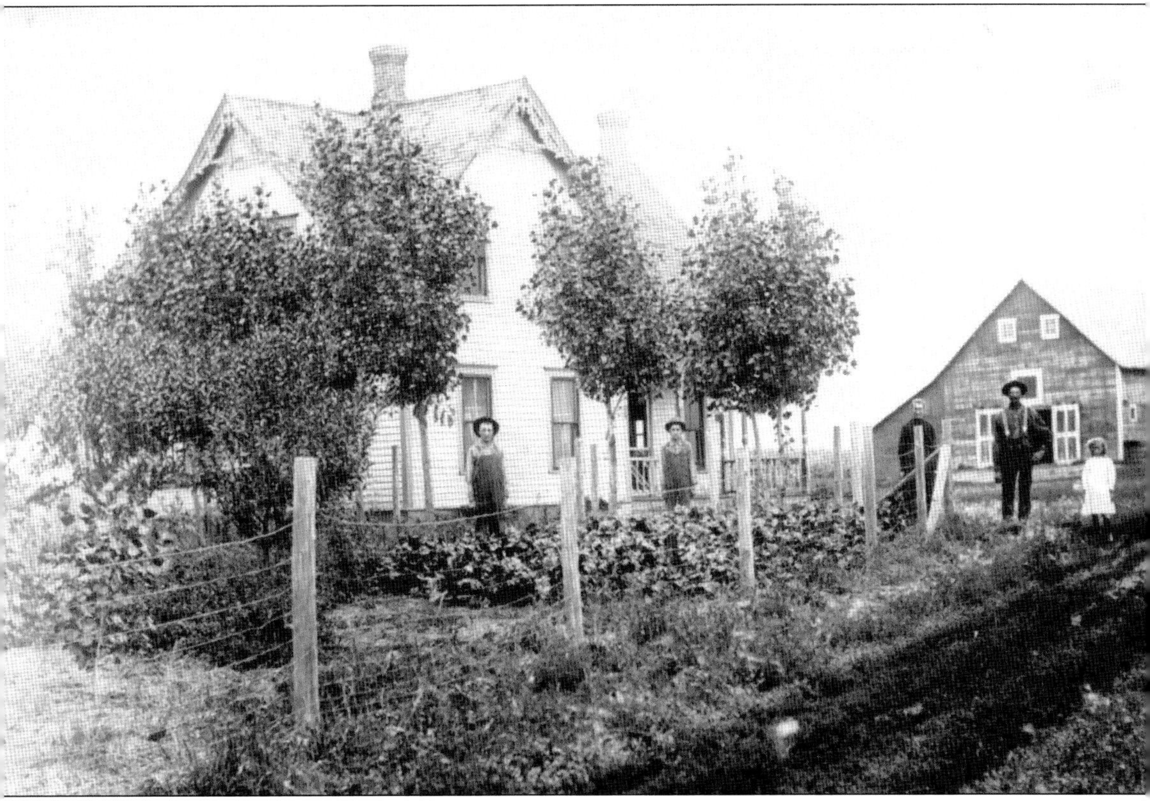

Frank Blasl and family stand outside their farm near Alice around 1909. One year after his birth in Germany, Frank and his parents immigrated to the United States and settled in Yankton, the capitol of Dakota Territory. His future wife, Emilie, who was born in the same town as Frank, also came to America with her family, settling in Minnesota. They eventually married and purchased a farm in Cass County. When the Northern Pacific Railroad built a station near their farm in 1900, Frank platted the town of Alice. They moved their farmhouse and barn several times as the town grew. Their oldest son, Gus, is standing on the left of the photograph in the vegetable garden with their younger son Hank. Emilie is next on the left with Frank standing in front of the family's barn. Young Hattie stands next to her father on the right of the picture.

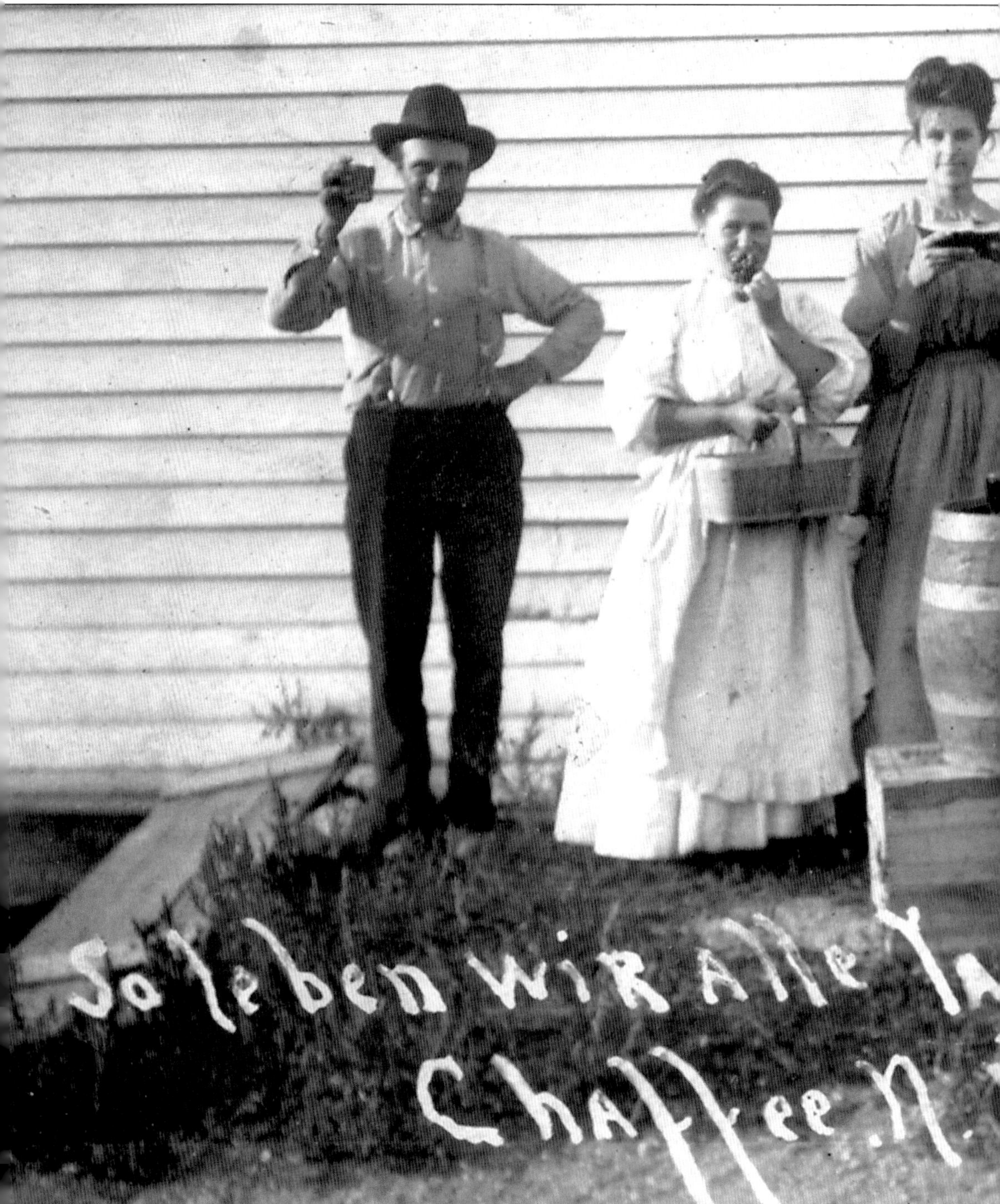


Scandinavians, mostly from Norway and Sweden, are the most prevalent ethnic group in Cass County. Germans, however, comprise the single largest ethnic group. In Cass County, the largest settlements of Germans were in Arthur, Amenia, Casselton, and Pontiac Township. This photograph was taken near Chaffee and reads, "This is how we live every day." The only

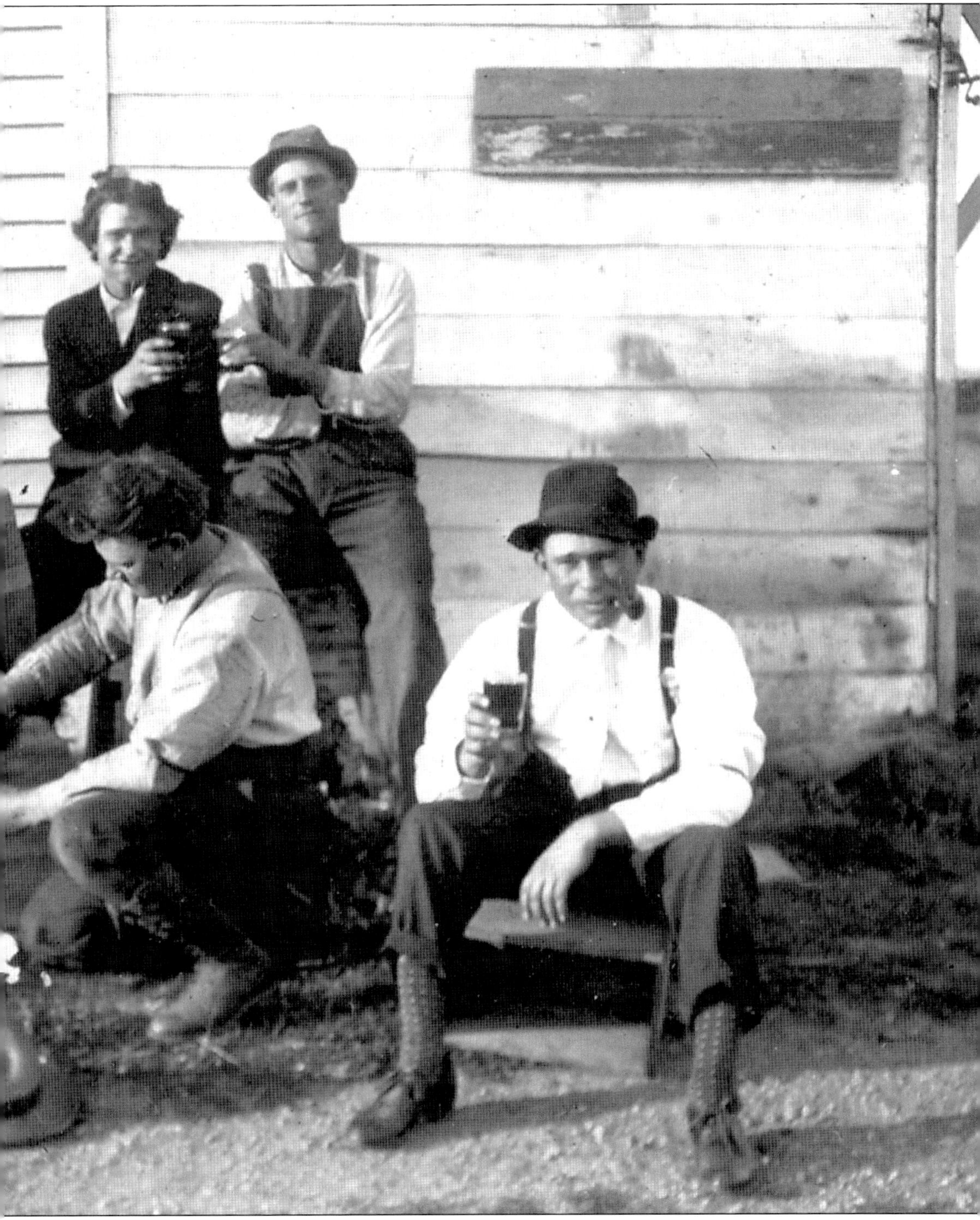

information on photograph is the date, July 4. The men are enjoying beer from a keg while the women eat fruit. The photograph was used as a postcard and probably sent to relatives to show how prosperous life was in North Dakota. Picture postcards like this one were frequently used to encourage further immigration and settlement.

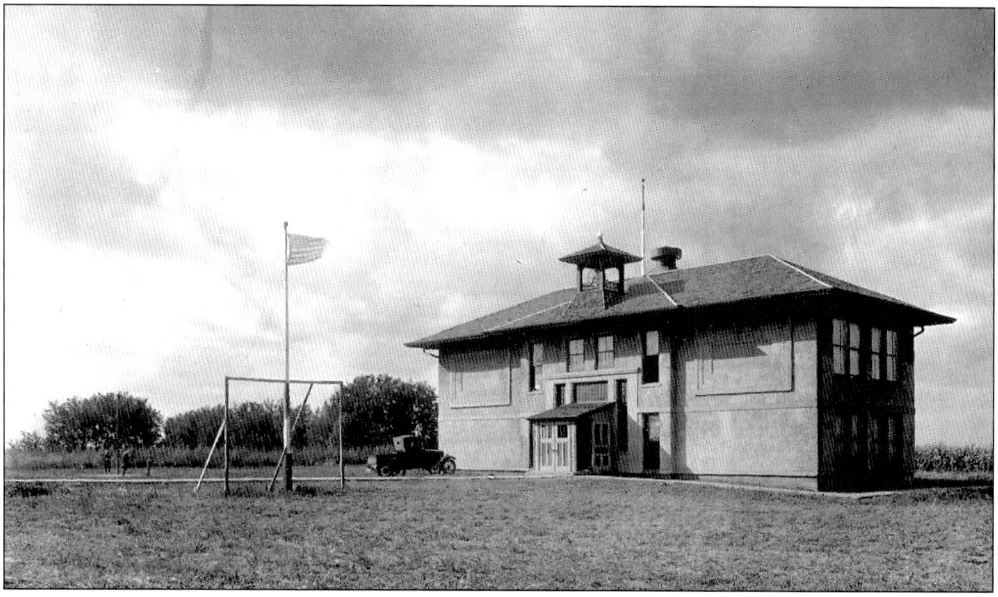

The Chaffee Public School is pictured here around 1926. The school district was organized in 1879 and operated a one-room schoolhouse until this building was constructed in 1911. The new school had four rooms and offered three years of high school until 1927, when the first high school class graduated from the Chaffee School.

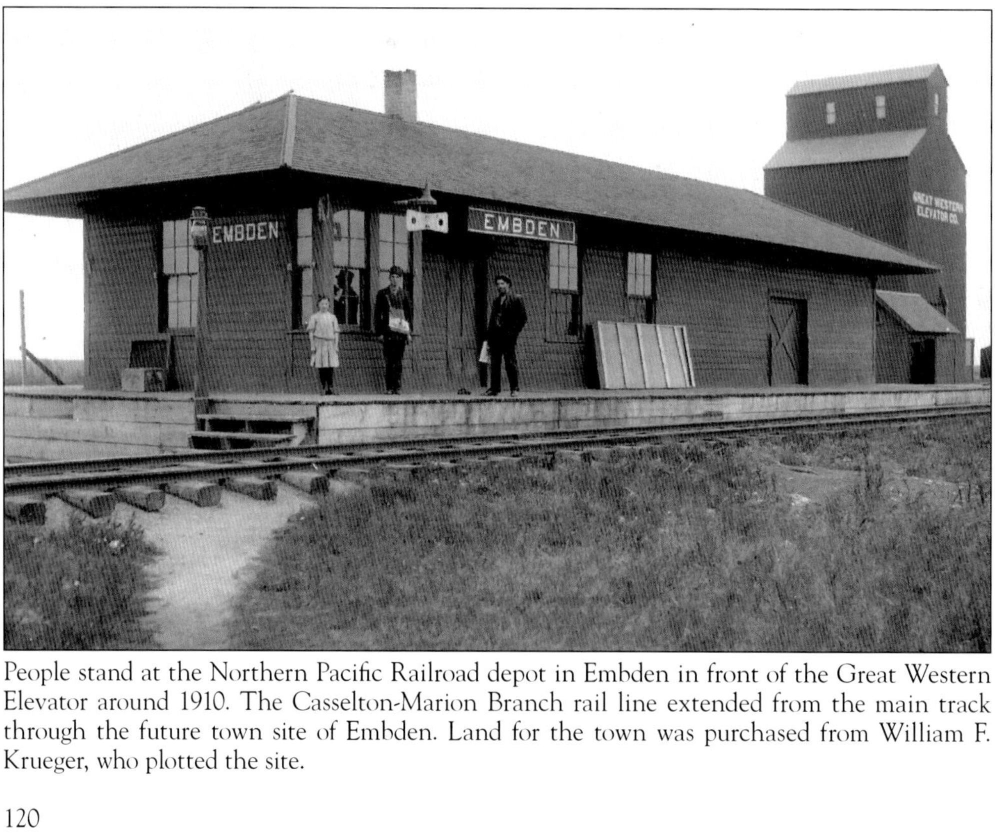


People stand at the Northern Pacific Railroad depot in Embden in front of the Great Western Elevator around 1910. The Casselton-Marion Branch rail line extended from the main track through the future town site of Embden. Land for the town was purchased from William F. Krueger, who plotted the site.

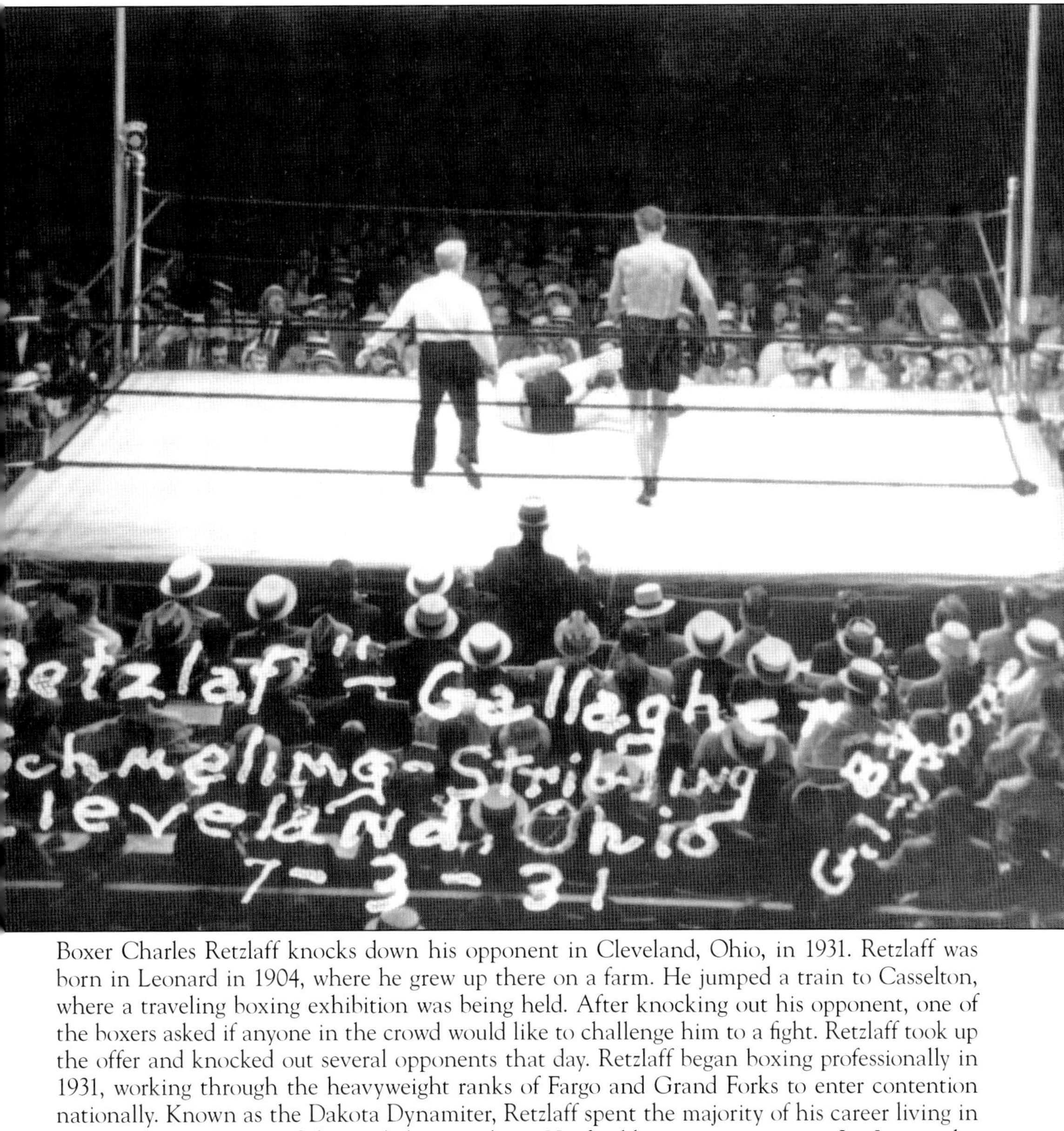


Boxer Charles Retzlaff knocks down his opponent in Cleveland, Ohio, in 1931. Retzlaff was born in Leonard in 1904, where he grew up there on a farm. He jumped a train to Casselton, where a traveling boxing exhibition was being held. After knocking out his opponent, one of the boxers asked if anyone in the crowd would like to challenge him to a fight. Retzlaff took up the offer and knocked out several opponents that day. Retzlaff began boxing professionally in 1931, working through the heavyweight ranks of Fargo and Grand Forks to enter contention nationally. Known as the Dakota Dynamiter, Retzlaff spent the majority of his career living in Duluth. He fought in 87 fights, only loosing three. His final loss was to rising star Joe Louis, who knocked out Retzlaff during the first round of a fight in Chicago in 1936. After the fight, Retzlaff returned to farming near Leonard.

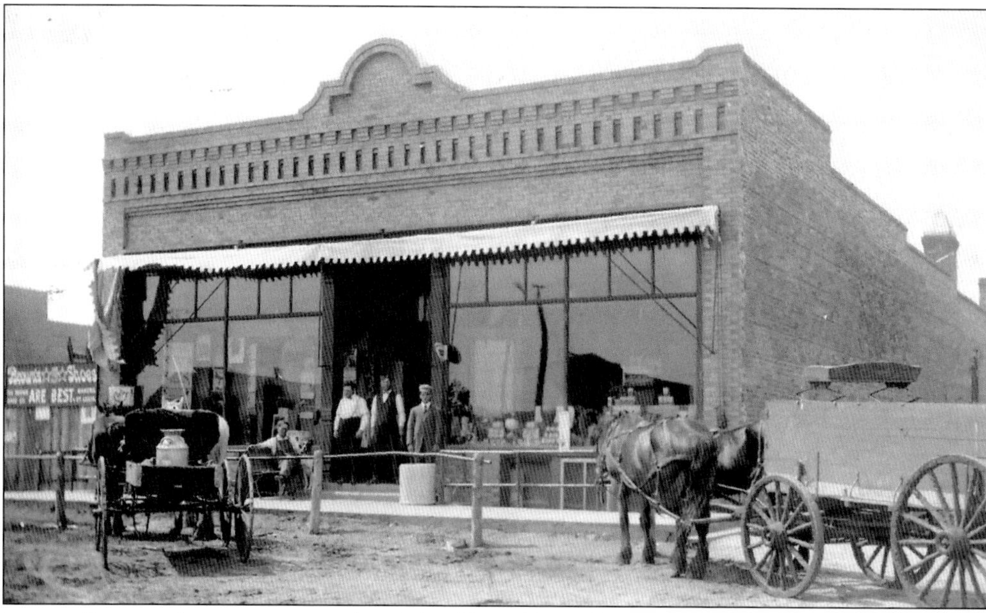

Leonard's general store was owned by John Philip Boos. Boos was one of the earliest settlers in the community of Leonard. He was born in northern Minnesota before moving to Leonard. Boos and his wife, Louise, opened the town's first boardinghouse, which housed men building the railroad. They later opened a general store that burned down twice before moving into this building in the 1890s.

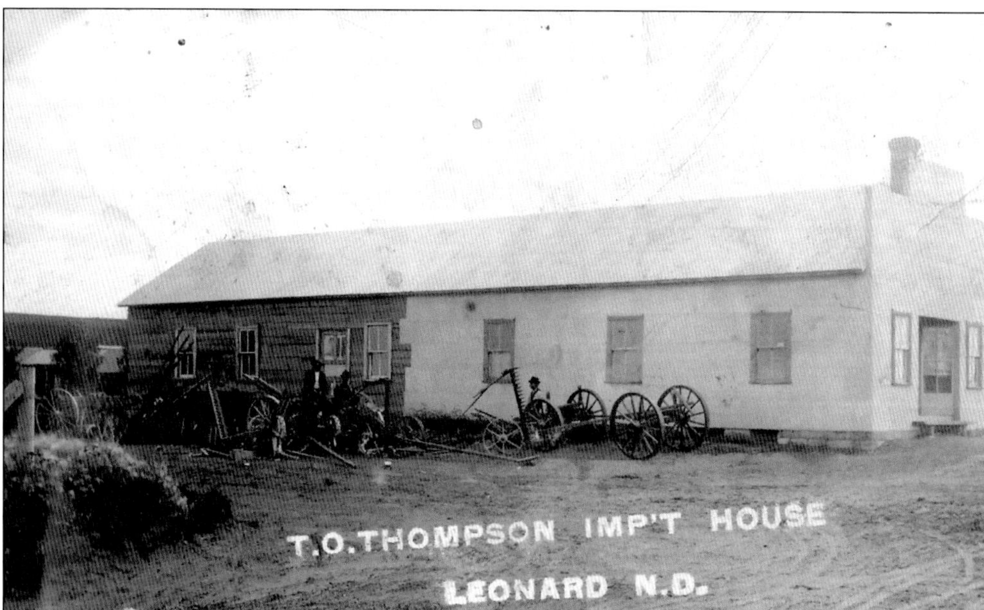


Targe O. Thompson opened this machine shop in Leonard, in the early 1900s, where he sold implements from International Harvester and John Deere. He owned and operated the first steam thresher in the area and would help neighbors harvest and plow their fields. Thompson eventually bought and operated a furniture store and telephone office in Leonard.

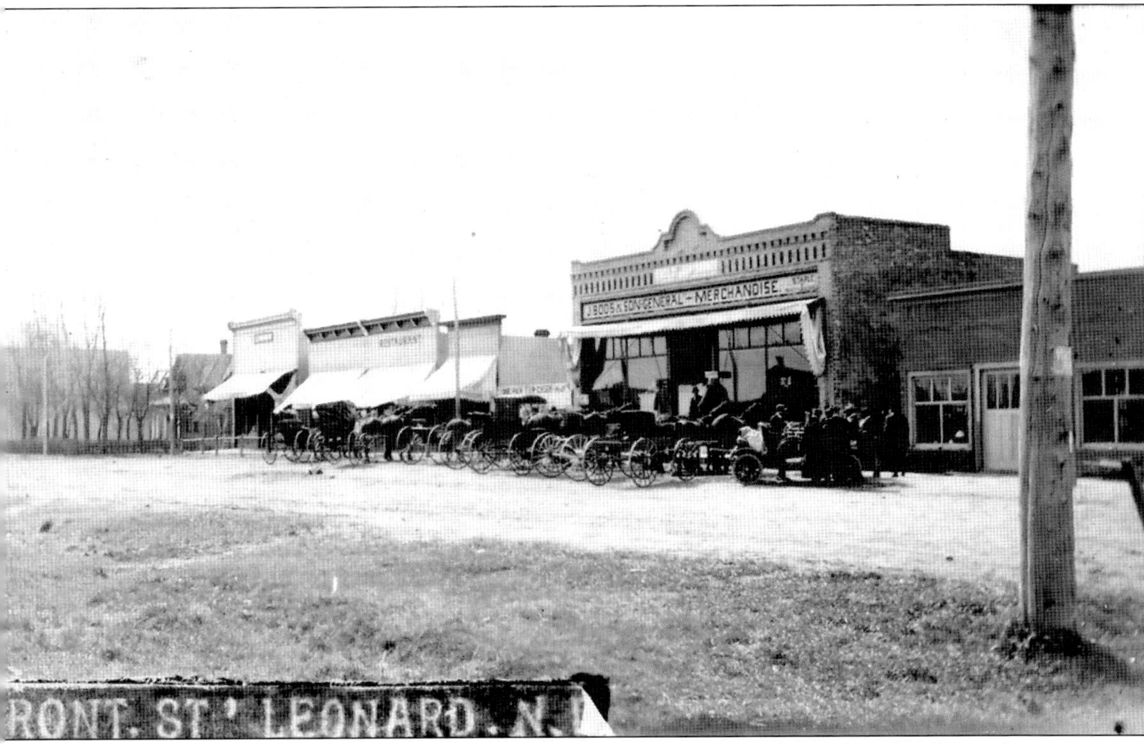


Horses and buggies are parked in front of the J. Boos and Sons General Merchandise Store along Front Street in Leonard around 1913. A crowd of people swarm around an early automobile parked next to the building. The car may have belonged to Targe O. Thompson, who owned an implement dealership in town. Thompson had the first automobile in the area. It was said that his wife, Inger, could see the headlights of his car six miles from their farm just outside of Leonard. When she saw the headlights of her husband's car on his way home from town she would know to put dinner on the table. Thompson was instrumental in plotting the land that was to be used for the construction of Highway 46 that runs from east to west along the southern edge of Cass County. The highway now begins west of Kindred at the interchange with Interstate 29 and runs 120 miles to the west.

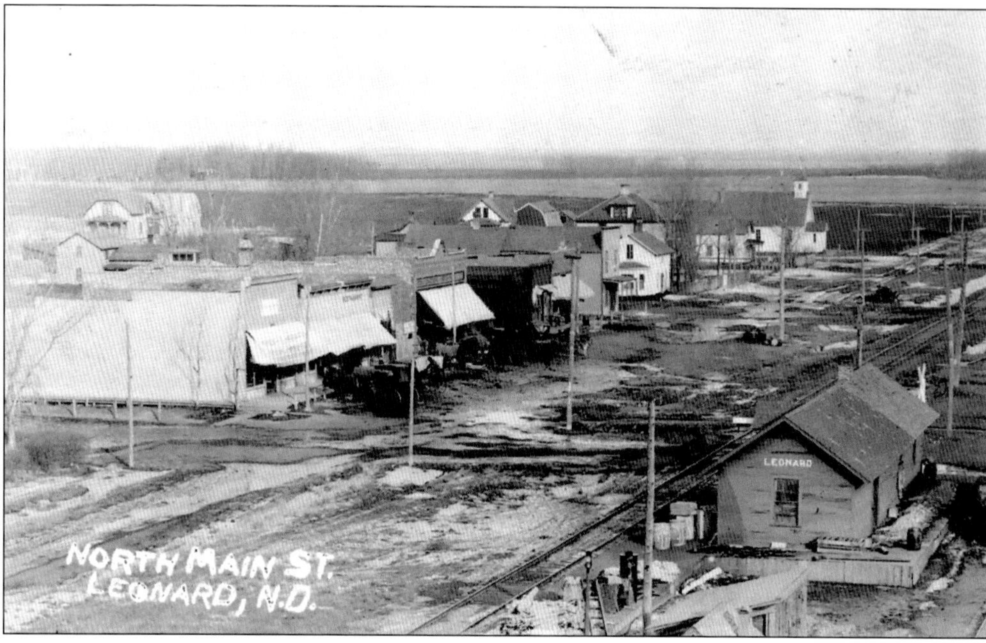


This is a photograph of North Main Street and Railroad Avenue in Leonard taken from a grain elevator along the Northern Pacific Railroad line around 1910. Northern Pacific Railroad built the train station in Leonard in 1882 where it stood until it was bought by a local resident and moved to his property. The station is still in use today as a shop and garage.

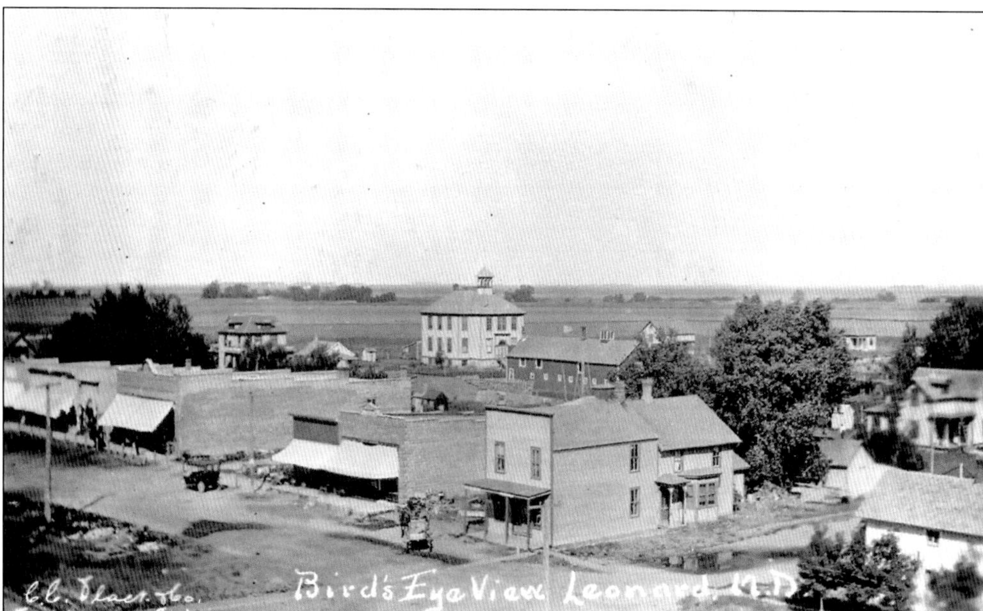


The top of a grain elevator provides a good view of Leonard in the 1920s. How Leonard got its name is still up for debate. One story credits the town's name to Leonard Stroble, who was a pioneer settler in the township. Another version credits the name to the town's first postmaster in 1881, Leonard C. Stiles.

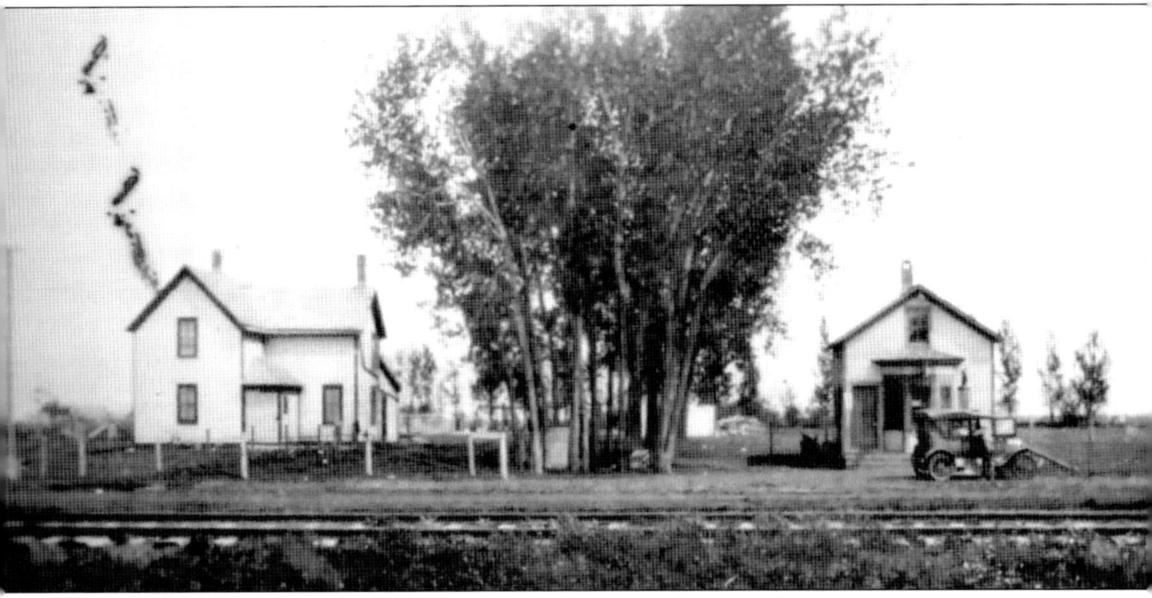

The home of Mr. and Mrs. William Kennicke is pictured on the left next to their store in Lynchburg around 1926. The Kennickes moved into their home in 1911. The house was built by Frank Lynch, who was president of the Red River Valley and Western Railroad, which was the train line running through the area at the time. They operated a store in Lynchburg, which also had a gas pump. People gathered at the store from miles around to drink beer, play cards, and talk. Kennicke worked at the elevator in town for nine years and at the lumberyard for five years. His wife operated the town's first telephone exchange. The town had a few other homes and stores throughout the years. There was never a train station in Lynchburg, only a small building that was used by railroad workers to find warmth. Only a few buildings were left in the town by the end of the 20th century.

# Bibliography


Cass County Historical Society. *Rural Cass County: The Land and the People*. Dallas: Taylor Publishing, 1976.

Danbom, David B. and Claire Strom. *Fargo, North Dakota, 1870-1940*. Chicago: Arcadia, 2002.

Drache, Hiram. *The Challenge of the Prairie: The Life and Times of Red River Pioneers*. Fargo, ND: North Dakota Institute for Regional Studies, 1970.

Drache, Hiram. *The Day of the Bonanza: A History of Bonanza Farming in the Red River Valley of the North*. Danville, IL: Interstate Printers and Publishers, 1964.

Fite, Gilbert. *The Farmers' Frontier, 1865-1900*. New York: Holt, Rinehart, and Winston, 1966.

Madison, James H. ed. *Heartland: Comparative Histories of the Midwestern States*. Bloomington: Indiana University Press, 1988.

Murray, Stanley Norman. *The Valley Comes of Age: A History of Agriculture in the Valley of the Red River of the North, 1812-1920*. Fargo, ND: Institute for Regional Studies, North Dakota State University, 1967.

Robinson, Elwyn B. *History of North Dakota*. Fargo, ND: Institute for Regional Studies, North Dakota State University, 1995.

Sherman, William C., et al. *Plains Folk: North Dakota's Ethnic Heritage*. Fargo, ND: Institute for Regional Studies, 1988.

Tweton, D. Jerome, and Theodore B. Jelliff. *North Dakota: The Heritage of a People*. Fargo, ND: North Dakota Institute for Regional Studies, 1976.

Wilkins, Robert P., and Wynona H. *North Dakota: A Bicentennial History*. New York: Norton, 1977.

Woodward, Mary Dodge. *The Checkered Years: A Bonanza Farm Diary, 1884-1888*. St. Paul: Minnesota Historical Society Press, 1989.

# INDEX